D1117648

# WORLD
## VEGETARIAN
# CLASSICS

# WORLD VEGETARIAN CLASSICS

## CELIA BROOKS BROWN

### WITH PHOTOGRAPHY BY GUS FILGATE

PAVILION

# Contents

# Introduction

For this monumental project, I set out on an odyssey to discover the 230 greatest vegetarian dishes in the world. I was determined to elect dishes which, wherever possible, were genuinely vegetarian, from genuinely vegetarian cultures or aspects of culture, rather than conversions without meat. London is one of the best places to be to gain access to world food, as one of the most cosmopolitan cities on earth. I interviewed experts, ate in dozens of restaurants, grilled taxi drivers and complete strangers on the tube, phoned relatives and friends of friends of friends. I read until I was blue in the face and, often, just when I had given up on one path, a whole new strand of exciting information would suddenly reveal itself. As Confucius said, "Real knowledge is to know the extent of one's ignorance."

Once I had determined what these classic recipes would be, the lab work began. I collected as many versions of each dish as possible, through written recipes – some published and others offered to me by enthusiastic cooks; others based on my conversations and reading. I took this information into my kitchen and refracted it through the prism that is my own culinary logic and passion. I tried to recreate each dish to what I thought to be a first-class result, easily achievable in modern Western kitchens, whilst trying to adhere to authenticity as closely as possible. Some dishes didn't meet the standard; others were just too complicated to expect the home cook to execute, so I sought replacements. Ultimately I arrived at what I hope is a definitive collection. There are regions missing and no doubt recipes too, but I did my best to give a well-rounded global interpretation in the given time. One thing that sets this book apart from similar

classic (klas'ik) 1 Belonging to the highest rank or class. 2 Serving as the established model or standard. 3 Having lasting significance or worth; enduring. 4 Adhering or conforming to established standards and principles. 5 Of a well-known type; typical. 6 Formal, refined, and restrained in style. 7 Simple and harmonious; elegant.

predecessors is that I have given equal weight to every area of the world, with roughly two chapters devoted to each continent.

The odd thing about food, especially dishes that are enduring, legendary and world-class, is that every cook's version will be different. The best cooks are always tweaking and improving on their repertoire, and ironically every true cook's definitive version of a recipe is considered by them to be the best one. Once the origin of a dish is traced (which is often impossible), a host of new questions beckon. If so-and-so invented the dish, had it been perfected by them beyond improvement? Or perhaps it was an abberation, or an accident? So often the best recipes are the result of necessity being the mother of invention.

I hope you find here some recipes which you recognise, and others which surprise and inspire you. Heaven knows I've been bowled over with surprises and inspiration and I hope it is evident in the contents of this book. I cooked every single recipe between these covers, several of them many, many times over in order to get them right. In retrospect, I set out to complete a project in a given time which would conclude with the book rolling off the press. I swiftly realised that this is not the end. This is just the beginning of a project that could last a lifetime. I have laid the foundations and now you, the reader, cook, taster and enthusiast, and I, can make it grow together.

I've set up a website: www.worldvegclassics.org – I invite you to go there and offer your comments, experiences and recipes and I will happily interact with you and your input. I'll be running World Vegetarian Classics-themed events and demonstrations and you can keep up with my activities on my personal website, www.celiabrooksbrown.com
Please join me on this continuing voyage.

Celia x

# My notes on ingredients

• All eggs are medium size. I recommend organic as they come from healthy chickens who have been given a happy life, fed on a totally vegetarian and chemical-free diet. They also taste better and perform better in cooking.
• Olive oil is not extra virgin unless specified. Non-extra virgin is safer for high temperature cooking.
• Pizza mozzarella, unless otherwise specified, is the drier, grateable type, sold in vacuum packs, as opposed to buffalo or cow's milk mozzarella sold packed in liquid.
• Always use garlic "degermed". By this I mean that if the clove is sprouting in the middle, completely remove the sprout or germ, as it has a bitter flavour which is particularly invasive when using garlic raw.
• All salt used should be sea salt.

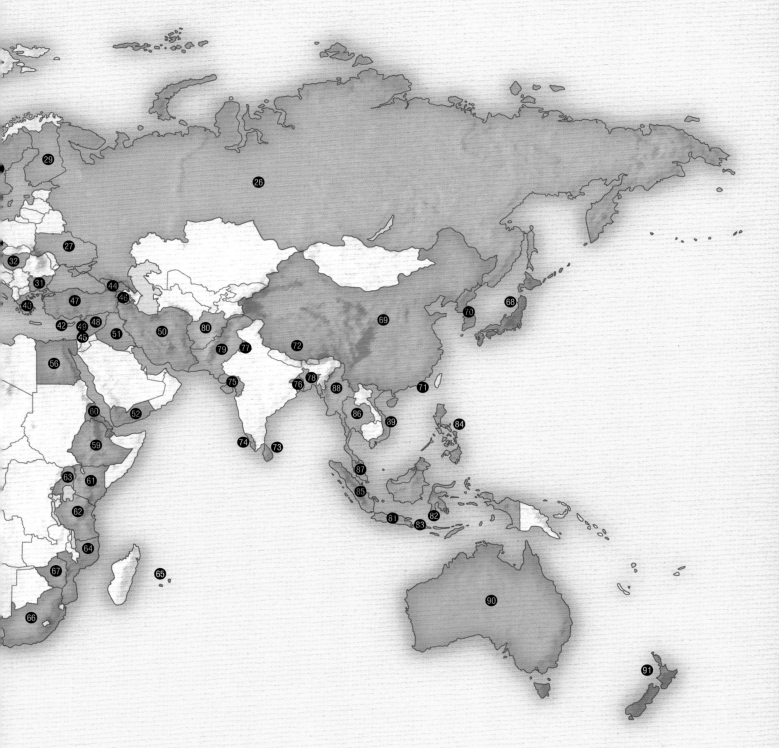

**The Middle East, Asia Minor and the Caucasus:**
44 Georgia
45 Palestine
46 Armenia
47 Turkey
48 Syria
49 Lebanon
50 Iran
51 Iraq
52 Yemen

**The Maghreb, Northern and West Africa:**
53 Algeria
54 Morocco
55 Tunisia

56 Egypt
57 Ghana
58 Nigeria

**Central, East and Southern Africa:**
59 Ethiopia
60 Eritrea
61 Kenya
62 Tanzania
63 Uganda
64 Mozambique
65 Mauritius
66 South Africa
67 Zimbabwe

**Japan and China:**
68 Japan
69 China
70 Korea
71 Hong Kong
72 Tibet

**The Indian Subcontinent and Central Asia:**
73 Sri Lanka
74 Kerala
75 Gujarat
76 Bengal
77 Punjab
78 Bangladesh
79 Pakistan
80 Afghanistan

**Southeast Asia:**
81 Java
82 Indonesia
83 Bali
84 Phillippines
85 Sumatra
86 Thailand
87 Malaysia
88 Myanmar
89 Vietnam

**Australasia:**
90 Australia
91 New Zealand

# chapter one
# North America and Canada

The classic dishes of North American cuisine have evolved out of the world's largest and newest proverbial melting pot of cultures. Many of the oldest American recipes started out as classics in their home culture and became Americanised by the use of ingredients found in the pioneers' new surroundings. Pumpkin Pie is a good example – this was probably an English cook's version of a custard tart, but using the newly discovered pumpkin in lieu of spiced fruits or "tartstuff" as it was then called. Similarly in Canada, a baked French brie married a cranberry chutney, creating an international hit.

Of course, Native Americans had a rich culinary culture before the initial invasion of the French and English. At Thanksgiving, Americans pay homage mainly to their European forefathers who struggled in the 1600s to adapt to their new environment; it seems just as fitting to thank the Native Americans who showed the new settlers what they could eat (corn, beans and pumpkin) and taught them how to cultivate it.

In my whistle-stop tour of vegetarian North American cuisine in this chapter, influences from the French are evident in Canada, while in the US, Mexican, African and Native Indian influences dominate. Fused with local ingredients, a uniquely American style reveals itself.

"In eating, if nowhere else, we celebrate the unity that comes from diversity."

Elizabeth Rozin, *Blue Corn and Chocolate*

# meet the expert:
# Marlena Spieler – Californian Cuisine

I met up with Marlena Spieler on a sunny August day. Marlena, herself a ray of sunshine, had just visited a Greek cheese distributor and was laden with cheese. Our mission was to shop for some gorgeous fresh ingredients, take them back to my house and cook up a feast for two in a California style, this time with a theme of salty Greek cheeses!

This, Marlena explained, was typical of how Californians cook. A visit to the farmer's market is transformed into a "veritable feast of simplicity", based on what's available and what's seasonal. While we rustled up a salad of fresh figs, mint, rocket (arugula), shaved fennel and slices of soft, white Manouri sheep's milk cheese, Sacramento-born Marlena and I discussed the ingredients that personify Californian cuisine. "A salad of local ingredients", she says, "would have to be the very embodiment of California food." A satisfying assembly of wild mesclun leaves, multi-coloured tomatoes, alfalfa sprouts, marinated tofu and artichokes, crisp fried noodles and a toasted sesame-balsamic dressing would be an ideal example of making the most of good, fresh, healthy ingredients, whilst fusing Italy with China.

California is blessed with the perfect climate for growing food, and this is fundamental to the appreciation Californians have for fruit and vegetables. That combined with a plethora of mixed ethnic influences, plus the natural foods movement, neo-Buddhism, and a desire to be beautiful like the Hollywood stars, forged a rich culture of modern vegetarianism. "Even in the 1950s, while those in the Midwest were eating canned vegetables, Californians were feasting on guacamole, artichokes, tacos and chow mein."

Marlena explained how California came to be such a melting pot of culinary influences, perhaps more than anywhere else in the States. Spanish missionaries brought ingredients from Mexico in the late 1700s and laid a strong foundation of Mexican influence over the Native American tribes already living there. Then one big day in 1848 changed everything – gold was discovered in the Sierra Nevada mountains. Within weeks, California was tranformed into a metropolis of fortune-hunters from all over the globe. A few got rich, and the rest stayed on to apply their original trades as

farmers, cheesemakers, winemakers and cooks. By the late 1800s, a rail infrastructure was emerging to support this sea-change, and thousands of Chinese rail workers immigrated, bringing their culinary influence and customs with them.

By the 1960s, California cuisine had evolved from a hotch-potch into a cuisine of distinction. "California cuisine is the blueprint for modern food", Marlena declares. Several modern food phenomena have sprung from California, such as salad bars, juice bars and the Raw Food movement. And of course McDonald's. But that's the dark side of the story.

As we sat down to our feast of fig and Menouri salad, amongst other delights, Marlena talked about her grandfather, a Russian immigrant and classic California dreamer who was always on health kicks. "As far back as the 1950s, he went through juicing, fasting and detoxing. He had a beautiful organic garden, and subscribed to an organic gardening magazine from the Rodale Press. I remember the corn which was as sweet as sugar, and the watermelon which was big and crisp-fleshed and juicy ... he loved his garden, which was a fixture of our lives until near the time of his death, when I was about eleven or so." A pity, I said, that he never got to see how his granddaughter grew up to become the World Ambassador of Californian Cuisine.

*Marlena Spieler has over 50 cookbook titles to her credit and has won many awards. She writes a bi-weekly column in* The San Francisco Chronicle.

# focus on ingredients

Wild rice – This long, slim, nearly black grain is an aquatic grass, which is actually not related to rice but is more similar to wheat. It is the only native North American grain and has been harvested in the wild by the Native Americans for centuries. For early European settlers, it was an important foodstuff, which they learnt how to gather from the Native Americans. Today it is both cultivated and wild. It has a distinctive nutty flavour with a hint of smokiness and is cooked by boiling, but takes considerably longer to soften than ordinary rice. Wild rice thrown dry into hot oil, then drained and salted makes a fabulous nibble.

Maple syrup – The sap of the maple tree is boiled down to make the syrup. The tree must be tapped at the right time of year, and it will then produce several gallons of sap, though 40 are needed to produce 1 gallon (4½ litres) of precious syrup. This was another Native American practice which was passed on to the settlers. For years it was the North Americans' only source of sugar until sugar cane replaced it as a cheaper form, but maple syrup remained a delicacy. It is a source of great gastronomic pride in Canada, especially Quebec.

**Cranberries**

**Wild Rice**

Cranberries – These little red tree fruits, native to Northern Europe and North America, are important in US culinary tradition – cranberry sauce has accompanied the Thanksgiving turkey since the earliest feasts. Unlike other berries, they must be cooked with sugar before they are palatable. Cranberry trees are grown in bogs, and are harvested by flooding the bogs and floating the cranberries to a collection area – the blinding red streams are a magnificent sight to behold. Cranberries store remarkably well and this has made them easily exportable on long ocean journeys for centuries. An early method for sorting cranberries was to throw buckets of them down a flight of stairs – the good ones bounce all the way down, the bad ones stay put. Because of this they also earned the nickname "bounce berry".

Sprouts – Just about any edible seed or bean can be sprouted and eaten, but the most common types are alfalfa, mung bean, broccoli and mustard seed. Asian immigrants probably introduced sprouting to the Americans, and it took off in a big way, especially in California during the natural foods movement of the 1950s. Sprouts are considered a super food. Alfalfa is used only as cattle feed in other parts of the world, but in North America the sprouted seeds are found in every salad bar and supermarket vegetable section, and are frequently found in sandwiches and *burritos* (see Grilled Vegetable Burritos on page 32 and Maple Roasted Mushroom Burger on page 16).

Okra – ladies' finger, *bamia*, *bindi*, gumbo, gombo – This vegetable is native to Africa and also much loved in India. During the days of the slave trade, okra made its way to the West Indies and America where it became a major ingredient in Creole cooking (see *Gumbo Z'Herbes* on page 25). It's hard to convince some people to like okra, as it is undeniably slimy. This mucilagenous quality is useful for thickening soups and stews, and acts as a glue, much like egg white, for coatings. The larger the okra, the more gummy it becomes, as well as being quite tough, so small pods are always best. My favourite way with okra is to slice into small pieces, toss in a bag with seasoned cornmeal, and shallow-fry until totally crisp – munchy heaven.

Blue cornmeal – Blue corn is rapidly gaining popularity in the US, mostly in the form of blue corn tortilla chips, but it is still a fairly eclectic ingredient. In the UK it is available in specialist and health food shops. It is appreciated mostly in the Southwestern US, where it has long been cultivated by Hopi and Pueblo Indian tribes. Today it is mostly grown in New Mexico and Colorado. It is special because it really is

**Blue Cornmeal**

**Alfalfa Sprouts**

blue – the pigment in the casing of the dried kernel makes the kernel appear dark blue, but inside it is white, so the ground meal appears much paler. When cooked, it turns an astonishing bright purple colour. It has a wonderful, complex corn flavour with a hint of sweetness, and has a protein content at least 30 per cent higher than ordinary corn, making it an ideal vegetarian food, and a power-packed breakfast food (see Blue Corn Blueberry Pancakes on page 22).

Beans – There are hundreds of varieties of beans. American bean varieties were brought back to Europe from the Americas by Columbus, but other types were already deeply rooted in Chinese and Japanese culture (see soya bean under Tofu on page 196) as well as Indian (see dal on page 222). Dried beans have a long shelf life, but it is worth remembering that the older they are, the longer they will take to cook. When buying dried beans it is not possible to determine their age, so keep tasting towards the end of cooking. All large dried beans (not lentils) must be soaked in cold water for at least 4–6 hours or overnight, before being boiled in fresh water until thoroughly tender. Salt is best added halfway through cooking as it can toughen the beans if added early. Some cooks add a little bicarbonate of soda (baking soda), which does have a softening effect, but is thought to reduce the nutritional qualities of the magnificent, high-protein bean.

This festive recipe is a wonderful example of European heritage meeting indigenous North American ingredients. When French Brie met Canadian cranberries, sparks flew, and a world classic combination was born. Here, pecans and herbs lend an extra dimension to the oozing cheese, and the flavour is lifted and enhanced by the zingy chutney. Carole Dulude, an enthusiastic employee of the bookshop and culinary hub that is Barbara Jo's Books to Cooks in Vancouver, dug this out of her entertaining repertoire for me. It is fabulous to serve at Christmas drinks parties.

# Baked Brie with Cranberry Chutney British Columbia, Canada

First make the chutney. Combine the cranberries, apricots, sugar, wine and salt in a small saucepan. Bring to the boil then leave to simmer for about 20 minutes until thick. Remove the chutney from the pan, leave to cool then chill in the refrigerator until required.

Preheat the oven to 200°C/400°F/Gas Mark 6. In a small bowl, combine the pecans and herbs with a little salt and pepper. Place the Brie or Camembert in an ovenproof serving dish. Brush the egg over the top of the cheese, then coat evenly with the nut mixture. Bake in the oven for 8–10 minutes, or until liquefying in the centre but not collapsing. Serve hot with plain crackers and the cold cranberry chutney.

**For the chutney:**

250 g/9 oz/2½ cups cranberries

6 ready-to-eat dried apricots, coarsely chopped

3 tbsp dark brown sugar

100 ml/3½ fl oz/generous ⅓ cup white wine, vermouth or dessert wine

pinch of salt


2 tbsp crushed pecans

1 tbsp chopped fresh parsley

2 tsp chopped fresh oregano or 1 tsp dried

sea salt and freshly ground black pepper

1 x 200–300 g/7–10½ oz Brie or Camembert

1 egg, beaten

plain crackers, to serve

**Serves 4–6**

Here's an immensely satisfying soup with a silky texture from the home of wild rice, where much steaming, hearty sustenance is needed to survive the harsh Canadian winters. The comforting earthy flavour of the rice really shines through, especially if you use water rather than vegetable stock, which makes it that much simpler to cook. (See notes on wild rice (page 12), and the origin of Chowder (page 19).)

# Wild Rice Chowder Manitoba, Canada

Wash the rice in a sieve (strainer) under cold running water. Place in a saucepan with the water, some salt and the bay leaves, cover and bring to the boil. Keep covered and leave to simmer for 50 minutes, or until the rice is tender and slightly fluffed. Do not drain.

Meanwhile, heat a large saucepan over a medium heat and add the oil. Add the onion and cook until translucent, then add mushrooms, celery and peppers and a little salt. Cook until soft.

Stir the flour into the vegetables and cook, stirring, for 3 minutes. Pour in the rice and its cooking water and keep stirring while it thickens. Add the milk and cream and heat until boiling. Now judge the consistency: add water if you feel it is too thick, and reheat. Taste for seasoning, adding a good grinding of pepper, and serve hot. It will thicken as it stands.

190 g/7¾ oz/1 cup wild rice
1 litre/1¾ pints/4 cups water
Salt
2 bay leaves
2 tbsp olive oil
1 large onion, chopped
2–3 flat field (portabello) or other
  flavourful mushrooms,
  about 200 g/7 oz, chopped
2 celery sticks (stalks), chopped
1 green (bell) pepper, finely chopped
1 red (bell) pepper, finely chopped
Sea salt and freshly ground
  black pepper
4 tbsp plain (all-purpose) flour
375 ml/13 fl oz/1½ cups milk
125 ml/4 fl oz/½ cup cream

**Serves 4–6**

Mushroom "burgers" can be found on restaurant menus all over Canada. These are not burger imitations, but rather a celebration of the juicy field (portabello) mushroom in its own right. They're a sweet, garlicky filling enhanced by a host of posh trimmings stacked between sesame buns, making a truly gourmet sandwich. What a great idea! Maple syrup provides a uniquely Canadian touch, and a creamy slab of Oka cheese completes the picture. The village of Oka is about a half hour's drive west of Montreal, where Trappist monks from Brittany in France settled in the late 1800s and started making this mild, semi-soft cheese, a close relative of Port Salut. To this day, Father Jerome sells the cheese in the monastery after Gregorian mass on Sundays, alongside iconic paraphernalia.

# Maple-roasted Mushroom Burgers Canada

Preheat the oven to 200°C/400°F/Gas Mark 6.

Wipe the mushrooms with a clean, damp kitchen paper (paper towels). Cut out the stem. Mix the olive oil and garlic together in a cup. Brush some oil over the mushroom caps. Lay the mushrooms gill-side up on a baking sheet. Score the mushrooms by making a grid pattern with the tip of a sharp knife, taking care not to cut all the way through the cap.

Drizzle maple syrup and vinegar over the gills, then sprinkle with thyme, salt and pepper. Lay the oily garlic slices over the surface and finish by drizzling with the remaining oil. Roast in the oven for 15–20 minutes, or until soft, juicy and sizzling. Serve hot with the trimmings of your choice.

4 large flat field or portabello mushrooms
4 tbsp extra virgin olive oil
4 garlic cloves, sliced
2 tbsp pure maple syrup
2 tsp cider vinegar
Large pinch of dried thyme
Salt and freshly ground black pepper

**For the trimmings:**
4 best-quality round bread rolls or buns, split and warmed or toasted
Sliced creamy cheese such as Port Salut or Oka

Thick slices of ripe tomatoes

Ripe avocado slices

Thinly sliced red onion

Alfalfa sprouts

Condiments such as good quality mayonnaise, chilli (chili) sauce, ketchup

**Serves 4**

I came across this "old-time breakfast speciality" in the *Laura Secord Canadian Cook Book*, published in 1966. I can't imagine anything more simple, or more Canadian. Rather alarmingly, the original recipe calls for a 4-cm/1½-inch depth of maple syrup in the pan! I suppose if you have the precious nectar on tap, you can afford to be so extravagant. In my reworking, I discovered that a small amount works absolutely fine. Just make sure that you choose a frying pan that is the right size to accommodate your eggs, or else you risk wasting some syrup.

Incidentally, Laura Secord was not a cookbook author, but a courageous Canadian heroine who, during the War of 1812, travelled 20 harrowing miles to warn a small British regiment of an American attack, and thus altered the course of history. On the centennial of her symbolic act, her name was chosen to become the corporate logo for a confectionery company, which then became hugely successful, and later produced the best-selling cookbook.

# Eggs Poached in Maple Syrup Quebec, Canada

Choose a frying pan with a lid, exactly large enough to accommodate the number of eggs you will be cooking. Pour a shallow puddle of maple syrup in the pan – enough to coat the surface. Place the pan over a medium heat and bring to boiling point, then reduce to a simmer. Crack the eggs, one at a time, into a saucer or teacup, then slide into the syrup. Season with salt and pepper to taste. Cover and cook until the eggs are done to your liking. Turn the eggs over in the syrup if you like them well done. Remove the poached eggs from the syrup and serve with hot buttered toast.

Any spare syrup can be cooled, strained and stored in the refrigerator for up to 3 days.

1–2 eggs per person
Pure maple syrup
Sea salt and freshly ground
    black pepper
Hot buttered toast, to serve

**Serves 1**

The word "chowder" is thought to derive from the French *chaudiére*, a cooking pot brought by early French settlers to Canada. It is most commonly associated with clams, but early settlers in America were making chowders out of whatever they had to hand in abundance, and corn was an important staple introduced by the Native Americans. Chowders are always thick and substantial, sometimes thickened with flour or ground maize (polenta), or in this case, potatoes. The cream cheese in this recipe imparts a wonderful richness with a slight acidity that complements the sweetness of the fresh corn, as well as enhancing the texture.

# Corn Chowder New England, USA

In a large bowl, stand each corn-on-the-cob upright and strip the kernels by cutting downwards with a sharp knife and set aside. Place the stripped cobs in a large saucepan and add the water, a generous sprinkle of salt and the bay leaves. Bring to the boil and simmer, covered, for 15 minutes. Discard the cobs and bay leaves.

Heat the oil in a separate saucepan. Add the onion and cook until translucent. Add the herbs and remaining vegetables and cook for about 5 minutes, or until softened. Add the cob stock and simmer until the potato is collapsing. Meanwhile, place the corn kernels in another saucepan and pour in enough cold water to barely cover. Bring to the boil and cook for 2 minutes. Do not drain; set aside.

Add the cream cheese and milk to the soup mixture, then purée until smooth, ideally with a hand-held blender. Stir in the corn kernels with their cooking liquid. Give the chowder one more whiz if desired, to break up corn kernels slightly. Reheat and adjust the seasoning with salt and pepper.

4 fresh corn-on-the-cobs
    (ears fresh corn)
500 ml/16 fl oz/2 cups water
Sea salt and freshly ground
    black pepper
2 bay leaves
2 tbsp olive oil
1 large onion, chopped
½ tsp dried sage, crushed
1 tsp fresh thyme leaves or ½ tsp
    dried thyme
1 medium carrot, chopped
2 celery sticks (stalks), chopped
1 large potato, peeled and chopped
200 g/7 oz/generous
    ¾ cup cream cheese
125 ml/4 fl oz/½ cup milk

**Serves 6**

These knockout beans are sweet, sweet, sweet! Beans and sugar are old friends – New Englanders learnt about cooking beans in maple syrup from the Native Americans. The Boston adaptation was to use molasses, which was gushing from the ports on the shipping routes from the Caribbean, during the days of slavery on the sugar plantations in the 17th and 18th centuries. It was part of what was known as triangular trade: sugar cane in the form of molasses was shipped to Boston to make rum, the rum was sent to West Africa to buy more slaves, who were in turn sent to the Caribbean to work in the sugar cane fields.

Long, slow cooking is the key here. It's worth tasting halfway through cooking to note the difference the length of time makes – eventually the beans become quite a different "animal" from how they started, as the rich, balmy aromas fill the house. It's crucial that you use a heavy-based, ovenproof dish that you are not too worried about staining.

# Boston Baked Beans New England, USA

*If using dried beans*, soak the beans in plenty of cold water overnight. Drain, place in a large saucepan, cover in plenty of fresh water and bring to the boil. Let them roll furiously for 10 minutes, then reduce the heat and simmer for 50 minutes, or until tender but not falling apart too much. Alternatively, follow the packet (package) instructions. Do not add salt. When they are tender, remove the saucepan from the heat but do not drain.

Preheat the oven to 150°C/300°F/Gas Mark 2. Place the beans in an ovenproof dish with a lid and pour in just enough of the hot cooking water to cover them. Stir in the molasses, mustard, tomato purée, onion, bay leaves, 2 tsp salt (or to taste) and a grinding of pepper.

*If using canned beans*, preheat the oven to 150°C/300°F/Gas Mark 2. Pour the beans with their liquid into an ovenproof dish with a lid. Check the ingredients of the beans – if they contain salt, you will probably not need to add more. Place over a medium heat (if the pan is suitable for cooking on the hob (stove) – otherwise use a saucepan, then transfer to your selected dish when ready to go in the oven). Add the molasses, mustard, tomato purée, onion, bay leaves and pepper. If the beans are unsalted add salt, then bring to the boil.

Place the dish in the oven and cook for 3 hours. Check the beans every hour. At some point, you will have to add more water, just enough to cover, to stop them drying out. Eventually they will be thick and caramelized, with a slightly burnt crust around the edges. This is good – it adds flavour. Once cooked, leave the beans to stand, covered, for at least 10 minutes, then serve with plain rice and fresh steamed vegetables.

400 g/14 oz/2¼ cups dried white beans such as cannellini or haricot or 3 x 400 g/14 oz cans, not drained

125 ml/4 fl oz/½ cup molasses or black treacle

2 tsp dry mustard

2 tbsp tomato purée (paste)

1 large onion, chopped

2 bay leaves

Sea salt and freshly ground black pepper

**Serves 4–6**

Here's another old classic from New England, the origin of which is a bit muddled. Beetroot red is Harvard's school colour, so that's good enough for me. It appeared in *Fannie Farmer's Cookbook* from her Boston Cooking School in 1896, so it goes back that far at least. I first tasted these at a Thanksgiving feast, when they are a traditional dish, but be warned – once on the plate, everything becomes psychedelic pink – they even dominate the cranberry sauce. I advise serving in separate bowls.

This delicious way with beetroot is almost more like a confection. I'll let you in on a secret. One night at home, we were enthusiastically tucking into some Harvard Beets, slurping the gorgeous sweet sauce with spoons. My friend Paul suggested vanilla ice cream. I'm telling you, it was a stroke of genius. Try the blinding fuchsia sauce over ice cream and you'll be astounded…

# Harvard Beets Boston, USA

If using fresh beetroot, bring a large saucepan of water to the boil. Scrub the beetroot but leave their roots and stem intact. Boil until tender throughout, then cool and rub off the skins, roots and stems.

In a lidded saucepan, combine the sugar, cornflour, cold water, vinegar and salt together. Bring to the boil and simmer for 5 minutes, or until thickened and clarified.

Slice the cooked beetroot and stir through the sweet-sour syrup. Cover and leave to stand for 30 minutes.

Just before serving, reheat the beetroot and stir in the butter. Once melted, it's ready to serve.

12 small or 6 large beetroot (beets), about 600 g/1 lb 5 oz

100 g/3½ oz/½ cup sugar

2 tsp cornflour (cornstarch)

60 ml/2¼ fl oz/¼ cup cold water

60 ml/2¼ fl oz/¼ cup white wine vinegar

Pinch of salt, or to taste

30 g/1 oz/2 tbsp butter

**Serves 4–6**

If you have never tried blue corn, you are in for a treat, not least for the excitement of the unfathomable colour and how it changes as you cook with it (see page 13). These true blue pancakes are a personal favourite, and my very own mother is a master of these. Whenever I'm visiting my home in Colorado Springs, she makes these for breakfast on the day I have to set off back to London, a farewell token of love, from the heart.

# Blue Corn Blueberry Pancakes

Colorado, USA

Preheat the oven to 110°C/225°F/Gas Mark ¼ for keeping warm. Choose your best non-stick frying pan and heat over a low to medium heat. Add the butter and leave to melt. Pour the melted butter into a bowl and leave to cool slightly while you prepare the pancake batter. Set aside your buttery pan – it is now properly greased and ready to use.

Mix the blue cornmeal, sugar, baking powder and salt together in a bowl. In a largish measuring jug or bowl, mix the milk, eggs and cooled butter together. Add the dry mixture and combine quickly to make a batter. A few lumps won't hurt – it's best not to over-mix the batter. Fold in the blueberries.

Heat the buttery frying pan over a medium heat. Pour in the batter in batches to make pancakes, no more than about 7.5 cm/3 inches in diameter. Distribute the blueberries sensibly through the batch, as they tend to sink to the bottom of the batter. When the top of each pancake is dryish and bubbly and the underside is golden, about 3 minutes, flip over and cook the other side. Keep the pancakes warm in the oven while you cook the remaining batches.

To make the maple butter syrup, heat the syrup and butter together in a small saucepan until the butter liquefies. Alternatively, use a microwave. Stir and pour over the stacks of warm pancakes.

**For the pancakes:**
50 g/2 oz/4 tbsp butter
225 g/2 cups blue cornmeal (see page 13)
2 tbsp caster (superfine) sugar
2 tsp baking powder
½ tsp sea salt
180 ml–250 ml/6½–8 fl oz/generous ¾–1 cup milk
2 eggs
220 g/7¾ oz/1½ cups blueberries

**For the maple butter syrup:**
80 ml/2¾ fl oz/⅓ cup maple syrup
30 g/1 oz/2 tbsp butter

**Serves 4**

The word always conjures up images of Sylvester the Cat and his spluttering exclamation, "thhhufferin' thhhuccotash!" What a marvellous word it is, too. Succotash is one of the oldest surviving vegetarian classics belonging to the Narragansett Indians of the New England region, long before the English arrived. Their name for this nutritious lima bean and sweetcorn combo, *msickquatash*, became "succotash" to the English settlers who couldn't pronounce it properly. It does roll off the tongue rather nicely.

Old recipes always come in infinite permutations. After sifting through dozens, I found this version in Elisabeth Rozin's book *Blue Corn and Chocolate*, and I think it's the best. As she says, the addition of Parmesan is unorthodox, but good!

# Succotash New England, USA

First boil the kettle. Place the beans in a saucepan and pour enough boiling water over them to cover. Bring to the boil, add salt and cook until just tender, about 3–5 minutes. Add the sweetcorn and bring to a simmer, then remove the pan from the heat and drain.

Meanwhile, place a large saucepan over a medium heat and add the butter. When the butter has melted, add the onion and cook until translucent. Add the tomato and cook until it just collapses, then add the drained beans and sweetcorn, plenty of freshly ground black pepper, lashings of freshly grated nutmeg and the cream. Bring to simmering point. Remove from the heat and serve, with Parmesan cheese grated over each serving.

275 g/10 oz/2 cups fresh or frozen lima beans or broad (fava) beans

Sea salt and freshly ground black pepper

250 g/9 oz/generous 2 cups fresh or frozen sweetcorn (corn)

1 tbsp butter

1 medium onion, finely chopped

1 large vine-ripened tomato, coarsely chopped

Whole nutmeg, for grating

4 tbsp single (light) cream

Freshly grated Parmesan cheese, to serve

**Serves 4–6**

Most Creole food is heavy on the pork, shrimp and catfish, heavy on the fat, and heavy on the portions, in New Orleans at least. I met a man who gained 9½ kg/21 lb in one week's vacation there! This Green Gumbo is the antidote. It's a Lenten recipe, served after the Mardi Gras parties, from Shrove (Fat) Tuesday until Easter. Strictly speaking, it should never contain meat or fish, but still contains the most important gumbo ingredient – okra. If you're not partial to the slimy quality of okra, there is a solution! In this process, inspired by the Culinary Institute of New Orleans, the okra is cooked separately with vinegar, which seems to minimize that quality.

The greens are, of course, the fundamental aspect of this gumbo. The folklore is that the more different types of greens you use, the more friends you will make throughout the year. Any green goes, including lettuce, chicory, cabbage; you name it. Most New Orleans cooks will make up a batch of gumbo large enough to feed an army, so many more types can go in. I've tailored this recipe for just 4 people, but multiply as you wish.

# Gumbo Z'Herbes
# Green Gumbo Louisiana, USA

Heat a large, heavy-based pan over a low heat. Add 3 tbsp oil and the flour. Cook, stirring frequently, until the roux turns deep golden, the colour of peanut butter, about 8–10 minutes. Add the onion, green pepper, celery, turnip and garlic and increase the heat. Stir vigorously and cook until the vegetables are tinged with gold, about 5 minutes. Add the greens with a little salt and cook until they are just wilted. Next, add the parsley and thyme, then gradually stir in the hot stock. Simmer for 20 minutes.

Meanwhile, heat the remaining 1 tbsp of oil in a frying pan over a medium heat and add the okra. Stir-fry until golden then remove from the heat. Add the vinegar – it will hiss and splutter. Add the contents of the pan to the gumbo, together with hot sauce and black pepper to taste. Serve in warmed bowls with grated cheese passed around at the table.

4 tbsp olive oil

3 tbsp plain (all-purpose) flour

1 large onion, chopped

2 spring onions (scallions), chopped

1 green (bell) pepper, chopped

2 celery sticks (stalks), chopped

1 turnip, about 150 g/5 oz, peeled and chopped

2 garlic cloves, chopped

400 g/14 oz/4–5 cups shredded or chopped mixed greens

Sea salt and freshly ground black pepper

6 fresh parsley sprigs, chopped

½ tsp dried thyme or 1–2 tsp fresh thyme leaves

1 litre/1¾ pints/4 cups vegetable stock, heated through

100 g/3½ oz/1 cup okra, sliced

1 tbsp white wine vinegar

Louisiana hot sauce such as Tabasco, to taste

Freshly grated Cheddar or Parmesan cheese, to taste (optional)

**Serves 4**

Stuffed chilli pepper casserole is the correct translation of this quintessentially New Mexican recipe. All over the Southwest, especially in farmers' markets in late summer, the smoky aroma of roasting Anaheim chillies wafts over the landscape. Oil drums fashioned as chilli roasters rotate over hot coals, and the charred chillies are sold still warm in plastic bags, which you can take home and peel yourself. Canned whole roasted chillies are also widely available and can certainly be used in place of fresh ones in this recipe. For those unable to find the chillies fresh or canned, the humble green capsicum (bell) pepper is a suitable substitute. A further simplification is to skip the stuffing mixture and just place rods of cheese inside the chillies, though you'll miss out on the oozing, spiked creaminess of the filling below.

# Chile Relleno Casserole
# Stuffed Pepper Casserole New Mexico, USA

Heat the grill (broiler) to its highest setting. Grill the chillies or peppers, turning until black and blistered all over. Remove to a plastic bag and leave to cool. When cool enough to handle, peel.

Preheat the oven to 180°C/350°F/Gas Mark 4. Beat the grated Gruyère cheese, cream cheese, oregano and cayenne together in a bowl. Make one cut along the grilled peppers and lay flat. Stuff generously with a dollop of the cheese mixture and roll up. Oil the casserole or gratin dish and lay the stuffed peppers on the bottom, ideally spaced apart if the dish allows. Beat the flour, milk and eggs with salt and pepper to taste together in another bowl until completely smooth. Pour over the peppers then top with the grated Cheddar cheese. Bake in the oven for 45 minutes, or until golden, bubbling and set throughout.

8 fresh Anaheim or Poblano chillies (chilies), or green capsicum (bell) peppers, stems removed and de-seeded

250 g/9 oz Gruyère, Jack or Havarti cheese, grated

200 g/7 oz/generous ¾ cup cream cheese, softened

1 tsp dried oregano, rubbed

Cayenne pepper to taste

Olive oil, for greasing

30 g/1 oz/scant ¼ cup plain (all-purpose) flour

250 ml/8 fl oz/1 cup milk

6 eggs

Sea salt and freshly ground black pepper

150 g/5 oz Cheddar cheese, grated

20 x 30 cm/8 x 12 in casserole or gratin dish

**Serves 6**

This dish is certainly rooted in Mexico, but it is has been adopted as an American classic, from the US/Mexico border all the way to Chicago. It's a bit like curry becoming the National dish of Britain – a British curry will be a far cry from a genuine Indian one, but tasty nonetheless. The red *"salsa rojo"* sauce is the crucial part of the dish. The "mild chilli powder" is a common mixture of mild ground red chillies with oregano, cumin, garlic and a little salt thrown in. Check the ingredients – what you find may be just chilli powder, in which case you might have to adjust the flavour. Traditionally the eggs are poached directly in the sauce, but logistically it's a little easier to cook them separately. The sauce should be a pungent blanket draped over the eggs, but you can lighten it with a little chopped tomato if you wish.

# Huevos Rancheros
# Ranch Eggs Southwestern USA

First, make the *salsa rojo*. Heat a saucepan over a medium heat and add the oil. Add the garlic and cook until fragrant, about 1 minute. Add the flour and chilli powder and cook until the colour changes. Gradually stir in the water. Add the fresh or canned tomatoes if you wish and salt to taste. Stir until thick. Remove the saucepan from the heat and set aside.

Preheat oven to 200°C/400°F/Gas Mark 4. Brush 2 baking trays (sheets) with oil. Spread the refried beans over the tortillas and place on the oiled baking trays. Distribute cheese over each tortilla. Bake until melted, about 10 minutes.

Meanwhile, cook the eggs. Heat a large frying pan over a medium–high heat and add the oil. Crack in the eggs, in batches if necessary, and season with salt and pepper to taste. Cook sunny-side up or over-easy, to your liking.

Place the melted tortillas on each serving plate, then top with the eggs. Smother with sauce and serve, with or without avocado and fried tomatoes.

2 tbsp sunflower oil, plus extra for greasing

8 heaped tbsp refried beans from a can

8 small corn tortillas (store-bought or home-made, see recipe on page 42), or 6–8 small flour tortillas or 4 large flour tortillas

150 g/5 oz mature (sharp) Cheddar cheese, grated

8 eggs

Sea salt and freshly ground black pepper

**For the *salsa rojo*:**

3 tbsp olive oil

2 garlic cloves, finely chopped

2 tbsp plain (all-purpose) flour

6 tbsp mild chilli (chili) powder

300 ml/10 fl oz/1¼ cups water

2 vine-ripened tomatoes, finely chopped, or ½ x 400 g/14 oz can chopped tomatoes (optional – see recipe introduction)

Sea salt

**To serve: (optional)**

Ripe avocado slices
Fried tomato halves

**Serves 4**

The fact is, hard and sour green tomatoes are not nearly as palatable as sweet and juicy red ones. But the green ones are the only "tool" for the job in this Southern classic – the firmness is perfect, and the tart edge is the ideal foil for the crunchy fried coating. They also make a delicious chutney.

# Fried Green Tomatoes Deep South, USA

Preheat the oven to warm. Slice the tomatoes about 1 cm/⅓ inch thick.

Sprinkle the flour over a plate and place the polenta in a bowl. Season the polenta with salt and pepper and work through with your fingertips. In a small bowl, beat the eggs.

Heat a shallow pool of oil in a large frying pan over a medium heat. Dredge each tomato slice first in the flour, shaking off excess, then in the beaten eggs, then in the polenta to coat evenly. Fry in batches, turning over with tongs, until golden and crisp on both sides. Drain on kitchen paper (paper towels). Keep warm while you cook the remaining batches. Serve hot.

4 large green tomatoes, about 475 g/1 lb
4 tbsp plain (all-purpose) flour
200 g/7 oz/1⅛ cups dry polenta (cornmeal)
Sea salt and freshly ground black pepper
2 eggs, beaten
Sunflower or vegetable oil for frying

**Serves 4**

Cornbread originates from the Native Americans. Its popularity has never ebbed – it is an absolute institution in the South, where dinner just wouldn't be dinner without cornbread. Its many cousins include pone, johnnycakes, hoecakes and spoonbread. This recipe is a blend of several, which delivers cornbread the way I like it – crisp on the outside and fluffy within, with a hint of sweetness.

# Cornbread Deep South, USA

Preheat the oven to 200°C/400°F/Gas Mark 6. Use the 2 tsp of soft butter to liberally grease a 20-cm/8-inch square or round baking tin (pan). Put the tin in the oven to heat up while you mix the batter together – this will help give the cornbread a crisp crust.

In a large bowl, stir the cornmeal, flour, sugar, baking powder and salt together until evenly combined. Add the eggs and gradually stir in the milk, then the melted butter to make a batter.

Remove the hot tin from the oven and quickly pour in the batter. Bake for 20–30 minutes, or until golden and firm to the touch. Serve hot or cold.

70 g/2¼ oz/⅓ cup melted butter, plus 2 tsp soft butter
215 g/7½ oz/1¼ cups cornmeal (polenta)
75 g/3 oz/½ cup plain (all-purpose) flour
1 tbsp sugar
2 tsp baking powder
1 tsp sea salt
3 eggs, beaten
250 ml/8 fl oz/1 cup milk

**Serves 4–6**

Summertime in Texas. The thick heat is suffocating and all life dwells constantly in refrigerated chambers of air conditioning, except the armadillos and the cicadas buzzing in the trees. Growing up, I spent just about every summer vacation in Texas with my relatives, and at every gathering, the adults sipped mint juleps and gimlets (gin with lime syrup), while I gulped fresh limeade through endless games of gin rummy. Usually there was cornbread, beef brisket, peach cobbler and pecan pie. And there was always "Bayne Salit". Bean Salad means summer. The original recipe came via my Aunt Nonie, and whether it was she or someone else who suggested adding water chestnuts, it's pure genius.

# Bean Salad Texas, USA

Soak the dried beans in plenty of cold water overnight. Boil them in fresh water and let them roll furiously for 10 minutes, then reduce the heat and simmer for 50 minutes, or until tender, but not falling apart too much. Alternatively, follow the packet instructions. Do taste each type of bean to make sure that they are all tender enough. Drain thoroughly.

Bring another small saucepan of water to the boil. Blanch the green beans for 2 minutes, drain and refresh under cold running water or in a bowl of iced water.

Meanwhile, prepare the marinade. Pound the garlic with the coarse salt in a mortar until smooth. Alternatively, use a garlic press. Whisk the garlic, vinegar, sugar and pepper together in a bowl then beat in the oil gradually to emulsify.

Empty the drained cooked beans into a wide, shallow dish and pour over the marinade while they are still hot. Leave to cool, then add the blanched green beans, water chestnuts, green pepper and red onion. Stir thoroughly. Cover and leave to chill in the refrigerator for at least 24 hours, but preferably longer, stirring now and then. The salad will keep for several days in the refrigerator.

**For the salad:**

500 g/1 lb 2 oz mixed dried beans

200 g/7 oz French (green) beans or runner (string) beans, cut into bite-sized pieces

2 x 225 g/8 oz cans water chestnuts, drained

1 green (bell) pepper, cut into bite-sized pieces

1 red onion, very finely sliced

**For the marinade:**

2 garlic cloves, crushed

2 tsp coarse sea salt

125 ml/4 fl oz/½ cup red wine vinegar

90 g/3¼ oz/⅓ cup caster (superfine) sugar

Lots of freshly ground black pepper

125 ml/4 fl oz/½ cup olive oil

**Serves 6–8**

Beans, cheese, chillies and tortillas are the cornerstones of Tex–Mex food. There are infinite configurations of these ingredients with extra additions, in the form of Americanized *burritos*, *tostadas*, *enchiladas* … Here they become a wickedly moreish, warming dip that was probably dreamed up by Texas home cooks who had lots of hungry cowboys to feed at parties. It first appeared in *Helen Corbitt's Cookbook* (1957), the Texas housewives' bible. My copy, given to me by my Texan mother, is dog-eared, sticky, crammed with post-it notes and bound with silver duct tape. Nearly half a century on, I still use it for entertaining ideas. Of Prairie Fire, Ms. Corbitt says, "I never saw a place where everyone likes a hot *hors d'oeuvre* as well as they do in Texas. They should be hot, and I mean hot!"

# Prairie Fire
# Hot Bean Dip Texas, USA

First boil the kettle for the bain-marie. Purée the beans, onion, garlic, jalapeños, vinegar and smoked paprika, if using, together in a food processor until smooth. Alternatively, mash the beans with a potato masher, chop the rest finely and combine.

Scoop into a heatproof bowl and set over a saucepan of simmering water. Mix in the cheese and stir until the cheese has melted. Garnish the surface with any of the optional garnishes. Keep warm on a hot plate or food warmer. Serve warm with tortilla chips for dipping.

2 x 400 g/14 oz cans borlotti
  or pinto beans, drained and rinsed
1 small onion, coarsely chopped
2 garlic cloves, halved and degermed
  if old
Pickled jalapeño peppers, to taste
1 tsp jalapeño vinegar from the jar
2 tsp smoked paprika (optional)
250 g/9 oz extra-mature (sharp)
  Cheddar cheese, grated
Tortilla chips, to serve

**To garnish (optional):**
2 tbsp sour cream, crème fraîche
  or yogurt, stirred
2 tbsp *salsa rojo* (see *Huevos
  Rancheros*, page 27) or hot salsa
2 tbsp sliced black olives
2 spring onions (scallions), sliced

**Serves 6–8**

*Burritos* or "little donkeys" found their way from "El Norte", the northern territory of Mexico, via Baja California, up into the vegetable-loving hands of the Californians. The California *burrito* is an institution, dating back to the 1950s, sold at just about every *Taqueria* or taco stall in the land. The further north you get, the more vegetarian the *burritos* become – in San Francisco it would not be unusual to find a salad-only *burrito*.

# Grilled Vegetable Burrito California, USA

Preheat the grill (broiler) or oven to 220°C/425°F/Gas Mark 7. Place the vegetables and tofu in a roasting tin (pan) and add the oil, vinegar, salt, and pepper and oregano. Toss well with your hands to coat everything evenly. Grill or roast for 30–40 minutes, stirring from time to time, until the vegetables are soft and golden. Remove from the oven and stir the beans through the mixture. Turn the oven to 110°C/225°F/Gas Mark ¼ and put the mixture back in to keep warm. Separate the tortillas, then wrap in foil and place in the oven to warm as well.

Meanwhile, make the *pico de gallo*. In a bowl, mix the tomatoes, onion, chillies, coriander, lime juice and salt together. Set aside until required.

To make the guacamole, cut the avocado(s) in half and remove the stone (pit). Scoop the flesh out with a spoon into a bowl. Add the lime juice. Using a fork or potato masher, mash until fairly smooth. Pound the garlic with the salt in a mortar, or use a galic press. Stir into the avocado along with the chilli powder and Tabasco and taste for seasoning. Set aside until required.

To assemble each *burrito*, lay out a warm tortilla and place a spoonful of vegetables and tofu towards the bottom. Top with a handful of lettuce and alfalfa sprouts. Fold the sides over, then roll up. If the tortillas are small, it may be easier to simply roll up without folding the sides. It may help to secure the burritos with a cocktail stick (toothpick).

Place on a serving plate and top with *pico de gallo*, guacamole and sour cream or Ranch Dressing.

**For the filling:**
2 medium courgettes (zucchini), cut into small chunks
1 red, 1 green (bell) pepper, cut into chunks
1 red onion, cut into wedges
200 g/7 oz fresh plain or smoked tofu, cut into cubes
2 tbsp olive oil
2 tsp red wine vinegar
Salt and freshly ground black pepper
1 tsp dried oregano
1 can pinto or borlotti beans, drained and rinsed

**For the *pico de gallo* (salsa):**
3 ripe vine-ripened tomatoes, finely chopped
1 small red onion, finely chopped
1–2 fresh red chillies (chilies), or to taste, de-seeded if large, finely chopped
Handful of fresh coriander (cilantro), finely chopped
1 tbsp lime juice
¼ tsp salt, or to taste

**For the guacamole:**
1 large or 2 medium ripe avocados
1 tsp lime juice
1 garlic clove
½ tsp coarse sea salt
1 tsp Mexican chilli (chili) powder
Tabasco sauce, to taste

**To serve:**
4 large or 8 medium flour tortillas or "wraps"
Shredded lettuce
Alfalfa sprouts
Sour cream or Ranch Dressing (see page 34)

**Serves 4–6**

Bottled Ranch dressing is the best-selling salad dressing in the USA. As with most things, home-made tastes much better. The story of the dressing is an all-American success story. "Hidden Valley Ranch" in California was a popular tourist spot and the chef who devised the dressing recipe was unable to meet the demands of the punters who went absolutely crazy over it and wanted to take jars of the stuff home with them. So, he made up a dry mix of seasoning, which could then be added to buttermilk and mayonnaise at home. He sent his customers away with sachets of the mix – much more portable and spoil-proof. He spotted an entrepreneurial opportunity and started manufacturing the mix as well as the bottled dressing. The tourism income at Hidden Valley Ranch was rapidly replaced by the dressing, which eventually took over the continent! Ranch dressing is delicious with everything, from a plain, crisp leaf salad to hot foods like pizza and *burritos* (see Grilled Vegetable Burrito on page 32).

# Ranch Dressing California, USA

Mash the garlic and salt to a paste in a mortar. Alternatively use a garlic press. Whisk the garlic paste, mayonnaise, buttermilk, parsley, chives, spring onions, vinegar and pepper to taste together in a medium-sized bowl.

Thin the dressing with a little water until it is a pouring consistency. Taste and add a pinch of salt if necessary. Use immediately or refrigerate, covered, for up to 3 days. Serve with crisp salad leaves.

2 garlic cloves, halved and degermed if old

½ tsp coarse sea salt

250 ml/8 fl oz/1 cup prepared or home-made mayonnaise

125 ml/4 fl oz/½ cup buttermilk or natural (plain) yogurt

2 tbsp finely chopped fresh flat-leaf parsley

2 tbsp finely chopped fresh chives

2 spring onions (scallions), thinly sliced

1 tbsp white wine vinegar

Pinch of salt

Freshly ground black pepper

Crisp salad leaves (greens), such as cos (romaine)

**Serves 6–8**

Orzo is tiny rice-shaped pasta, which has been embraced by Americans in recent times in both hot and cold pasta dishes – "pasta salad" is surely an American invention, which can be a class act when done with orzo. The best orzo comes from Greece, as does the feta, but this has strong Italian undertones too, reflecting the cultural collage of California. This perfect and clever little recipe, adapted from Marlena Spieler's book *The Flavour of California*, can be assembled lickety-split for a really scrumptious summer lunch or supper. Or, Marlena suggests an alternative: serve it as an elegant first course by hollowing out tomato halves, seasoning with salt and balsamic vinegar, stuffing with warm pesto orzo, then sprinkling with pine nuts, feta and basil.

# Pesto Orzo with Balsamic Tomatoes, Pine Nuts and Feta

California, USA

To cook the orzo, bring a saucepan of water to the boil and salt it well. Add the orzo and cook, stirring frequently as it's very fond of sticking to the base of the pan, until tender, about 6–8 minutes. Drain, retaining a little moisture, then return to the pan, add the pesto and stir through well. Cover and keep warm.

Meanwhile, toast the pine nuts by swirling them around in a small, hot frying pan until patched with gold.

Place the tomatoes in a bowl and toss with balsamic vinegar and salt and pepper to taste.

Divide the orzo between 4 serving plates. Add a pile of tomatoes to one side then sprinkle the feta and toasted pine nuts over. Finish by ripping basil leaves over the top.

250 g/9 oz/1 cup orzo
Sea salt and freshly ground black pepper
4 heaped tbsp pesto, or to taste
3 tbsp pine nuts
6 ripe but firm vine tomatoes, about 700 g/1 lb 5 oz, cubed
1–2 tsp top-quality balsamic vinegar, or to taste
125 g/4 oz feta cheese, crumbled or cubed
Handful of fresh basil leaves

**Serves 4**

# chapter two Latin America and The Caribbean

When the Old World merged with the New, it forged the greatest gastronomic revolution in history. Christopher Columbus may have been responsible for the pillage and butchery of whole cultures, and had the arrogance to claim to "discover" places that had been inhabited for millennia, but it is undeniable that without him, the tables of the world would be colourless. The culinary gifts from Latin America and the Caribbean – sweetcorn (corn), (bell) peppers and chillies (chilies), tomatoes, potatoes and chocolate to name but a few – were bestowed on the rest of the world as a direct result of Columbus' efforts with the backing of the Spanish empire. What would pizza be without tomatoes? Thai green curry without chillies? Irish *Colcannon* without potatoes? Life without chocolate?

The New World, in turn, absorbed ingredients from the Old with zeal, primarily wheat, meat and dairy products, which form an essential part of its cuisine today. Although there are few vegetarian traditions in the region, there has been deprivation, which has led to the elevation of the bean to god-like status, and some fantastic ingenuity with vegetables, fruits and grains.

"The culinary life we owe Columbus is a progressive dinner in which the whole human race takes part, but no one need leave home to sample all the courses."

Raymond Sokolov, *Why We Eat What We Eat*

# meet the expert:
# Sofia Craxton – Mexican Cuisine

Mexican-born Sofia Craxton is a chef, teacher, author and expert on the food of Latin America, living in London. Sofia admits, "Mexico is a meat-eating country – vegetarian is a bad word unless you are a hippie!" Though she points out that, before the Spanish arrived with animals in the late 1400s, Mexico had no dishes with beef, pork or lamb, and no dairy products. Of course, they all took off in a big way. "However, a diet of lots of vegetable dishes is common – our diet is based on beans and maize (corn) and rice. It is the imaginative ways of using these ingredients that define Mexican cuisine. Being a poor country, we rely a lot on meat alternatives, and a diet based on indigenous Mexican ingredients can have all the amino acids required for a protein-rich diet without meat."

It seems in modern Mexico there is actually an abundance of vegetarian foods. "Many of our most delicious stall foods are vegetarian," she says, "like *tamales* (see page 41) and *quesadillas* (fried tortillas filled with melting cheese). Also, there are more and more vegetarian places to eat in towns like Tepotzlan, Oaxaca and San Miguel de Allende, where people are quite alternative."

If one item could personify Mexican food, it would have to be the tortilla, without which a Mexican meal would not be complete. Proper tortillas (see page 42) are made with masa harina, a particular type of ground maize with an added alkali that gives it special nutritional properties (see page 39). Maize originated in Mexico. Sofia explains, "Maize is our staple grain – we make everything out of maize. It is nutritious, gluten-free, and it has the classic flavour of Mexican food. You can actually smell Mexico when you make tortillas, and Mexicans smell of maize!"

Maize combined with beans make a complete protein that is ideal for vegetarians. Mexico produces many types of beans, but the pinto bean reigns supreme. "Along with tortillas," says Sofia, "a meal is simply not complete without refried beans or *frijoles de la olla* (cooked in the pot) – there is always a pot of beans simmering away at the back of the hob (stove) in every Mexican household." Of course in modern times, busy people rely on canned, dehydrated or supermarket-ready beans.

Chillies (chilies), though they originated in Peru, are the defining flavour element of Mexico's cuisine, and there are hundreds of varieties, each with unique qualities. Mexicans appreciate their subtle nuances, and know their pasilla from their cascabel. "They can be very mild or scorchingly hot, and they are loved by all," says Sofia. "It makes no difference who you are – rich or poor or beautiful or ugly, everybody in Mexico loves chillies. Even some children's sweets and candies have chilli in them." I remember this very clearly from when my father took me to Mexico for the first time aged eight – I became addicted to a sweet tamarind candy dipped in chilli powder.

Of all the culinary gifts the Mexicans have given to the rest of the world, Sofia is proudest of one. "Tomatoes – need I say more?" The importance of the tomato in cuisine universally simply cannot be overstated. It changed the way the world eats. "Mexican tomatoes are especially delicious because of the climate where they grow. They are fleshy, juicy without being watery and you can feel the warmth of the earth when you taste them." These qualities are sadly lacking in the greenhouse-grown bullets that are so often found on Western supermarket shelves, but where there is demand, supply will follow...

seeds and membranes. A general rule of thumb is that the smaller the chilli, the hotter it is, though this does not apply to the hottest chilli of all, the habanero, which is lantern-shaped and roughly the size of a walnut or larger. These are called many names including "Madame Janette" in parts of the Caribbean. Scotch Bonnets are almost identical, and yes, they are searingly hot, but they also have a wonderful fruity character. Chillies are anti-bacterial and the hot experience of eating chillies causes the brain to release endorphines, so you get a natural high when eating them! If you find the sensation uncomfortable, drinking water won't do a thing – capsaicin is inhibited by sugar, so drink juice, alcohol, milk or yogurt. ALWAYS wear gloves when handling chillies. I store chillies in the freezer, so I always have some to hand – just run under hot running water to thaw instantaneously.

**Habanero Chillies**

Chillies (chilies) – Ancient Peruvians were probably the first to cultivate chillies and sent them north to Mexico. The chilli pepper was mistakenly called "pepper" by Columbus who likened it to black pepper. There are dozens of varieties of chilli, each with its own unique character, not just heat. The heat in chillies comes from the chemical capsaicin, concentrated in the

**Plantain**

Plantain – A type of banana, which is used as a starchy vegetable and is not suitable for eating raw. Plantains are most popular throughout Latin America and the Caribbean, as well as Africa and Asia. They can be used at every stage of ripeness – when the skin is quite black all over, they become quite sweet, but even then they are still cooked – boiled and served like potatoes, mashed, lightly sautéed or fried crisp – like potatoes, they take very well to frying (see *Tostones* on page 50). They can also be served as a sweet; in Southeast Asia, ripe plantains are poached in coconut milk with sugar and a pandanus leaf (see page 249). The skin is also used in cooking.

Ackees – The fruit of a tree introduced by Captain Bligh to Jamaica, which seems to be the only place in the world where they have been absorbed into the daily cuisine, usually as part of the favourite Jamaican dish ackee and salt fish. Not all parts of the fruit are edible and they are quite poisonous when under-ripe, so most often they are found ready-prepared in cans. They have a surprising appearance – bright yellow and fluffy like scrambled eggs. Ackees have a wonderful creamy texture, literally melt-in-the-mouth, and a

nutty flavour, and though they are a fruit, their flavour lends itself best to savoury dishes (see Ackee Soufflé on page 47).

Maize (corn, sweetcorn) – There is some controversy over where maize originated, but the generally accepted view is that it is native to Latin America and reached the rest of the world after Columbus brought it back. Cultures throughout the world rely on it as a staple, though its protein content is considerably less than wheat or rice. Ancient Mayan and Aztec civilizations, perhaps unwittingly, had a remarkable remedy for this flaw: they added alkaline ashes to soften the corn, and this process, called nixtamalization, unlocks proteins, making the maize a super food. This might have contributed to the advancement of these superior civilizations. Masa harina is the name for a special flour for making tortillas – ground corn with added calcium hydroxide, which has the same nutrition-boosting effect and creates a unique flavour. As soon as corn is picked from the plant, the sugars in the kernels start to convert to starch, so fresher corn will always be sweeter. When buying fresh corn, try to get it with the husk on as it maintains freshness. Frozen corn is the next best thing as it's frozen soon after harvesting. Canned corn is a last resort.

Palm hearts (hearts of palm) – These are the core of the coconut palm tree which are a great delicacy in Latin America and Asia especially, usually sold in cans. Their texture is rich and they are a fantastic addition to salads (see *Insalata Tropical con Palmitos* on page 57) as well as cooked (see *Palmito Revuelto con Huevos* on page 54). Fresh, raw hearts can be large, faintly pink, and quite crunchy with a delicate floral flavour. Unfortunately, an entire tree has to die to extract the heart, which makes them rather controversial as they are subject to poaching.

Cassava (*manioc, yuca*) – An important root vegetable in Africa and Latin America, cassava is prolific and easily cultivated as it grows fast and resists pests. It is a good, cheap source of energy, but, nutritionally, little else as it is almost pure carbohydrate. Its extreme starchiness does make

**Ackee**

for good eating though – it's delicious deep-fried like potatoes, though it can be cooked in every way imaginable, savoury or sweet (see *Enyucado* on page 59). It is also processed into meal and flour and is most familiar to Westerners in the form of tapioca; it is also used commercially as a laundry starch. Frozen cassava is convenient to use. Some cassava is toxic and must be cooked before consumption.

**Cassava**

Mexicans like to make many foods "drunken", including eggs, meat and seafood, using either beer or tequila. These classic, soupy beans are really not that intoxicating as most of the alcohol evaporates in the cooking. These beans are satisfying in themselves, but can be served with warm corn tortillas (see page 42) or, better yet, with *quesadillas*: sprinkle grated Cheddar cheese and perhaps a few chopped spring onions over tortillas and bake in an oven preheated to 200°C/400°F/Gas Mark 6 until melted and crisp.

# Frijoles Borrachos
# Drunken Beans Mexico

Heat a large saucepan over a medium heat and add the oil. Add the onions and fry until soft and translucent. Add the garlic and chillies and fry until fragrant, then add the tomatoes. Drain one can of beans and add to the pan, then add the other can with their liquid. Add the cumin, vinegar or lime juice, 200 ml/7 fl oz/scant 1 cup lager and salt and pepper to taste. Bring to the boil, then reduce to a simmer and cook for about 30–40 minutes, or until thickened but still a soupy consistency. Taste for seasoning.

Add the remaining 200 ml/7 fl oz/scant 1 cup lager and the coriander. Return to the boil and serve in bowls with a dollop of sour cream. Continue simmering if you prefer it thicker.

2 tbsp olive oil

2 large onions, finely chopped

3 plump garlic cloves, finely chopped

2 fresh red and 2 fresh green chillies (chilies), de-seeded if large, finely chopped, or to taste

2 large tomatoes, about 250 g/9 oz, chopped

2 x 400 g/14 oz cans pinto or borlotti beans

2 tsp ground cumin

1–2 tbsp jalapeño vinegar from the jar or lime juice, to taste

400 ml/14 fl oz/1¾ cups lager

Salt and freshly ground black pepper

Generous handful of fresh coriander (cilantro), chopped

Sour cream, crème fraîche or thick yogurt, to serve

**Serves 4**

*Tamales* could be called the quintessence of Mexican food. They have been around since time immemorial, a staple food of the Aztecs long before the Spanish invaded. In modern Mexico they remain an important part of the diet, enjoyed particularly at festival times, with much ritual surrounding their preparation. Made from the same masa dough as tortillas (see page 42), there are innumerable different fillings throughout Mexico – from pumpkin to pineapple to peanuts. Here is a very basic cheese-stuffed *tamale*. Use your imagination with the stuffing – add oregano, chopped chilli, beans or vegetables. Just remember that the buttery *masa* should not be a vehicle for the filling, rather the filling should be there to enhance the dough. An alternative dough can be made with ordinary polenta (cornmeal), or simply with sweetcorn (corn). See *Humitas Chilenas* on page 63.

# Tamales
# Steamed Cornmeal Parcels Mexico

If using dried corn husks, soak them for several minutes in boiling water. If using banana leaves or baking paper (parchment), cut them into 16 x 6 cm/2½ inch wide and 20 cm/8 inch long strips.

Beat the butter in a food processor until light and fluffy. Beat in the masa harina, salt and baking powder. Gradually add the vegetable stock until you have a soft, pliable dough. Divide the dough into 8 pieces. (For *Humitas Chilenas*, use dampened hands to form *tamale*-shaped lumps of corn purée without the cheese.)

Mould each piece of dough around each rod of cheese, enclosing it completely.

*If using corn husks*, place the dough in the middle of the husk and wrap it up, using an extra piece if necessary to cover. Tear strips of husk and use to tie up the ends of the parcel (package).

*If using banana leaves or baking paper*, place the *tamale* at the bottom of a strip and roll up, then wrap the other strip around the ends, and stick a cocktail stick (toothpick) through the *tamale* to secure in place.

Place the *tamales* in a steamer set over a saucepan of simmering water. Steam for about 1 hour, or until the dough is no longer sticking to the wrapper – check after about 45 minutes. Serve hot with refried beans, rice and salsa. Allow each diner to unwrap his or her own *tamales*, and provide a plate for discarded wrappers.

Fresh or dried corn husks, or fresh banana leaves, or baking paper (parchment)
100 g/3½ oz/7 tbsp butter
175 g/6 oz/1½ cups masa harina (see page 39) or fine polenta (cornmeal)
Pinch of salt
1 tsp baking powder
125 ml/4 fl oz/½ cup vegetable stock
175 g/6 oz Cheshire, Wensleydale or Jack cheese, cut into 8 x 6 cm/ 2½ inch rods

**To serve:**
Refried beans
Freshly cooked rice
Hot salsa

**Makes 8, serves 4**

These are an essential accompaniment to every Mexican meal, as well as an ingredient in *Sopa de Tortilla* (see page 44), *Huevos Rancheros* (see page 27) and many other dishes, such as *tacos* and *enchiladas*. Even a complete novice can make them easily with the help of a little clingfilm (plastic wrap). The essential ingredient is masa harina, which is ground maize with added calcium hydroxide, or lime, a chalk-like mineral. These flat breads are not to be confused with the *Tortilla de Patatas* of Spain (page 112).

# Corn Tortillas Mexico

Place the masa harina and salt in a bowl and stir in the water. Cover the bowl with clingfilm (plastic wrap) and leave to rest for 15 minutes.

Using your hands, pull the mixture together then knead briefly to form a soft dough. It should feel like clay, but not sticky, crumbly or dry (add more water if this is so.) Divide the dough into 10–12 pieces and roll into balls.

Heat a dry non-stick or cast-iron frying pan over a high heat.

Form the dough into 10 cm/4 inch circles: either pat between your palms, or, my preferred method: roll out between 2 pieces of clingfilm. They may not look perfect but they will taste great!

Place one at a time gently in the hot frying pan, as you roll them. When dry and sliding around when you shake the pan, about 1–2 minutes, turn over with a pair of tongs. Remove from the pan when puffed. Serve immediately, or wrap in cling film and eat on the same day, or freeze.

250 g/9 oz/1⅞ cups masa harina
Pinch of salt
About 330 ml/11⅔ fl oz/1⅓ cups
   warm water

**Makes 10–12**

Every culture has its hand-held, protein and stodge-filled pastry parcel (package). This is Mexico's, not to be confused with the Spanish *empanada*, which is a flat pie cut into wedges (similar confusion happens with tortillas, see *Tortilla de Patatas*, page 112). In Cornwall, they might fill these with cheese, potato and onions. In Mexico, they do it with black beans, cheese and chillies.

# Empanadas con Frijoles Negros
# Black Bean Pasties Mexico

To make the dough in the food processor, place the flour and salt in the bowl and pulse a few times to aerate. Add the butter and process until slightly crumbly. Gradually pour in the warm water until the dough draws together. Turn out on to a clean surface and knead a few times, then wrap in clingfilm (plastic wrap) and leave to rest at room temperature for 30 minutes. To make by hand, sift the flour and salt into a large bowl. Add the butter and rub it in with your fingertips until crumbly. Stir in the water to form a dough then knead and rest as above.

Preheat the oven to 180°C/350°F/Gas Mark 4. To make the filling in the food processor, process the black beans, chipotle, water, oregano, vinegar, honey and salt until fairly smooth, leaving a little texture. Add the cheese and pulse until combined. Alternatively, mash everything together thoroughly in a bowl. Taste for seasoning, adding a little more chilli, vinegar, honey or salt as you see fit.

Line a baking sheet with non-stick paper. Divide the dough into 6 pieces. Roll into balls, then roll into flat circles about 12 cm/4½ inches in diameter. Place a rounded tablespoon of the filling in the middle of each circle. Don't be tempted to overfill them or they might burst in the oven. Pull the top and bottom edges up around the filling, then seal by pressing the edges together, forming a wavy crescent-shaped edge. Place on the baking sheet, brush with beaten egg, and bake for 20–25 minutes, or until golden all over. Eat warm.

**For the dough:**
175 g/6 oz/1⅓ cups plain
  (all-purpose) flour
½ tsp salt
30 g/1 oz/1 tbsp butter
90 ml/3 fl oz/⅓ cup warm water

**For the filling:**
150 g/5 oz/¾ cup cooked
  black beans
1 dried chipotle chilli (chili),
  reconstituted in hot water for
  20 minutes, or 2 tsp chipotles
  in adobo
2 tbsp water
½ tsp dried oregano
1 tsp white or red wine vinegar
1 tsp honey
Pinch of salt
70 g/2¼ oz pizza mozzarella (see note
  on page 7), chopped
1 egg, beaten, for brushing

**Makes 6**

This is one of the quickest and easiest soups south of the border. The only tricky bit might be finding fresh corn tortillas, as flour tortillas become too doughy in this recipe – it's the flavour and grainy texture of the masa harina (see page 39) in the corn tortilla that makes this soup unique. They are extremely simple to make, however, if you can find the proper masa flour (see page 39).

Alas, there IS a simple substitute! Plain, salted corn tortilla chips for dipping (not "chilli" or "ranch" or any other flavour), which are available just about everywhere now. These are very salty, so use a well-flavoured but virtually salt-free stock.

# Sopa de Tortilla
# Tortilla Soup Mexico

In a blender or food processor, purée the tomatoes, onion and garlic until smooth, adding a small amount of vegetable stock if necessary to get the blades moving. Heat a large saucepan over a medium heat and add the oil. Pour in the tomato mixture and cook, stirring frequently, for about 5 minutes, until slightly thickened.

Add the vegetable stock and oregano to the pan, cover and bring to the boil. Taste for seasoning and add a little salt if needed (this will all depend on how salty your stock is to begin with). Reduce the heat and simmer for 5 minutes.

To prepare the garnish, slice the chilli, if using, into little rings, shaking out the seeds as you go. Discard the seeds. Heat a small frying pan over a medium heat and add the oil. Add the dried chilli and fry very briefly until puffed and crisp. Drain on kitchen paper (paper towels).

To assemble each bowl, line the bottom of each with tortilla wedges then top with cubes of cheese. Ladle over the tomato stock and top with diced avocado and fried chillies, if you like.

3 ripe vine-ripened tomatoes, about 350 g/12 oz, quartered

1 small onion, coarsely chopped

2 garlic cloves, coarsely chopped

1 tbsp vegetable oil

1 litre/1¾ cups/4 cups vegetable stock

1 tsp dried or fresh oregano

Sea salt

4 corn tortillas (see page 42), cut into wedges, or corn tortilla chips (see introduction)

250 g/9 oz mature (sharp) Cheddar or Jack cheese, cut into 5 mm/¼ inch cubes

**To garnish:**

1 large dried chilli (chili), such as chipotle or ancho (optional)

1 tbsp vegetable oil

1 ripe Hass avocado, stoned (pitted), peeled and diced

**Serves 4**

Here's my version of this exotic Mayan recipe from Pre-Columbian Mexico. The original recipe demands the painstaking operation of extracting the pumpkin seed oil first, to use as a garnish later. Having tried it, I assure you it would drive most home cooks to tears. Many hundreds of pumpkin seeds were sacrificed in the perfecting of this recipe, which captures the exotic flair of the original. This is surely a modern classic for the twenty-first century, packed with flavour, nutrition and plenty of "wow" factor. And it's a fast one, if you use store-bought tortillas and salsa.

# Papadzules Tortillas with Pumpkin Seed Paste Yucatan, Mexico

Preheat the oven to 110°C/225°F/Gas Mark ¼ to warm the tortillas. Wrap them in foil and leave in the oven. Place 4 plates in the oven as well.

To make the paste, first place the pumpkin seeds in a large frying pan and toast over a medium–high heat, shaking frequently while they pop and crackle, until golden and puffed. Transfer to a tray or flat dish and leave to cool completely.

Place the seeds in a blender with the chillies, garlic, spring onions, cumin, lime juice, salt, pepper, coriander and half the water. Start the motor and gradually pour in the rest of the water, stopping when a smooth thick paste forms.

Scoop the paste into a heatproof bowl and set it over a saucepan of simmering water. Warm the paste through, stirring frequently, but do not over-heat as it will go lumpy.

To assemble the *papadzules*, take a warm tortilla, spoon some paste in the middle, then sprinkle with a little mashed egg. Roll up the tortilla and place seam-side down on a warmed plate or serving dish. Repeat with all the tortillas, reserving some egg to sprinkle over the top. Spoon some salsa over the tortillas and finish with mashed egg.

8 small tortillas, or 4 large, ideally real corn tortillas made with masa harina (see page 42)

6 eggs, hard-boiled (hard-cooked), shelled and mashed

Hot tomato salsa, to serve, either store-bought or home-made (see *pico de gallo* on page 32)

**For the paste:**

200 g/7 oz/1⅓ cups hulled pumpkin seeds

1–2 fresh green chillies (chilies) or to taste, de-seeded if large, coarsely chopped

2 garlic cloves, coarsely chopped

3 spring onions (scallions), sliced

1 tsp ground cumin

2 tbsp fresh lime juice

½ tsp sea salt, or to taste

Freshly ground black pepper

Large handful of fresh coriander (cilantro), stems and leaves coarsely chopped

About 300 ml/10 fl oz/1¼ cups water

**Serves 4**

What's an ackee, I hear you say? It's the national fruit of Jamaica, but has made its way around the world in cans (see page 38), and will be easy to find in any African or Caribbean grocery store. I was dubious about the sound of this recipe when I first came across it in two separate Caribbean cookbooks, but my curiosity was aroused, as ackees are almost always paired with salt fish. I was so surprised! This soufflé is a revelation – easy to make and sumptuous, yet light.

# Ackee Soufflé Jamaica

Separate the eggs and place the yolks in a large, non-metallic bowl, and the whites in another large bowl.

In a wide frying pan, melt the butter over a low–medium heat. Add the flour and stir for a couple of minutes until bubbling. Then add the warm milk a little at a time, stirring constantly until you have a thick roux or sauce. Add the salt and Maggi seasoning or soy sauce. Remove the pan from the heat and cool briefly, then stir into the egg yolks. Stir in the ackees gently, then leave to cool.

Preheat the oven to 180°C/350°F/Gas Mark 4. Generously grease a medium casserole or soufflé dish with butter.

Beat the egg whites until stiff then gently fold into the ackee mixture, keeping it light. Scoop into the prepared dish and bake on the middle shelf of the oven for about 30 minutes, or until golden and puffed. Do not be tempted to open the oven during cooking or you risk the soufflé collapsing. Eat immediately.

4 organic eggs
40 g/1½ oz/3 tbsp butter, plus extra for greasing
3 tbsp plain (all-purpose) flour
250 ml/8 fl oz/1 cup milk, warmed in the microwave or gently in a saucepan
½ tsp salt
½ tsp Maggi seasoning or dark soy sauce
1 x 540 g/1 lb 4 oz can ackees, drained

**Serves 4**

"*Ital*" is a Rastafarian concept, which means the essence of things in their natural state. *Ital* foods are super-healthy and free from animal products, unrefined and generally contain no salt. They rely on natural flavours, chilli in particular, to provide enough excitement for the sense of taste, along with a sense of well-being. Wholegrain rice and no salt is correct for this dish, but you can use any rice and salt, though then it wouldn't be strictly *Ital*. If you are able to find short-grain brown rice, this is best, as it makes a wonderfully creamy "Rasta Risotto". Serve on its own or with a bean dish such as *Caraotas Negras* (see page 54).

# Ital Rice Coconut Okra Rice Jamaica

Choose a large, heavy-based saucepan with a lid. Heat it over a medium heat and add the oil. Add the onion and fry until translucent. Add the garlic and rice and cook until the garlic is fragrant, about 1 minute. Add the okra, red pepper, chilli, coconut cream and water. Stir, cover and bring to the boil. Simmer, covered, until all the liquid is absorbed and the rice is tender. Stir the spinach in at the end and continue cooking until it wilts, about 2 minutes. Serve immediately in warmed bowls.

1 tbsp sunflower oil

1 medium onion, halved and sliced

2 garlic cloves, chopped

200 g/7 oz/1 cup wholegrain rice, washed and drained

50 g/2 oz okra, stem removed, sliced

1 red (bell) pepper, chopped

½ fresh habanero chilli (chili) or other chilli to taste, chopped (wear gloves!)

100 ml/3½ fl oz/generous ⅓ cup coconut cream

750 ml/1¼ pints/3 cups water

100 g/3½ oz/generous 2 cups fresh spinach, washed and chopped

**Serves 4**

The name, meaning "Moors and Christians" describes the black and white aspects of this dish, symbolic of the suppression of blacks by whites, both in Spain in Columbus's time, and throughout the Caribbean. Though many versions exist throughout the region, Cuba has embraced this dish with particular enthusiasm, and it is considered "typical Cuban food". It rarely has any meat added, and the classic accompaniments are fried plantains and eggs. It makes a perfect partner for *Colombo au Giraumon* (see page 53).

# Moros y Cristianos
# Black Beans and Rice Cuba

Heat a large saucepan with a lid over a medium heat and add the oil. Add the onion and green pepper and cook until the onion is translucent.

Add the garlic and tomatoes, together with salt and pepper to taste. Cook for a few minutes, until the tomato collapses and thickens. Add the cooked black beans and raw rice. Stir until mixed, then pour in the water and stir. Bring to the boil, cover the saucepan, reduce the heat to a simmer and cook until all the water is absorbed, about 10–25 minutes, depending on the type of rice used. Fluff with a fork and serve.

2 tbsp olive oil

1 medium onion, chopped

1 green (bell) pepper, chopped

1 large garlic clove, chopped

2 medium tomatoes, chopped

Sea salt and freshly ground black pepper

200 g/7 oz/1 cup cooked black beans

175 g/6 oz/scant 1 cup raw long-grain rice, rinsed under cold running water

425 ml/14¾ fl oz/1¾ cups water

**Serves 4–6**

On a recent trip to the minute and stunning island of Curaçao in the Dutch Antilles, I discovered this habanero relish (see Chillies on page 38). Jars of it were sitting on every table in a local workers' café, ready to spoon over rice and beans and plantains and whatever else you might be eating. It's one of the best showcases I know for the complex floral flavour of the magnificent habanero. Any chilli sauce seems to be called *Madame Janette* in Curaçao, which is also their name for the chilli itself.

In Curaçao they prefer their plantains soft, ripe and sweet, unlike these crispy little *Tostones* from the opposite side of the Caribbean. However, they are perfect with the relish. This combo is a killer snack or appetizer and, I warn you, once you get started, it's hard to stop.

# Tostones con Madame Janette
# Fried Plantains with Habanero Relish Puerto Rico/Curaçao

To make the *Madame Janette*, place the vinegar, sugar, salt, carrot, onion and chilli in a screw-top jar, cover and shake well. Alternatively, whisk in a bowl until the sugar dissolves. The flavour improves and intensifies with time. Store in the refrigerator for up to a week.

To make the *Tostones*, peel the plantain, using a small knife to cut the peel off if necessary. Cut into 1 cm/½ inch pieces. Soak in a bowl of salted water for about 30 minutes. This step is not essential but it will produce crisper *tostones*.

Heat a shallow pool of oil in a large frying pan over a low–medium heat. Add the plantain pieces and fry on both sides, turning with tongs, until tender but not brown, about 2–3 minutes each side. Drain on kitchen paper (paper towels) and cool slightly. While still warm, place them on a chopping board with some space in between. Stretch a piece of clingfilm (plastic wrap) over them. Using a mallet or the back of a large spoon, gently flatten the pieces to about half as thick. The edges will fluff out slightly – this is fine.

Reheat the oil, this time slightly hotter – over a medium heat. Add the flattened plantains and fry until crisp and golden on both sides. Drain on kitchen paper and serve warm with the *Madame Janette*.

**For the *Madame Janette*:**

100 ml/3½ fl oz/generous ⅓ cup white vinegar (rice or malt)

1 tbsp caster (superfine) sugar

½ tsp sea salt

5-cm/2-inch piece carrot, peeled and finely chopped

½ small onion, finely chopped

1 Madame Janette/habanero/Scotch Bonnet chilli (chili) (see page 38), de-seeded and finely chopped (wear gloves!)

**For the *tostones*:**

2 large green plantains, just beginning to ripen but not yet yellow

Sea salt

Sunflower or vegetable oil for frying

**Serves 4**

If you know your aubergines, you'll know how they love to absorb flavours and fats like a sponge. In this comfortingly low-labour recipe, the sweet and − let's face it − quite fatty coconut milk has a wonderful effect on the texture of the aubergines. This is a rich dish, which loves the company of plain rice, *Moros y Cristianos* (see page 49), a baked potato or even better, a baked sweet potato.

# Berehein na Forno Roasted Coconut Aubergines (Eggplants)

St. Maarten

Preheat the oven to 180°C/350°F/Gas Mark 4. Arrange a layer of aubergines in the base of a large casserole or gratin dish, measuring about 20 cm x 30 cm/8 x 12 inches. Scatter over some chopped onion then season with salt and pepper to taste and add some chilli. Make 2 or 3 layers, then pour the coconut milk over.

Cover tightly with foil and bake in the oven for 45 minutes–1 hour, or until the aubergines are meltingly soft. Uncover and cook for a further 10–15 minutes until the liquid is slightly reduced and the aubergines are light golden. Serve hot or warm.

1 large or 2 medium aubergines (eggplants), about 500 g/1 lb 2 oz, sliced into 5-mm/¼-inch thick circles

1 large onion, finely chopped

Salt and freshly ground black pepper

1 large fresh red chilli (chili), de-seeded and finely chopped, or 1 tsp hot dried chilli (red pepper) flakes

1 x 400 g/14 oz can coconut milk

**Serves 4**

*Colombo* is a loose term for a Caribbean-style curry, originating from the name of the Sri Lankan capital, introduced to the islands below by migrant Hindus who brought their spice mixtures with them in the mid-1800s. Though Caribbeans use a lot of pork in their cooking, it's quite likely that the original Hindu version would have been vegetarian. This is based on a recipe from Elizabeth Lambert Ortiz's *Caribbean Cooking*, which calls for a special *Colombo* "curry powder". Instead, I have elected five spices, which seem typical of *Colombo* curries. The result is sublime, especially if you use a sweet, dense-fleshed pumpkin (see page 171).

# Colombo au Giraumon
# Pumpkin Curry Martinique/Guadeloupe

Heat a large saucepan over a medium heat and add the oil. Add the onion and pepper and cook until the onion is translucent. Add the spices and cook until fragrant, about 1 minute. Add the pumpkin and tomatoes and cook until the tomato softens. Add a little salt (more is added with garlic at the end) and pepper and the coconut milk. Bring to the boil, then simmer for about 20 minutes, stirring occasionally and keeping the cinnamon stick submerged, until the pumpkin is soft and beginning to collapse. Depending on the type of pumpkin used, further cooking may reduce to a smooth purée, so choose your consistency – chunky or smooth.

To finish, crush the garlic with the salt in a mortar until smooth and stir into the curry. Simmer for a further 5 minutes. Serve with plain boiled rice or with *Moros y Cristianos* (see page 49).

2 tbsp sunflower or vegetable oil
1 large onion, chopped
1 green (bell) pepper, chopped
Large pinch of cayenne pepper
1 tsp coriander seeds, crushed, or 1 tsp ground coriander
½ tsp ground allspice (pimiento)
1 cinnamon stick
Large pinch of saffron threads
500 g/1 lb 2 oz pumpkin, cut into 2 cm/¾ inch cubes
2 medium tomatoes, chopped
Salt and freshly ground black pepper
1 x 400 g/14 oz can coconut milk
1 large garlic clove
½ tsp coarse sea salt
Freshly cooked plain rice, to serve

**Serves 4**

The name simply means "black beans", but this bean dish is also referred to as "native caviar". Indeed, the ingredients here add up to more than the sum of their parts in terms of flavour, which may be how this dish got its glorified caviar tag. It could also simply be the appearance of the shiny, round black beans. Eat this as a cold salad with lettuce leaves, or warm with boiled rice and fried plantains.

# Caraotas Negras
# Black Bean Caviar Venezuela

If using dried beans, soak them in plenty of cold water for 4 hours or overnight. Drain the beans and place in a saucepan with plenty of fresh water and bring to the boil. Boil vigorously for 10 minutes then reduce the heat to a simmer. Cook until very tender, about 45 minutes–1 hour. Add a little salt halfway through cooking. Drain.

In a large frying pan that will accommodate the beans, heat 2 tbsp of oil over a low heat. Add the onion and cook until translucent. Crush the garlic, chilli and cumin seeds in a mortar until smooth-ish. Scrape into the saucepan and cook until fragrant, about 1 minute. Add the drained beans with the remaining 2 tbsp of oil. Stir until thoroughly mixed and cook until heated through. Serve hot, warm or cold.

200 g/7 oz/1 cup dried black beans, or 475 g/3 cups cooked or canned (drained weight) black beans

Salt

4 tbsp olive oil

1 large onion, chopped

3 garlic cloves, de-germed

1 or more small fresh red chillies (chilies), stem removed, deseeded if large

2 tsp cumin seeds

½–1 tsp coarse sea salt (depending on how salty your beans are)

**Serves 4–6**

Palm hearts, with their mild, nutty flavour and creamy texture, have a surprising affinity with eggs. This nifty recipe is adapted from Elisabeth Lambert Ortiz's *Caribbean Cookery*.

# Palmito Revuelto con Huevos
# Palm Heart Scramble Dominican Republic

Heat a large frying pan over a low heat and add the butter. When the butter has melted, add the palm hearts and cook until warmed through. Lightly beat the eggs with a little salt and pepper then pour into the pan. Allow the bottom surface to set, then stir until scrambled but not dry. Serve immediately on hot buttered toast.

1 x 400 g/14 oz can palm hearts (page 39), drained and coarsely chopped

30 g/1 oz/2 tbsp butter

4 organic eggs

Salt and freshly ground black pepper

Hot buttered toast, to serve

**Serves 4**

*"Huancaina"* refers to the Huanca Indians of Peru, enemies of the Incas, collaborators with the Spanish conquistadores, and celebratory cultivators of the potato at its origin in the Andes. The key ingredient of this velvety, moreish sauce, and many Peruvian dishes, is a chilli by the name of *aji amarillo*, a large, thin-fleshed pod with a distinctive fruity sweetness and searing heat. The closest common substitute would be a Scotch Bonnet or habanero, the world's hottest chilli. Proceed with caution and always wear gloves when handling chillies, especially her majesty the habanero (see page 38). A Bolivian recipe by the same name uses a peanut sauce.

# Papas a la Huancaina
# Potatoes in Creamy Onion Sauce Peru

Heat a frying pan over a medium heat and add the oil. Add the onions and fry until soft and slightly golden. Add the garlic and chilli and cook until fragrant, about 1 minute. Remove the pan from the heat and cool briefly.

In a blender combine the cream crackers, cottage cheese, evaporated milk and lemon juice. Add the onion mixture and purée until smooth and velvety. Leave to cool to room temperature.

When ready to serve, arrange the potatoes, eggs, olives, lettuce and tomatoes on individual serving plates, smother with the sauce and serve.

**For the sauce:**

2 tbsp sunflower oil

3 large onions, about 500 g/1 lb 2 oz, chopped

1 garlic clove, crushed

1 fresh yellow habanero chilli (chili), de-seeded and chopped, or fresh red chillies, to taste

3 cream crackers or soda crackers, lightly crushed

3 heaped tbsp cottage cheese

250 ml/8 fl oz/1 cup evaporated milk

1½ tbsp fresh lemon juice

**To serve:**

1 kg/2 lb 4 oz new potatoes, boiled until tender

Hard-boiled (hard-cooked) eggs, sliced

Black olives

Lettuce

Sliced tomatoes

**Serves 4–6**

An American friend discovered this salad in Peru, a country well-known for embracing foods of other cultures, Asia in particular. The Chinese influence is evident here, with soy sauce, sesame oil and water chestnuts enhancing a colourful palate with a myriad of textures and flavours in this magnificent platter. Hummus makes a tasty substitute for a purée of manioc or cassava (see page 39), and if palm hearts are not available, use canned artichoke hearts, halved, instead.

# Insalada Tropical con Palmitos
# Palm Heart Salad Peru

First toast the almonds by shaking them about attentively in a hot, dry frying pan until tinged with gold. Alternatively, cook in an oven preheated to 200°C/400°F/Gas Mark 6 for 5–7 minutes until golden. Leave to cool.

Mix the hummus, garlic, 1 tbsp of oil and soy sauce together in a bowl. Select 3 plump palm hearts and cut in half lengthways. Using a teaspoon, spoon the hummus mixture into the chicory leaves. Sprinkle with the toasted almonds. Set aside.

To make the dressing, whisk the lemon juice, water chestnuts and salt and pepper to taste together in a bowl. Gradually whisk in the oils to emulsify.

Arrange the salad leaves on a large platter. Decorate the platter as you wish – though a nice arrangement is to have avocado slices on one side, tomato slices on another, stuffed chicory and palm hearts fanning out over the tomatoes, and carrots and olives distributed throughout. Drizzle the dressing over everything and serve immediately.

50 g/2 oz/½ cup flaked or slivered almonds
300 g/11 oz/1 cup hummus
1 garlic clove, crushed
1 tbsp olive oil
½ tsp soy sauce
1 x 400 g/14 oz can palm hearts, drained (see page 39)
6 chicory leaves

**For the dressing:**
2 tbsp fresh lemon juice
4 water chestnuts from a can, chopped
Salt and freshly ground black pepper
3 tbsp olive oil
1 tsp sesame oil

**For the platter:**
200 g/7 oz baby salad leaves (greens) or other salad leaves
2 medium avocados, peeled and sliced
2 ripe vine-ripened tomatoes, sliced
1 medium carrot, peeled and grated
Handful of good quality black olives, such as Kalamata

**Serves 6**

I am lucky enough to live a five-minute walk away from a Colombian café called "*El Parador Rojo*" (The Red Parrot). Here I always get a warm welcome, the best coffee in London, a rocking earful of funky Latin music and a *Plátano con Queso*, their *especialidad*. The cooks at the café showed me how it's done, emphasizing how important it is that the plantain is fully ripe (the skin will appear deep yellow with streaks of black). Now I make them at home in minutes, and so can you. They are a rather indulgent snack for late morning, teatime or midnight, worth every wicked mouthful. Wash down with strong coffee or beer.

I am also lucky to have access to ripe plantains in my local store, which you may not. I have tried this with a slightly under-ripe banana. Trust me, it is NOT the same.

# Plátano con Queso
# Cheese-stuffed Plantain Colombia

Preheat the oven to 180°C/350°F/Gas Mark 4. Peel the plantain, using a paring knife to assist you if necessary. Heat a shallow pool of oil in a large frying pan over a medium heat. Leaving the plantain whole, fry gently, turning frequently, until golden all over (the inside curve will remain a little pale), and softened. Drain on kitchen paper (paper towels) and leave until cool enough to handle.

Place the plantain on a baking tray (cookie sheet). Using a small knife, make a slit from the top to the bottom of the plantain, cutting almost all the way through but not quite. Gently pry the plantain open. Sprinkle all over with a little salt. Cut the mozzarella into fingers which will fit in the slit, then nestle them in.

Bake in the oven for 10 minutes, or until the cheese is melted but not running out of the plantain. Serve warm.

1 ripe plantain per person
Sunflower or vegetable oil, for frying
Sea salt
50 g/2 oz pizza mozzarella (see note on page 7) per person

**Serves 1**

I became intrigued by the sound of this dish while reading Raymond Sokolov's enlightening book, *Why We Eat What We Eat*. I wanted to include a recipe using cassava or manioc in this collection, and his description of *Enyucado* captivated me: "In my experience the best place to witness the highest form of manioc cuisine is in Cartagena … a sort of pastry … or candy, except that it was being consumed as a side dish with main courses in a downtown saloon … It is an unctuous thing to eat and a triumph of man against manioc."

I did my best to re-create the dish, using what I hope are accessible ingredients. I am delighted with the result, and some Colombian cooks I fed it to congratulated me. So here it is…enjoy as a weird and wonderful accompaniment to a piquant bean dish such as *Frijoles Borrachos* (see page 40) or *Caraotas Negras* (see page 54) or as a dessert.

# Enyucado Cassava, Cheese and Coconut Paste Cartagena, Colombia

Bring a large saucepan of water to the boil. Cut the peeled cassava into large chunks (if using fresh) and boil until completely tender, about 30–40 minutes. Drain and leave to cool. Remove any tough strings and mash. Set aside until required.

Preheat the oven to 180°C/350°F/Gas Mark 4. In a food processor, combine the cooked cassava, both cheeses, coconut, butter, milk and sugar. Rub the anise seeds and add to the mixture. Process until completely smooth.

Liberally grease the baking dish with butter. Scoop the mixture in and smooth the top. Bake for 30–45 minutes until deep golden. Eat warm or cold.

600 g/1 lb 5 oz fresh peeled or frozen cassava (manioc) (see page 39)

180 g/6½ oz/generous ¾ cup ricotta cheese

75 g/3 oz pizza mozzarella (see note on page 7)

50 g/2 oz block creamed coconut, chopped

100 g/3½ oz/7 tbsp butter, plus extra for greasing

160 ml/5⅔ fl oz/generous ⅔ cup milk

50 g/2 oz/¼ cup sugar

½ tsp anise seeds

20 x 25 cm/8 x 10 inch baking dish

**Serves 6–8**

There is a virtually identical pie from Liguria in Italy by the same name, made with Swiss chard or artichokes. That recipe requires 33 layers of home-made filo (phyllo) pastry – one for every year of Christ's life. This one is far simpler, though symbolism is still abundant, with three whole eggs cooked in the torte, which I suspect represents the Holy Trinity. This is a rather magnificent centrepiece for the Easter table. I have thrown in a handful of uncooked rice, a trick I learned from a Greek cook, which absorbs extra moisture from the spinach while baking. This should help keep the bottom pastry layer nice and crisp.

# Torta Pascualina Easter Torte Argentina/Uruguay

Preheat the oven to 180°C/350°F/Gas Mark 4. Generously grease the springform cake tin (pan) with butter.

On a lightly floured surface, roll the pastry out quite thin. You should have enough to line the base and sides of the tin as well as having a lid. Make one circle to fit the base, then another slightly larger for the lid – leave this one to chill in the refrigerator until required. Cut out 2 or 3 strips to fit the sides of the tin, running horizontally. Press the base circle firmly inside the cake tin, then the side strips, sealing well. Chill.

To make the filling, first thaw the spinach in a microwave or in a covered saucepan over a medium heat. Once thawed, drain thoroughly then place on a clean tea (dish) towel, wrap up and squeeze, releasing as much moisture as you possibly can.

Meanwhile, heat a large frying pan over a medium heat and add the oil. Add the onions and fry until translucent. Add the garlic and cook until fragrant, about 1 minute. Transfer to a large bowl and add the spinach, peppers, olives, grated Parmesan cheese and plenty of freshly grated nutmeg. Mix thoroughly, then taste for seasoning. Add salt and pepper to taste if necessary. Beat 2 eggs together, then add to the bowl along with the rice and mix well. Beat another egg and brush some over the bottom pastry layer; reserve the remaining beaten egg. Spoon the filling into the pastry-lined cake tin and smooth the surface. Make 3 indentations with the back of a spoon and break 3 eggs into them.

Place the chilled pastry lid on top and seal the edges. Make a cross-shaped incision in the middle. Brush the reserved beaten egg over the surface. Bake in the oven for about 1 hour, or until the pastry is deep golden. To test that the middle is cooled, insert a skewer briefly, then quickly press it against the inside of your wrist. If it feels hot, it's done.

Butter, for greasing

1 packet (package) shortcrust pastry (unsweetened pie dough), about 500 g/1 lb 2 oz

1 kg/2 lb 4 oz frozen leaf spinach

2 medium onions, finely chopped

2 garlic cloves, finely chopped

200 g/7 oz grilled (broiled) peppers in brine or oil, drained, (about 4), coarsely chopped

20 good quality black olives, stoned (pitted) and coarsely chopped

100 g/3½ oz Parmesan cheese, grated

Freshly grated nutmeg

Salt and freshly ground black pepper

6 eggs

2 tbsp raw long-grain rice

24-cm/9½-inch springform cake tin (pan)

**Serves 8**

*Pupusas* are unique to El Salvador and are considered the "national snack", sold at *pupuserias* across the land. They are not complete without the pickled cabbage relish (*curtido*) and a hot tomato sauce, so I can't help comparing them to the All–American hot dog with sauerkraut and ketchup. But there's no question which I'd rather eat! Cheese and onion are just one of the many fillings for *pupusas*. I've used three cheeses here to emulate native Salvadoran white cheese, with the guidance of my friend Blanca, a talented chef and expert in Latin cooking, who's eaten many a *pupusa*.

# Pupusa con Curtido Stuffed Pancakes with Pickled Cabbage El Salvador

To make the *curtido*, first boil the kettle. Pour a little boiling water in a large preserving jar and swirl to sterilize, then drain. Place the cabbage, carrot and onion in a colander and pour boiling water over them. Place the vegetables in the sterilized jar with the oregano, salt, vinegar and water and mix well. Seal tightly and store in the refrigerator for 1 week (if you can wait that long, it does make a fantastic pickle!), then serve with the *pupusas*.

To make the *pupusas*, mix the masa harina or cornmeal with the salt in a small bowl. Pour in the warm water and quickly mix thoroughly. Cover with clingfilm (plastic wrap) and leave to stand for 15 minutes.

For the filling, place the feta, Cheddar and mozzarella cheeses in a food processor and process until crumbly. Alternatively, grate finely. Stir in the spring onions.

Using your hands, mix the masa harina mixture together until a dough forms. It should be like clay and not sticky. Divide the dough into 12 walnut-sized pieces and roll each into a ball. There are two ways of doing this. Take one ball and place in your palm, cupping your palm around it. Push the thumb of the other hand into the centre and form into a small cup shape. Fill with 1 tbsp of the filling and enclose the dough around the filling. Flatten the cake, patting it round and round, until about 0.5 cm/¼ inch thick and about 7.5 cm/3 inch in diameter.

Alternatively, divide a ball into 2 pieces. Roll out to a 7.5 cm/3 inch diameter ball between sheets of clingfilm. Top with 1 tbsp of the filling, cover the filling with the other small flattened ball, then cover with the clingfilm and roll flat. Heat a dry non-stick frying pan over a medium heat. Add the *pupusas* and cook on both sides until dry and flecked with black, about 4–5 minutes each side. Serve hot straight from the pan, with the *curtido* and chilli sauce.

**For the curtido:**
100 g/3½ oz/1 cup cabbage,
    finely chopped
1 medium carrot, grated
1 medium onion, halved and
    finely sliced
1 tsp dried oregano
1 tsp sea salt
100 ml/3½ fl oz/generous ⅓ cup white
    wine vinegar
100 ml/3½ fl oz/generous ⅓ cup water

**For the pupusas:**
250 g/9 oz/1½ cups masa harina (see
    page 39) or very fine cornmeal
½ tsp salt
350 ml/12 fl oz/1½ cups warm water

**For the filling:**
25 g/1 oz feta cheese
25 g/1 oz Cheddar cheese
75 g/3 oz mozzarella cheese (any type)
2 spring onions (scallions), finely sliced

Chilli (chili) sauce, or tomato ketchup
    spiked with cayenne pepper to taste,
    to serve

**Serves 4–6**

A Chilean cook assured me: *Pastel de Cholco* is all about the delectable sweetcorn layer. No matter what goes underneath the mixture – chicken, beef or in this case, eggs and mushrooms, it plays second fiddle to the creamy, crusty topping with a slight sugar crunch. The typically Chilean accents of cumin seed, oregano, raisins and olives can be applied to whatever filling you choose downstairs. The same cooked sweetcorn mixture is often cooked alone encased in a corn husk, much like the Mexican *Tamales* (see page 41). These are called *Humitas Chilenas* (instructions below).

# Pastel de Choclo
# Sweetcorn (Corn) Pie Chile

Preheat the oven to 200°C/400°F/Gas Mark 6.

Heat a large frying pan over a medium heat and add 2 tbsp of the oil. Add the spring onions and fry until fragrant, about 2 minutes.

To thaw the sweetcorn, boil the kettle. Place the sweetcorn in a bowl and pour boiling water over it. Stir, then drain thoroughly.

Place the sweetcorn in a food processor with the spring onions and oil in the pan and process to a thick purée. Alternatively, use a hand-held blender to purée the corn in a bowl. Scoop the purée into the frying pan and place over a medium heat. Add a little salt and cook, stirring, for about 5 minutes until thickened slightly. The texture will differ depending on the corn – add a little milk if the mixture is too stiff – you want to achieve a spreading consistency, a bit like mashed potato. (For *Humitas Chilenas*, this mixture can now be formed into *Tamale* shapes, wrapped and steamed as for *Tamales*, see page 41.)

Heat another frying pan over a medium heat and add the remaining tbsp of oil. Add the mushrooms with a generous pinch of salt and pepper to taste and fry until the mushrooms collapse.

Oil the casserole or gratin dish. In it, combine the mushrooms, hard-boiled eggs, raisins, cumin seeds, oregano and olives. Spread the corn mixture over the top, to cover edge to edge. Smooth the top and sprinkle evenly with the sugar. Bake in the oven for 45 minutes–1 hour, or until well browned on top, then serve.

3 tbsp olive oil, plus extra for greasing
5–6 spring onions (scallions), sliced
750 g/1 lb 10 oz/5½ cups frozen
  sweetcorn (corn)
Sea salt and freshly ground black pepper
500 g/1 lb 2 oz mushrooms, sliced
  (about 6 cups)
6 hard-boiled (hard-cooked)
  eggs, sliced
70 g/2¼ oz/⅜ cup raisins
1 tsp cumin seeds
1 tsp dried oregano
About 20 black olives, stoned (pitted)
1 tbsp granulated sugar

20 x 30 cm/8 x 12 inch casserole or
  gratin dish

**Serves 4–6**

# chapter three
# Northern Europe and Russia

The factor that unites every country in this region is the cold winters. For nearly half the year, Russians and Northern Europeans traditionally rely on carbohydrate-heavy foods like breads, noodles, dumplings and especially potatoes, enhanced with bone-clinging fats, cheeses, creamy gravies and steaming hot broths to sustain them. Natural refrigeration has great advantages, too, which explains the heavy reliance on butter and dairy products, unheard-of in some tropical diets. Dairy products make an appearance in almost every recipe in this chapter, and this region boasts a staggering range of the most sophisticated and delicious cheeses in the world. Not only is cheese a wholesome and nutritious staple and an essential protein source for vegetarians, but the sensory pleasure it delivers is incomparable. Without it, the bleak winter or any other time of year would be even harder to bear.

"What I say is that, if a man really likes potatoes, he must be a pretty decent sort of fellow." A.A. Milne

# meet the expert:
# Denis Cotter – Irish Cuisine

Denis Cotter established Café Paradiso, Ireland's most renowned vegetarian restaurant, in 1993 in Cork. He is also the author of *The Café Paradiso Cookbook* and *Paradiso Seasons*. It had been my ambition to meet Denis at his esteemed restaurant to talk about Irish food, perhaps over a glass of Merlot and a Gratin of Asparagus and Gabriel cheese with chive and mustard cream, or some such delicacy that I had drooled over in his marvellous cookbooks. As it happened, we met in the car park of a service station off the M1 motorway. He was only in London for the day and was rushing back to the airport. We agreed that the food and coffee on offer was best avoided, and time was of the essence, so we sat in my camper van and I boiled up a brew.

While familiar with the fairly static vegetarian scene in the UK, I was curious about the Irish restaurant business from a vegetarian perspective. "I think it is worse than it was in the 1980s," was the surprise answer from Denis. "Then, in Dublin, there was one very good restaurant and a number of others at least trying to push the standards along. 'Vegetarian' is now simply one of many different marketing strands, and what we have now is a health food industry rather than a vegetarian one. The good thing is, now you would be hard pushed to find a menu anywhere in the country, from five-star hotels down to country pubs, that didn't allow for the fact that a vegetarian might walk in the door any minute."

The Irish attitude towards food is intrinsically linked to recent history. Denis explains, "In a country with a relatively recent memory of poverty and starvation, to deliberately deprive yourself of meat was initially seen as daft, possibly dangerous." At the time Ireland was hit by the Great Famine of 1845, a third of the Irish population was dependent on the potato for sustenance. "The introduction of the potato facilitated landlords keeping tenants on increasingly small plots, since an acre could, just about, almost, feed a family. It didn't need a lot of work, so the tenants had plenty of spare time for watercolouring, walking on the hills, reading poetry and discussing philosophical matters. Oh, and working 18-hour days growing grain for the landlord."

Within six years, the potato famine took a million Irish lives, and a million more had emigrated – more than a fifth of the entire population was lost. It was an unforgettable lesson on the importance of crop diversity, and led to an obsession with a "good square meal" of meat, two veg and potatoes. Generally Irish food remained unadventurous, but local and good. "People trusted their food and were proud of it," says Denis. "The miracle of moving from famine to a good rural economy was, somehow, pulled off impressively."

Dairy produce is an ancient pride of the Irish. "The cow in Ireland is practically sacred," says Denis. "I sometimes moan that if the Irish agriculture industry was less focussed on milk, we might have a stronger vegetable one, and we'd be less dependent on heroic – but unrewarded – growers. But there is no denying the power of milk in our economy."

Potatoes, not least for their affinity with milk, continue to dominate Irish food. "Ah, potatoes," muses Denis, "we still love them and discuss them more than any other food. They have kept us alive for more generations than they let us down, and to the Irish, food *is* potatoes. In the countryside, you are still likely to hear someone say at two minutes to one 'I'm going home for the spuds'."

Irish people, at home and eating out, have always loved their vegetables. "They see them as the diverting colour in an otherwise dull cuisine," says Denis. "For a while, expensive restaurants began to trade in exotic stuff – baby sweetcorn and mangetout all over the place – but lately, there is a growing movement to return to an emphasis on quality, mirroring similar changes elsewhere, driven by Slow Food, organics and markets."

Modern Irish food, as reflected by Denis' style, began to take shape after an influx of foreign immigrants arrived in the early 1970s introducing new ingredients and a spirit of culinary adventure, though it remains fundamentally Irish. "When people ask me what is Irish about my food, I tell them that I am an Irish cook working creatively in an Irish town, using produce grown or made by people that I know personally and who live in Ireland. You may recognize the seasoning of a dish as vaguely North African or Italian, but everything about the way it is put together is related to where it is happening. The best of Irish food is like that now: we are not working to Irish traditions, but we are cooking in a way that relates to where we are."

# focus on ingredients

Mushrooms (edible fungi) – Wild mushrooms have had a place in this region's cuisine for centuries, though many a life has been sacrificed in the attempt to distinguish the edible from the poisonous. Ceps (cèpes), chanterelles, girolles and morels are some of the best in the world, and the mushroom hunt itself is a widely practised recreation, especially in France, Germany, England, Austria and the Czech Republic. Cultivated mushrooms are now big business, particularly in Eastern Europe. Avoid washing mushrooms as they are like sponges and will retain water, which alters the cooking process; simply wipe with a damp cloth. True wild mushrooms that have been plucked from the forest floor may well be muddy and can be rinsed under cold running water and laid out to dry on kitchen paper (paper towels). Avoid cleaning mushrooms until just before you use them. Store in a paper bag in the refrigerator.

Mustard – The yellow, white, brown or black seeds of a plant which is a member of the cabbage family. Valued throughout Europe and Asia since time immemorial, it is a fantastically easy plant to grow. The whole seeds are used as a spice in Asia; in Europe they are generally used mixed into a condiment; in Russia, the world's largest producer, mustard oil is common for cooking. The pungent, sinus-tingling heat of mustard is activated by first breaking down the seeds, then adding cold water. Ten minutes must then pass in order for a chemical reaction to take place, which suppresses bitterness and releases the pungency – an essential step, before adding other flavourings.

Beetroot (beets) – This root vegetable with passionate pink pigment can also be yellow or striped with gold and red. It was written about by the Greeks as early as 300 BC. The sugar beet is a very important crop for making sugar; the red beetroot is the common root vegetable, much loved by some and much maligned by others. Cooking beetroot from fresh delivers its best qualities, in particular a cool, earthy flavour beneath sweetness. They should not be trimmed before boiling in order to keep all that red juice locked up inside. Ready-cooked beetroot, usually sold in vacuum-packs, is a convenient product, though a little inferior to fresh, as are canned, bottled and pickled beetroot.

**Beetroot**

**Chervil and Dill**

**Dill** – This feathery herb is extremely versatile and can be used in abundance in salads and with bean and grain dishes. The name comes from an Old Norse word, and while dill is also greatly loved in the Middle East, Northern Europeans and Russians probably use it the most.

**Chervil** – This thoroughly feminine herb has the quaintest looking leaves and a wisp of aniseed (anise) flavour. It is so delicate that heat spoils it – use only fresh or sprinkled in at the end of cooking. In Eastern Europe and Germany, a different type of chervil is grown for the root only. It is also much loved in France where it forms part of the mixture called *fines herbes*, along with parsley, chives and tarragon.

**Paprika** – The red pepper was embraced with great enthusiasm when it eventually reached Hungary, after crossing the Atlantic from the New World. *Capsicum annuum* is the variety used to make paprika; it is a cone-shaped pepper up to 12 cm/4½ inches long and about 2.5 cm/1 inch wide. The climate in the paprika producing region in the south is perfect for peppers, and at the end of the hot, dry summers, the red-ripe peppers are harvested, dried and ground into paprika powder. There are dozens of grades of Hungarian paprika,

and the name of the very finest, *különleges* means "exquisite delicate". Paprika is generally mild, though some grades are quite hot. It contains natural sugars and is therefore susceptible to burning, so it's best added towards the end of cooking. (*See also* pimentón on page 92.)

**Cheddar Cheese** – This cheese is a personal favourite, and indeed the most popular hard cheese in the world. Good Cheddar has everything a cheese should: creaminess with a tang that dashes through and fabulous melting ability. Originally made in Cheddar, near a gorge by the same name in Somerset, England, it's now produced all over the UK as well as in North America and Australia. Traditionally it's made with animal rennet, but vegetarian Cheddars are now available.

**Yeast extract** – Marmite™, Vegemite®, Vitam-R™ – An absolute must on buttered toast in the UK and Australia, yeast extract is also used as an ingredient in cooking. It tastes a little like beef extract and is used as a flavouring in many vegetarian recipes where extra flavour is required. It is treacle-brown and extremely salty, though the German version Vitam-R™ is less salty and a pale copper colour. It's an excellent source of B vitamins – another boon for vegetarians who miss out on the B vitamins in meat.

**Chanterelle Mushrooms**

**Mustard Powder and Mustard Seeds**

This timeless salad is ubiquitous in the whole region adjoining Russia, including the Caucasus and Turkey, and has travelled across the world with many waves of immigration. It is often served from a can (!), but made fresh it is quite delicious. The name derives from the supposed creator of the salad, the famous French chef Olivier, who had a restaurant in Moscow in the late nineteenth century. Though this recipe has the classic flavour one expects, it has mutated quite severely since that time, as Olivier's obscured original is known to have been based on game.

# Salat Olivier
# Russian Salad Russia

First boil the kettle. Place the potatoes in a large saucepan and pour in enough boiling water to cover. Add a little salt. Cover and cook for about 8–10 minutes, or until nearly tender, then add the peas and return to the boil. Cook for 1 minute, or until potatoes and peas are tender. Drain and cool completely.

Meanwhile, mash the eggs with a fork until well crumbled, then whisk in the mayonnaise, yogurt, vinegar and salt and pepper to taste. Stir in the pickled cucumbers and spring onions.

When the potatoes and peas are cool, stir the creamy mixture through them and mix well. Scoop into a serving bowl and garnish with tomatoes and olives.

450 g/1 lb potatoes, peeled and cut into 1 cm/½ inch cubes

Sea salt and freshly ground black pepper

75 g/3 oz/¾ cup fresh or frozen peas

3 hard-boiled (hard-cooked) eggs, shelled and rinsed

3 tbsp mayonnaise

3 tbsp natural (plain) yogurt

2 tsp white wine vinegar

1 large or 2 medium dill pickled cucumbers, finely chopped

2 spring onions (scallions), finely chopped

**To garnish:**

1 medium vine-ripened tomato, halved and sliced

12 good quality black olives

**Serves 4**

Adaptations of this aubergine purée pop up throughout the Middle East and the Mediterranean, but it almost certainly got its "Poor Man's Caviar" moniker from somewhere around the Caspian and Black Seas, where the Russians and Iranians have cultivated caviar from sturgeons for centuries, though the word caviar derives from the Turkish *kavyar*. So what does an aubergine purée have in common with real caviar? It may be that the seedy appearance of the aubergine flesh resembles fish eggs. I prefer to think that it's because the mixture tastes so sublime – who needs caviar when you can eat this?

# Baklazanaya Ikra
# Poor Man's Caviar Russia

Prick the aubergines several times. Microwave on High power for 5 minutes, or until thoroughly soft. Alternatively, boil, steam or bake in an oven preheated to 200°C/400°F/Gas Mark 6 until soft. Cool.

When the aubergine is cool enough to handle, remove the stem and scoop the flesh away from the skin. Chop the flesh finely.

Heat a large frying pan over a medium heat and add the oil. Add the onion and green pepper and cook until the onion is soft and translucent. Add the aubergine flesh, tomato paste, water, salt and pepper. Reduce the heat as low as possible and cook, stirring frequently, until the mixture thickens, about 20–30 minutes. Place in a bowl and stir in lemon juice to taste. Cool, then leave to chill in the refrigerator. Serve well chilled with dark rye bread.

2 medium aubergines (eggplants), about 450 g/1 lb
2 tbsp olive oil
1 small onion, finely chopped
1 small green (bell) pepper, finely chopped
2 tbsp tomato purée
4 tbsp water
Salt and freshly ground black pepper
1–2 tbsp fresh lemon juice
Dark rye bread, to serve

**Serves 4**

Russians are serious eaters. They are passionate about their food, and emphatic about the importance of preparing good food for friends and family. And they serve a lot of food – enough is never enough. Of course, Russians eat a lot of meat and fish nowadays (little meat was eaten until the 19th century), but during Lent and certain other religious periods, believers shift to vegetarian dishes, entirely or at least part of the time. *Borshch* is a firm favourite during this period.

There are multiple variations of *Borshch* throughout Eastern Europe and Russia, but the Ukraine claims sovereignty over the soup. Their version is distinctively chunky, with many types of vegetables and beans – so chunky that a spoon should stand upright in the pot, as this recipe demonstrates. Ukrainians also prefer their *Borshch* hot and aromatic, whereas a smooth Russian *Borshch* can be served cold. *Piroshki* (see page 72) are the desired accompaniment to this already substantial potage.

# Borshch
# Beetroot (Beet) Soup Ukraine

Place the beetroot, potatoes, carrot and celery in a large saucepan with the water and add plenty of salt and pepper. Bring to the boil then reduce to a simmer and cook until the vegetables are tender.

Meanwhile, heat a frying pan over a medium heat and add the butter. When the butter has melted, add the onion and green pepper and cook until soft. Add the garlic and cook until fragrant, about 1–2 minutes. Add to the soup pan with the tomato juice and return to a simmer. Add the cabbage and red kidney beans and cook until the cabbage is barely tender, about 5 minutes. Add the vinegar and sugar. Taste and adjust seasoning if necessary. Serve each bowl hot, with a generous dollop of sour cream.

3 medium/2 large fresh beetroot (beets), about 500 g/1 lb 2 oz, peeled and cut into small dice

2 medium waxy, red-skinned potatoes, about 300 g/11 oz, peeled and cut into small dice

1 medium carrot, peeled and chopped

2 celery sticks (stalks), ideally from the heart with leaves, chopped

1 litre/1¾ pints/4 cups water

Sea salt and freshly ground black pepper

50 g/2 oz/4 tbsp butter

1 large onion, about 250 g/9 oz, chopped

1 green (bell) pepper, cored and chopped

3 garlic cloves, chopped

500 ml/16 fl oz/2 cups tomato juice

200 g/7 oz shredded Savoy cabbage (about ¼ trimmed head)

1 x 400 g/14 oz can red kidney beans, drained and rinsed

1 tbsp red wine vinegar

1 tbsp soft brown sugar

Sour cream or crème fraîche, to serve

**Serves 6–8**

Traditionally, these are an essential accompaniment to *Borshch* (see page 70). My stepmother, Inna, is Ukranian and an outstanding cook, and these are one of her specialities. Before I knew how to cook, I was baffled that she could prepare something so delicious by hand. As a matter of fact, they're easy to make. I've always been enamoured with her *Piroshki*, but until I started putting this book together I had never succeeded in extracting the recipe from her, mostly because she's always cooked it by heart. At last, I got it, fiddled with it, devoured it, and wrote it down for you. Enjoy.

# Piroshki
# Little Stuffed Pies Ukraine

Preheat the oven to 190°C/375°F/Gas Mark 5.

To make the dough, place the flour, baking powder and butter in a food processor and whiz until the butter is incorporated and it appears crumbly. Add the salt, 1 egg and sour cream or crème fraîche and process until it draws together as a dough. Remove from the machine and knead for a couple of minutes until smooth. Wrap in clingfilm (plastic wrap), then leave to rest for about 30 minutes, while you prepare the filling.

Heat a large frying pan over a medium heat and add the butter. When the butter has melted, add the spring onions and mushrooms with a generous sprinkling of salt and pepper. Cook until the mushrooms are collapsed and most of the liquid has evaporated. Cool briefly, then place in the rinsed-out food processor with the eggs, sour cream or crème fraîche and dill and pulse until everything is well chopped, but not a totally smooth purée. Taste for seasoning.

On a lightly floured surface, take golf ball-sized pieces of dough and roll out into flat circles. Fill each with a heaped teaspoon of filling in the middle. Pull up the edges like a sack and press to seal, making round parcels (packages). Place seam-side down on an oiled baking tray. Brush with beaten egg. Bake in the oven for 15–20 minutes, or until golden. Serve warm.

**For the dough:**
275 g/9 oz/1¼ cups plain (all-purpose) flour
½ tsp baking powder
4 tbsp cold butter, cubed
½ tsp sea salt
1 egg, plus 1 egg, beaten, for glazing
125 ml/4 fl oz/½ cup sour cream or crème fraîche

**For the filling:**
30 g/1 oz/2 tbsp butter
3 spring onions (scallions), sliced
500 g/1 lb 2 oz mushrooms, coarsely chopped
Sea salt and freshly ground black pepper
2 hard-boiled (hard-cooked) eggs, shelled and quartered
2 tbsp sour cream or crème fraîche
3 tbsp fresh dill, chopped
Oil for greasing

**Makes 15**

Cabbage, sour apples and walnuts have always been a harmonious trio. Before modern air-freight, the Scandinavians, like many Northern Europeans, relied upon the cold storage power of apples, cabbages and root vegetables to sustain them through the winter. Etel, a life-long vegetarian Swedish friend, remembers salads like this from her childhood, growing up in Jönköping, east of Gothenburg. She admits it was quite unusual to be vegetarian back then – she took after her father who had become one through a 1930s health movement. Her mother developed some very creative ways with nuts and she enjoyed plenty of Sweden's fantastic dairy products.

# Vinter Sallad
# Winter Cabbage Salad Sweden

Finely grate the red cabbage and Chinese leaf – a food processor will make light work of this task with a 2 mm/¹⁄₁₆ inch blade – and place in a large bowl. Combine the cabbages with apple, leek, parsley, sultanas and walnuts.

To make the dressing, beat the mustard, honey, salt and pepper together thoroughly in a bowl or shake in a jar. Add the oil gradually to emulsify. Toss through the salad and leave to stand for at least 30 minutes before serving.

500 g/1 lb 2 oz red cabbage

300 g/11 oz Chinese leaf (Napa cabbage), about ½ head

1 large green sour apple, cooking apples or Granny Smith, cut into small pieces

1 small leek, very finely sliced

2 tbsp chopped fresh parsley

4 tbsp sultanas (golden raisins)

4 tbsp chopped walnuts

**For the dressing:**

4 tbsp cider vinegar

2 tbsp Dijon or coarse grain mustard

2 tbsp honey

1 tsp salt

Freshly ground black pepper

3 tbsp olive oil

**Serves 4–6**

# Laatikot **A Trio of Christmas Bakes**

Finland

These unusual root vegetable bakes are serious comfort food. There is no particular significance to the trio, it's just that swede, potatoes and carrots are just about the only vegetables that will survive in storage in the bitter Finnish winters. These recipes are a triumphal achievement, showing how you can make something worthy of the Christmas table out of practically nothing. The Potato Bake is particularly interesting with its brief fermenting process, which converts some of the potato starch to sugar and creates an entirely different "animal".

All three have a distinct sweetness, which complements the traditional Finnish Christmas ham. My suggested vegetarian accompaniments would be Mrs. Myrtleberry's Roast (see page 86), *Houbovy Závin* (page 76), Glamorgan Sausages (page 84) or *Spanakopita* (page 108). There is no need to wait for Christmas – these rib-clinging bakes are wonderful for any chilly day.

# Lanttulaatikko
# Swede (Rutabaga) Bake

Preheat the oven to 180°C/350°F/Gas Mark 4.

To cook the swede, bring a saucepan of water to the boil and salt it well. Add the swede and cook until tender. Drain, reserving some of the water.

Meanwhile, soak the breadcrumbs in the cream for at least 5 minutes. While the swede is still warm, combine with the breadcrumb-cream mixture. Use a hand-held blender or masher and some of the reserved cooking water to make a smooth paste, the consistency of thick porridge. Beat in the golden syrup or honey and nutmeg and taste for seasoning. Leave to cool, then beat in the eggs.

Scoop into the well-greased casserole or gratin dish, smooth the top and bake in the oven for 1 hour. Serve hot.

1 large swede (rutabaga), about
   1.25 kg/2¾ lb, peeled and cubed
Salt and freshly ground black pepper
50 g/2 oz/1 cup fresh breadcrumbs
150 ml/5 fl oz/⅔ cup double
   (heavy) cream
1 tbsp golden syrup or honey
½ nutmeg, finely grated
2 eggs

20 x 30 cm/8 x 12 inch casserole or
   gratin dish

**Serves 6**

# Imeletty Perunalaatikko
# Potato Bake

Preheat the oven to 150°C/300°F/Gas Mark 2.

To cook the potatoes, bring a large saucepan of water to the boil and salt it well. Add the potatoes and boil until tender throughout. Drain thoroughly and leave in a colander until no longer steaming but still warm. Mash with the flour and combine thoroughly. Cover with a clean tea (dish) towel and leave in a warm part of the kitchen to ferment for 4 hours.

After fermenting, the potato should taste quite sweet. If not, leave for a while longer. Beat the milk, butter and salt to taste into the potato.

Scoop into the well-greased casserole or gratin dish, and bake in the oven for 2 hours. It will be very dark and crusty and that's just great! Serve hot.

1 kg/2 lb 4 oz potatoes, peeled
Salt
4 tbsp plain (all-purpose) flour
80 ml/2¾ fl oz/generous ⅓ cup milk
30 g/1 oz/2 tbsp butter, melted

20 x 30 cm/8 x 12 inch casserole
  or gratin dish

**Serves 6**

# Porkkanalaatikko
# Carrot and Rice Bake

Preheat the oven to 160°C/325°F/Gas Mark 3.

Bring the water to the boil in a saucepan and add the rice. Leave to simmer for 20 minutes. Add the milk, stir then cover and cook for 20–25 minutes, or until soft and creamy like rice pudding. Remove to a bowl and leave to cool.

Stir the grated carrot into the rice then stir in the golden syrup or honey and season with nutmeg, salt and pepper. Taste and adjust seasoning if necessary. Beat in the eggs until evenly combined.

Scoop into the well-greased casserole or gratin dish, smooth the top and bake in the oven for 1 hour. Serve hot.

500 ml/16 fl oz/2 cups water
215 g/7½ oz/1 cup pudding rice
500 ml/16 fl oz/2 cups milk
450 g/1 lb carrots, grated
1–2 tbsp golden syrup or honey,
  or to taste
Freshly grated nutmeg
salt and freshly ground black pepper
2 eggs

20 x 30 cm/8 x 12 inch casserole
  or gratin dish

**Serves 6**

My uncle Rickie Garza is Editor Emeritus of The Czech Heritage Society of Texas, and is also the proud owner of a Czech dance hall in Nelsonville, built in 1923. Though not himself of Czech origin (rather, an exotic combination of Mexican-American and Bavarian), he is an enthusiastic cook and collector of recipes. He described this classic strudel to me and here is the result. Don't be frightened of filo pastry. It is really easy to use if you work fast, while the dough is still moist. This technique of sprinkling breadcrumbs between the buttered layers makes the pastry flaky and light as fairy wings.

# Houbovy Závin
# Wild Mushroom Strudel Czech Republic

First, make the sauce to allow the flavours to infuse. Mix all sauce ingredients together in a bowl and leave to chill in the refrigerator until required.

Preheat the oven to 200°C/400°F/Gas Mark 6.

Heat a large frying pan over a high heat and add the oil. Add the mushrooms and salt and fry briskly, moving them around frequently, until the mushrooms are soft and golden, about 10 minutes. There should be no liquid left in the pan. Reduce the heat to medium and add the butter, garlic, thyme and plenty of pepper. Cook until the garlic is just soft and fragrant, about 1 minute, then remove the pan from the heat. Cool the mixture for a few minutes, then place in a food processor and pulse until finely chopped.

Lay one sheet of filo pastry out on a clean, dry surface. Keep the remaining pastry well wrapped or covered with a slightly damp cloth to prevent it going dry and brittle. Brush a little melted butter all over the pastry, then sprinkle about 2 tbsp breadcrumbs evenly over the surface. Add another layer of filo (phyllo), butter, breadcrumbs, etc. until you finish with a layer of pastry. Butter it, then make a 8-cm/3-inch wide pile of the mushroom mixture along one of the short edges of the pastry, leaving a 2.5 cm/1 inch border all round. Fold the top and bottom long edges inwards over the filling, then fold over the short edge and roll up the pastry tightly. Lay seam-side down on a baking sheet and brush with more butter.

Using a sharp knife, cut several diagonal slashes halfway through the pastry.

Bake the strudel in the oven for about 20 minutes, or until golden and crisp. Slice into portions and serve with the cold herb sauce.

**For the cold herb sauce:**
125 ml/4 fl oz/½ cup crème fraîche or sour cream
4 tbsp chopped fresh herbs, especially chives, dill, chervil
½ tsp coarse grain mustard
1 tsp white wine vinegar
Salt and freshly ground black pepper

1 tbsp sunflower oil
500 g/1 lb 2 oz mixed mushrooms, wild and cultivated, cleaned and coarsely chopped
1 tsp salt
30 g/1 oz/2 tbsp butter
2 garlic cloves, chopped
1 tsp fresh or ½ tsp dried thyme
Freshly ground black pepper
4 large sheets filo (phyllo) pastry
50 g/2 oz/4 tbsp butter, melted
6 tbsp fresh breadcrumbs (made from 1 average slice good quality bread)

**Serves 4**

A perfect soup, which simply cannot be improved upon, this is not to be confused with the Turkish garlic-walnut-bread sauce by the same name. The two are probably related, as Bulgaria and Turkey are neighbours. Also, that sauce is a delicious dressing for cucumbers – a good example of how certain ingredients are eternal allies.

# Tarator Yogurt and Cucumber Soup with Walnuts Bulgaria

Whisk the yogurt and water together in a bowl until smooth. Pound the garlic with a large pinch of coarse sea salt in a mortar until smooth. Alternatively, use a garlic press. Stir the garlic into the yogurt mixture. Add the cucumber and mint and season with salt and pepper to taste. Leave to chill in the refrigerator for about 10 minutes.

Pour into bowls and garnish with a drizzle of oil and chopped walnuts.

500 ml/16 fl oz/2 cups chilled Greek or thick and creamy yogurt

250 ml/8 fl oz/1 cup chilled water

1 garlic clove, de-germed

Coarse sea salt and freshly ground black pepper

2 medium cucumbers, chilled, peeled, de-seeded and finely diced

Handful of fresh mint leaves, chopped

**To garnish:**
Virgin sunflower or olive oil
3–4 tbsp chopped walnuts

**Serves 4**

This all-purpose ragout celebrates capsicum peppers, which are so adored in Hungary. It's often served for lunch with a fried egg on top or with *Spätzle* (see page 80).

# Lecsó Peppers in Tomato Sauce Hungary

Heat a wide frying pan or wok over a low–medium heat and add the oil and butter. When the butter has melted, add the onion and cook until soft and translucent.

Add the peppers and cook until they start to soften slightly, about 2 minutes. Add the garlic and cook until just fragrant, about 1 minute. Add the paprika and caraway, if using, and cook until the paprika changes colour. Add the chopped tomatoes, tomato purée and a good pinch of salt and pepper. Cover the pan and reduce the heat to a simmer. Cook for 10 minutes, stirring occasionally, then remove the lid and cook for a further 10 minutes. Serve hot, warm or cold.

1 tbsp sunflower oil

15/½ oz/1 tbsp butter

1 large onion (about 250 g/9 oz), chopped

3 large (bell) peppers, red, green and yellow, cut into bite-sized chunks

2 plump garlic cloves, chopped

1 tbsp paprika, preferably Hungarian

1 tsp caraway seeds (optional)

1 x 400 g/14 oz can chopped tomatoes

2 tbsp tomato purée (paste)

Salt and freshly ground black pepper

**Serves 4**

When the chilli pepper and her capsicum cousins came back from America with Columbus in the 16th century, they proceeded to conquer Asia and Africa, but not the timid palates of Northern Europe – with the exception of Hungary. The Hungarian climate and soil are perfect for pepper cultivation, and their enthusiasm soon developed into a world-dominating industry and a complex canon of celebrated dishes. Hungarian paprika, made from a particular red pepper, which is dried and ground, (see page 67), comes in more than 30 grades of sweetness and heat. A mild paprika will complement the subtle woody flavour of the mushrooms here, and make sure it's fresh and not a bottle of dust retrieved from the back of your cupboard.

Chanterelles are traditional for this simple yet luxurious dish, though I think a mixture of wild and cultivated makes for a more interesting texture. This is a phenomenally quick, easy and delicious dish, which has become an after-work favourite in my house.

# Houby Paprikás
# Mushrooms Paprika Hungary

Heat a large saucepan over a low heat and add the butter. When the butter has melted, add the onion and cook until soft and translucent.

Add the mushrooms, season with salt and pepper to taste, then increase the heat and stir. When the moisture from the mushrooms has been released, allow it to evaporate, concentrating the flavour. This might happen quickly or slowly, depending entirely on the type of mushrooms used.

Add the paprika and cayenne and fry for a few moments longer, until the paprika turns a shade darker. Finally, add the sour cream or crème fraîche and dill, and allow it to bubble gently for a further 5 minutes or so.

Serve immediately with rice, pasta or *Spätzle*.

30 g/1 oz/2 tbsp butter
1 medium onion, chopped
450 g/1 lb mixed mushrooms, cleaned, chopped chunky of large
Sea salt and freshly ground black pepper
1 tbsp paprika, ideally Hungarian
Generous pinch of cayenne pepper
250 ml/8 fl oz/1 cup sour cream or crème fraîche
3 tbsp chopped fresh dill
Rice, pasta or *Spätzle* (see page 80), to serve

**Serves 4**

*right Houby Paprikás* served with *Spätzle* (see page 80).

One of the world's easiest home-made noodles – much easier than Italian pasta, but just as delicious. They certainly don't score as high as their Italian cousins in the glamour department – more gutter than Gucci, but charming in a homely kind of way, and extremely satisfying. Unless you happen to have a special *spätzle*-maker, be prepared for making a bit of a mess with a conventional colander – one with a flat base works best. Great fun for kids. Serve with *Houby Paprikás* (see page 78), *Lecsó* (page 77) or any sauce you would spoon over pasta.

# Spätzle
# Noodle Dumplings Germany/Eastern Europe

Choose a large boiling pan and a large-hole colander, which will rest on top of the pan. Fill the pan with water and rest the colander on top, so that the base of the colander is at least 5 cm/2 inches above the surface. Bring to the boil, salt it well and reduce to a simmer.

Meanwhile, in a large bowl mix ½ tsp salt into the flour. Add the egg and gradually work in the milk. You may need more or less milk, but you want to achieve a consistency somewhere between a dough and a batter, though leaning towards batter – you should be able to push it through the holes of the colander quite easily.

Using a large metal spoon, scoop part of the batter into the colander and push it through into the simmering water. The *spätzle* will sink to the bottom, then rise when cooked. Remove the cooked *spätzle* with a slotted spoon and keep warm while you cook the remaining batches. Serve.
If keeping for any length of time, stir through a little oil to stop them sticking together.

Sea salt
250 g/9 oz/generous 1¾ cups
   plain (all-purpose) flour
1 large egg, beaten
200–250 ml/7–8 fl oz/⅞–1 cup milk

**Serves 4**

From rösti to hash browns, the marriage of grated potatoes and hot oil is a firm favourite throughout the potato-eating world. Starch and fat are just a match made in heaven, and it's a match that's sustained many a family through deprivation and cold winters. These are identical to Jewish potato *latkes*, but are made a bit larger as a main meal. Christian Germans have traditionally eaten vegetarian dishes on Fridays and this might be one of them, accompanied by vegetables and perhaps a fried egg.

# Kartoffelpuffer
# Potato Cakes with Caraway Cheese

Germany

To make the *kartoffelpuffer*, preheat the oven to 150°C/300°F/Gas Mark 2 for keeping them warm. Grate the potatoes. This is most easily done by pushing them through the rotary grater of a food processor. Place the potato in a sieve (strainer) to drain. Press all the excess moisture out of the potato and transfer to a bowl. Combine thoroughly with the onion, egg, flour and salt.

Heat a large frying pan over a medium heat and add a shallow pool of oil. Transfer the potato mixture back to the sieve and stand over the bowl, as moisture will continue to drain out. Take a heaped dessertspoon of the mixture at a time and flatten out in the hot oil, forming thin cakes about 7.5 cm/3 inches wide. Try not to overcrowd the pan. When crisp and golden underneath, flip over and cook the other side. Drain on layers of kitchen paper (paper towels) in an ovenproof dish, and keep warm in the oven while you cook the rest.

To make the caraway cheese, push the cottage cheese through a sieve into a bowl, using a ladle or the back of a large spoon. Stir through the milk, caraway seeds and seasoning.

Serve the hot *kartoffelpuffer* with the cheese in a bowl or spooned over them.

500 g/1 lb 2 oz potatoes, peeled
½ small onion, finely chopped
1 egg
2 tbsp plain (all-purpose) flour
½ tsp salt, or to taste
Sunflower or vegetable oil, for frying

**For the caraway cheese:**
200 g/7 oz/scant 1 cup cottage cheese
1 tbsp milk
1 tsp caraway seeds
Pinch of salt
Freshly ground black pepper

**Makes about 12–14, serves 4**

This "Green Sauce" can be spooned over whatever you like, but traditionally it's enjoyed with eggs and potatoes, or with meat. It is exclusive to Frankfurt, though I suspect versions have travelled the globe – it does bear some resemblance to California's Ranch Dressing (see page 34). There are several ways to make it and every way is, of course, the best way, as with so many classic recipes. All versions have exactly seven leafy herbs, some common, others more unusual and indigenous to their homes such as burnet, borage and lovage, if you can get hold of them. Goethe was a big fan of *Grüne Soße* and as he said, "One doesn't always lose when one has to do without." So use what's available to you, and lots of it.

# Frankfurter Grüne Soße
# Potato and Egg Salad with Seven Herb Sauce Frankfurt, Germany

Remove any tough stems from the herbs and chop very, very finely. This is really best done by hand, as a machine can bring out any bitterness. Stir together the sour cream or crème fraîche and yogurt. Add the chopped herbs, shallot, pickled cucumbers, a little salt and pepper, vinegar, mustard and oil, if using. Mix thoroughly and leave to stand for at least 1 hour, preferably overnight, to allow the flavours to infuse.

Meanwhile, boil the potatoes in a large saucepan until tender, then drain. Keep warm. You can hard-boil (hard-cook) the eggs if you like (about 11 minutes) or, for just-cooked "butter-yolked" eggs, cover with cold water, bring to the boil and simmer for 6 minutes. Leave to cool, then shell and cut in half.

Taste the sauce and add more seasoning if you like, including a drop more vinegar or oil if you feel it needs it.

Arrange a bed of watercress or rocket on a platter or individual plates. Top with the warm potatoes and egg halves. Spoon the green sauce over them and serve.

Choose 7 fresh herbs from this list, enough to make a substantial bouquet. The chopped herbs should represent a volume of about 500 ml/16 fl oz/2 cups: flat-leaf or curly parsley, chives, watercress, rocket (arugula), dill, tarragon, chervil, mint, basil, sorrel, burnet, borage, lovage

250 ml/8 fl oz/1 cup sour cream or crème fraîche

500 ml/16 fl oz/2 cups low-fat natural (plain) yogurt

1 medium shallot, very finely chopped

2 pickled cucumbers, very finely chopped

Sea salt and freshly ground black pepper

1 tbsp white wine vinegar

2 tsp Dijon mustard

2 tsp sunflower oil (optional, though it adds richness and gloss to the sauce)

1 kg/2 lb 4 oz new potatoes

6 organic eggs

Watercress or rocket (arugula) leaves, to serve

**Serves 6**

The true original vegetarian sausages with no high-tech meat mockery, these aren't far off modern "analogue meat" and have a remarkable texture and flavour. In his diary of Welsh adventures from 1862, *Wild Wales*, George Borrow ate them in Glamorganshire, South Wales. Waking up to a miserable morning and having to put on still-wet clothes, the sausages cheered him up: "The breakfast was delicious, consisting of excellent tea, buttered toast and Glamorgan sausages, which I really think are not a whit inferior to those of Epping." (Epping sausages were a renowned pork sausage of the time.)

# Selsig Morgannwg
# Glamorgan Sausages Wales

Mix the 150 g/5 oz/3 cups breadcrumbs, leek, cheese, parsley, salt, pepper and mustard together in a large bowl. Beat together 2 eggs plus one yolk, reserving the white separately in a small bowl. Add the eggs to the mixture and beat thoroughly. Squeeze some mixture in your palm – if it is still too crumbly to bind, dribble in a little milk.

Divide into 12 balls, then form into sausage shapes about 7.5 cm/3 inches long. Place the flour on a plate and toss each sausage in the flour, shaking off the excess. Beat the reserved egg white in a bowl until frothy, then brush over sausages. Toss each in the remaining breadcrumbs. Place the sausages on a plate and leave to chill in the refrigerator for at least 20–30 minutes.

Heat a shallow pool of oil in a large frying pan over a low–medium heat. Add the chilled sausages and fry gently, in batches if necessary, turning carefully with tongs, until golden all over. Serve with mustard and fruit chutney.

150 g/5 oz/3 cups fresh breadcrumbs, plus an extra 50 g/2 oz/1 cup for coating
1 small leek, white part only, or 1 small onion, finely chopped
75 g/3 oz Caerphilly or mature (sharp) Cheddar cheese, grated
1 tbsp finely chopped fresh parsley
Salt and freshly ground black pepper
½ tsp dry mustard or prepared mustard
3 organic eggs
Milk (optional)
3 tbsp plain (all-purpose) flour
Olive oil for frying
Mustard and fruit chutney, to serve

**Serves 4**

This recipe is thought by some to be an old English country recipe, possibly from Devon, as it's sometimes called Devon Pie. Some attribute its origins to the land girls who worked the fields during World War Two. It was thoroughly popularised by Cranks vegetarian restaurant, which opened in swinging London in 1961, capturing the zeitgeist of hippy gastronomy. It was a big hit at the restaurant as it personified the Cranks style of wholesome, home-made goodness. Homity Pie is a delicious concoction of humble ingredients – true comfort food. Serve with a crunchy green salad.

# Homity Pies
# Potato and Garlic Pies England

To make the pastry (pie dough), place the flour, baking powder, mustard powder and salt in a food processor. Pulse a few times to aerate. Add the butter and process until the mixture resembles fine crumbs. Alternatively, work the butter into the flour by hand. Add the water and process until the dough just draws together. Turn out on to a lightly floured board and press together. Do not knead or it will become tough. Wrap in clingfilm (plastic wrap) and leave to chill until required.

To make the filling, place the potatoes in a large saucepan and pour boiling water over them, adding a little salt. Cover and cook until tender, about 10–15 minutes, then drain, mash and place in a large bowl.

Meanwhile, heat a large frying pan over a low–medium heat and add the oil. Add the onions and cook until very soft. Add to the cooked potato with the butter, parsley, half the cheese, garlic, milk and salt and pepper, and mix very thoroughly. Taste for seasoning. Leave to cool.

Preheat the oven to 220°C/425°F/Gas Mark 7. Thoroughly grease pudding moulds, foil dishes, ramekins or springform cake tin (pan) with soft butter. On a lightly floured surface, roll out the pastry, then use to line your chosen mould(s). Fill with the cooled filling mixture, and top with the remaining cheese. Bake the individual pies in the oven for 20 minutes or a large pie for 25–30 minutes. Serve hot or warm.

For the pastry (pie dough):
200 g/7 oz/1½ cups 100% wholemeal (whole wheat) flour
2 tsp baking powder
½ tsp dry mustard or prepared mustard
Large pinch of salt
100 g/3½ oz/7 tbsp cold butter, cubed
3 tbsp water

**For the filling:**
350 g/12 oz floury (mealy) potatoes, peeled and cut into large chunks
Sea salt and freshly ground black pepper
2 tbsp olive oil
3 large onions, about 450 g/1 lb, coarsely chopped
30 g/1 oz/2 tbsp soft butter, plus extra for greasing
Generous handful of fresh parsley, 5–6 sprigs, finely chopped
100 g/3½ oz/scant 1 cup Cheddar cheese, grated
2 garlic cloves, de-germed and crushed
1 tbsp milk

6 x pudding moulds or 10 cm/4 inch foil dishes or large ramekins
OR
1 x 24 cm/9½ inch springform cake tin (pan)

**Serves 6**

Nut Roast is one of the all-time greats of vegetarian classic food, but if not done well it can be a big disappointment. I was delighted to have been given this recipe, which originated from a Mrs Myrtleberry who ran a B&B in Devon. My main adjustment was to toast the nuts, which brings out a wonderful flavour. This is rich, satisfying and choc-full of protein. Though it might not have the most elegant appearance, it fits well into a full roast dinner, ideal for Christmas. Serve with steamed vegetables or salad, and a rich tomato sauce or gravy.

# Mrs Myrtleberry's Roast Devon, England

Place the nuts in a dry frying pan over a medium heat. Toast, stirring gently, until golden and fragrant, taking care not to burn. Remove to a bowl and leave to cool. Whiz in a food processor until very finely chopped (the mixture should still be loose, not a purée).

Preheat the oven to 180°C/350°F/Gas Mark 4. Grease the loaf tin (pan) with butter and line with baking paper (parchment), then grease the paper.

In a large bowl, combine the ground nuts with shallots, tomatoes, eggs, cheese, herbs, yeast extract mixture, lemon juice and seasoning. Mix thoroughly. Scoop the mixture into the prepared tin and bake for 45 minutes–1 hour, or until firm and golden. Cool slightly, then turn out on to a serving plate and peel off paper. Decorate with herb sprigs and serve with a rich tomato sauce or gravy.

250 g/9 oz/1⅔ cups mixed nuts (walnuts, hazelnuts, sesame seeds, almonds, cashews)

Butter for greasing

100 g/3 ½ oz shallots (about 4 small), finely chopped

400 g/14 oz can chopped tomatoes, drained

3 organic eggs, beaten

150 g/5 oz Gruyère or mature (sharp) Cheddar cheese, grated

1 tsp fresh or ½ tsp dried thyme

2 tsp fresh chopped sage or ½ tsp dried sage

½ tsp dried mint

1 tbsp finely chopped fresh parsley

1 teaspoon yeast extract blended with 1 tsp boiling water (or use 2 tsp soy sauce)

1 tsp fresh lemon juice

Pinch of salt

Freshly ground black pepper

Herb sprigs, to decorate (optional)

Rich tomato sauce or gravy, to serve

loaf tin, at least 500 g/1 lb 2 oz capacity, or a springform cake tin (pan), 20 cm/8 inches in diameter

**Serves 4–6**

Sounds boring? Far from it. This recipe is pure ingenuity – how do you turn a few potatoes into a ludicrously delicious and satisfying meal? It's all in the technique of browning the small-cut potatoes first. This is based on a recipe given to me by Geraldine Hartman, author of *Not Just for Vegetarians*. The recipe came over to the Canadian prairies from Ireland and was used in Geraldine's family for years, and was much appreciated during the brutal winters of her childhood.

# Traditional Potato Soup Ireland

Heat a large, heavy-based saucepan with a lid over a low–medium heat and add the butter. When the butter has melted, add the potatoes and onion and cook, stirring frequently, until slightly browned, about 8–10 minutes. The starchy potatoes are fond of sticking to the base of the pan, so keep them moving, though a golden crust forming in the pan will contribute to the flavour – just avoid burning.

Pour in the boiling water, stir and bring to the boil. Reduce the heat to a simmer, add salt and plenty of pepper, cover and leave to simmer for 15–20 minutes, stirring occasionally, until the potatoes are very soft.

Mix the flour to a paste with a little cold milk in a bowl, then beat into the remaining milk. Gradually pour into the soup. Simmer for a further 5 minutes. Add more milk if you prefer a thinner consistency. Serve in warmed bowls with grated Cheddar cheese, parsley and more black pepper.

50 g/2 oz/4 tbsp butter
1 kg/2 lb 4 oz (about 6 medium) potatoes, peeled and diced
1 large onion, chopped
750 ml/1¼ pints/3 cups boiling water
1–2 tsp salt, or to taste
Freshly ground black pepper
4 tbsp plain (all-purpose) flour
500 ml/16 fl oz/2 cups milk

**To serve:**
Grated Cheddar cheese
Chopped fresh parsley

**Serves 4–6**

Denis Cotter (see page 65), in his book *Paradiso Seasons* gives this recipe for *Colcannon* and comments, "Nothing will cause more derision in an Irish household, even in the twenty-first century, than lumpy mash, so do go at it with some energy, but don't ever be tempted to put it in the blender – that's called thick soup."

*Colcannon* was a favourite dish for fast days in Ireland and was used for rituals around Halloween. One such ritual, according to Jane Grigson in her *Vegetable Book*, was to fry the *Colcannon* into a crusty mass and push a ring into it. The lucky person who chomped on the ring would be the next to marry.

# Colcannon
# Cabbage Mash Ireland

Place the potatoes in a large saucepan with a lid and cover with water and a generous pinch of salt. Cover, bring to the boil and cook until tender. Drain and leave in the colander.

Meanwhile, bring another saucepan of water – this time just a little water – to the boil and cook the cabbage until just tender. Drain and chop finely (this avoids it getting waterlogged).

Return the potato saucepan to the hob (stove) over a medium heat. Add the oil, then add the spring onions and garlic and fry for 2 minutes. Add the cabbage and fry for a further 1 minute. Add the milk and butter and, when the butter is melted, add the potatoes and mash until smooth. Season with plenty of salt and pepper and serve in individual bowls with a decent tablespoon of butter, if desired.

1 kg/2 lb 4 oz floury (mealy) potatoes, peeled
Salt and freshly ground black pepper
½ head of spring or pointed cabbage, cored and chopped
2 tbsp olive oil
4 spring onions (scallions), finely chopped
2 garlic cloves, finely chopped
200 ml/7 fl oz/⅞ cup cup milk
60 g/2¼ oz/4½ tbsp butter
Butter, to serve (optional)

**Serves 4–6**

# chapter four
# Southern Europe

"The Bishop smiled… 'A soup like this is not the work of one man. It is the result of constantly refined tradition. There are nearly a thousand years of history in this soup'."

Willa Cather, *Death Comes for the Archbishop*

The soup in question was French Onion with croûtons, but it could well be *La Soupe au Pistou* or *Ajo Blanco*, both recipes included here. Southern Europe, with its mild climate and long history of wealth and power, has spawned some of the world's most sophisticated and influential cuisines. The Roman Apicius wrote the first ever cookbook in the fourth century AD; subsequent works didn't come along until the Middle Ages, but most were from the aristocratic households of Italy, Spain and France.

But where there's wealth and power, there must be poverty too. There is no early written record of peasant cooking in the Mediterranean, and that's where the greatest vegetarian recipes of the region originate. It's the historically poorer regions of Provence, Southern Italy and Andalucia, for example, where the sun shines and the land is fertile, that the creativity with vegetable cooking was prolific, and still is today.

# meet the expert:
# Jenny Chandler – Spanish Cuisine

Jenny Chandler is the founder and owner of The Plum Cooking Company in Bristol, England. Having spent much time in Spain, she has a particular love for its cuisine, and she is the author of *The Food of Northern Spain*.

It may seem odd to focus on Spain in a vegetarian cookbook. Omnivores consider it to be "*Jamón* Heaven", and Jenny admits, "Vegetables are usually served up as a first course – the main dish will invariably be fish or meat." However, its vegetable cuisine has a fascinating history. Being vegetarian can be a bit of a challenge for the tourist, though Jenny points out that most visitors will miss out on the real Spanish cuisine, which exists in the home. She says, "A glance at the market places of Spain will give you an idea of the vast role vegetables play in the local diet. Vegetable dishes tend to be eaten at home, while restaurants serve meat and fish, considered to be more of an extravagant treat." Behind closed doors – that's where Spain's vegetable cookery abounds!

Historically, as in so much of the world, religion and poverty have dictated the Spanish diet. "There was in the past a very strict Catholic tradition of avoiding meat, not only on Fridays but on numerous Saints' days such as Lent. During the terrible years of poverty that followed the Spanish Civil war, beans and pulses were eaten on a huge scale, and they were often referred to as the *carne de los pobres*, meat of the poor."

Some classic dishes are vegetarian by default – take gazpacho for example. A tomato-based gazpacho is, as Jenny explains, "the story of Spanish food in one bowl, and Spain's most celebrated vegetarian dish." Though gazpacho is normally associated with tomatoes, it was made without them before the 16th century (see page 114). "Tomato gazpacho really does embody Spanish cuisine, with the olive oil (from olives introduced by the Carthaginians), vinegar (from grapes introduced by the Greeks), bread (from wheat cultivated in vast quantities by the Romans) and tomatoes (brought from the Spanish colonies) along with peppers (also from Latin America) and the beloved native garlic. Originally these were all pounded together with a pestle and mortar – a method borrowed from the Moors."

The Moorish Empire, which extended as far as the Pyrenees and ruled in Spain for over 700 years, left an indelible mark on the cuisine, not to mention the architecture, as well as the agricultural infrastructure. They built irrigation systems in the huge river valleys of eastern Spain, and introduced aubergines (eggplants), artichokes, apricots, dates and oranges to the region, which all flourished there, as well as rice. "Eastern Spain is renowned for its rice dishes," Jenny explains. "The most famous vegetable *paella* comes from Murcia, just south of Valencia where short grain rice is grown and where the *paella* originated. Murcia is one of Spain's most fertile vegetable growing regions, so the *Paella Huertana*, or 'vegetable patch *paella*' is a regional speciality."

It was the Spanish conquest of the New World, however, that shaped Spanish food the most, and indeed affected the way the whole world eats. Capsicum (bell) peppers have taken on particular importance over the centuries, and in Spain they are eaten raw in salads, roasted on the fire, pickled, puréed and dried. "Dried peppers are used in numerous sauces like Romesco, where they are combined with almonds and hazelnuts. But it's the taste of pimentón, the unique smoked paprika, that really transports me to Spain," says Jenny. "Those universally adored peppers, as well as tomatoes, potatoes, corn, certain beans and chocolate were all introduced into Europe via Spain." These ingredients have become utterly essential. "Now," says Jenny. "the Spanish kitchen would be bereft without them," as would every kitchen in the Old World.

# focus on ingredients

Pimentón (smoked paprika) – Spain's own paprika, made by the same method as the Hungarian (see page 67), with a slightly different type of red pepper, a round one called cascabel. The area where pimentón is produced, Extramadura in the southwest, has a mild climate, and the peppers are dried for several days over smoking oakwood to prevent rotting. This gives the resulting spice a pronounced smoke flavour that makes pimentón totally unique. This is the spice that gives Spanish chorizo sausage its distinctive flavour. It is fabulous for vegetarian cooking because it can be added to anything to give a hint of smoke in place of bacon. Stir into yogurt with a little lemon juice, crushed garlic and salt and you have an amazing sauce or dressing. There are varying degrees of heat with pimentón, as with Hungarian paprika. Mild is called sweet or *dulce*; hot is called *picante*.

Saffron –This has been an important spice throughout the Mediterranean since ancient times, and the saffron of La Mancha in Spain is held in particularly high regard. It is the most expensive spice in the world, worth more than its weight in gold; luckily it is used very sparingly in cooking. Saffron is the stigma of a particular crocus flower, and it takes 70,000 crocuses to produce 450 g/1 lb of saffron.

**Pimentón**

**Pimentón**

Each stigma must be harvested by hand, which makes the whole operation very expensive. A small amount will give food a brilliant yellow colour and a distinctive, delicate flavour. Saffron "brews" into cooking like tea. If using it for uncooked dishes, (it's divine in a creamy dressing with lemon on cold potatoes) it can be soaked first in a little hot water to bring out the colour and flavour.

Artichokes – Originating in the Mediterranean, these complex vegetables are actually flower heads, giant thistles to be exact. When they are just a young bud, the whole artichoke is edible; Italians even eat them raw. As the artichoke matures, the choke develops further, eventually becoming the purple heart of the flower if allowed to bloom. This hairy choke must be cut out of the artichoke as it is not pleasant to eat. Mature artichokes must be eaten before they start to open up and bloom, so choose tightly closed specimens. Artichokes contain cynarin, a liver-cleansing chemical, and they are grown for pharmaceutical as well as culinary use; they also have a reputation as an aphrodisiac. They have a tendency to alter the taste of other food and drink, making it taste sweeter, which is why wine connoisseurs insist they shouldn't be eaten with wine.

**Artichokes**

Celeriac (celery root) –This is the root base of a plant closely related to celery, though only the base is eaten and not the stems. It is large and knobbly, creamy white with shades or patches of green and a strong, sweet celery flavour offset by a creamy texture when cooked. Celeriac can be eaten raw as in the French classic *Remoulade*. It does have a tendency to oxidize and turn brown, so it is often soaked in acidulated water or blanched before use. It has a surprising affinity with tomatoes (see page 103).

Olives – Symbolic of the Mediterranean and worshipped by the ancient Greeks and Romans, olives are one of the most important plant foods, not least for the oil they provide. The olive fruit itself is very bitter and unpleasant and must be cured to become palatable, unless it is made into oil, in which case it can go straight to the press. Avoid ready-stoned (pitted) black olives in brine (often canned) as they are actually green olives, which have been turned black by soaking in lye baths – this also leaches out all the good olive flavour. Extra virgin olive oil is from the first cold pressing and is the tastiest, though for high-temperature cooking it is best not to use unrefined oil but rather to use a lower grade oil. Flavour varies greatly – as a very general rule, Spanish and Greek oils can be quite peppery in taste, while French and Italian are fruitier. Some of the most delicious olive oils come from Provence and Sicily. Andalucia in Spain produces the greatest amount in the world.

**Celeriac**

**Saffron**

Basil – This beautifully fragrant herb is indispensable for Mediterranean cooking. It is quite vulnerable once picked and certainly does not appreciate being refrigerated – it is best stored wrapped in paper and left in a cool part of the kitchen. The flavour and fragrance of basil is best released by tearing the leaves and it should always be added at the end of cooking to preserve its delicate nature. Dried basil has lost much of its heady fragrance, but retains a certain sweetness and stores well. Supermarket basil plants seem to have a planned obsolescence but are handy to have around in the short term. If grown from seed, the plant will thrive in a warm, sunny place.

Risotto rice (Arborio, vialone nano, carnaroli) – Risotto is a speciality of the rice-growing regions of the north of Italy. The three aforementioned types have unique characteristics, which cater to the regional tastes. All of them are special in that they produce a lot of creamy starch for a thick and flavourful risotto, while each grain retains a toothsome bite at the core. Arborio is a plump grain, which is preferred in the northwest, where they like a stickier, more compact risotto. Vialone nano is a smaller grain, which is less starchy and produces a loose risotto, as preferred in Venice. Carnaroli is a newer strain, which is a cross between Arborio and a Japanese type. It is considered the best rice for risotto, producing a perfect balance of creaminess and bite.

Risotto is one of the few rice dishes of the world which is not served as an accompaniment, but stands completely alone in solitary splendour. There are three basic elements in risotto, which, if they are of the highest standard, come together to conjure up the magic. First, the rice — it *must* be the correct Italian risotto rice (see page 93). Second, the liquid — a well-flavoured stock, as well as some wine. Third, the character of the dish — the flavour base, which is usually a vegetable, and usually with a potent flavour as here, a selection of fresh and dried wild mushrooms.

My favourite risotto-making lesson came from an article in *Saveur* magazine entitled "*Risotto Voce*". It explained how the sense of hearing is one of the most useful. The rice talks to you. When the rice first goes in, it needs to fry a little, and when it starts making a crackling noise, you know it's time to add the first ladle of stock. Once that's absorbed, you can tell by the faint hissing sound the rice makes each time it's ready for more liquid.

# Risotto con i Funghi
# Wild Mushroom Risotto Italy

Place the dried porcini in a small bowl and pour the boiling water over them. Leave to soak for about 20 minutes. Drain and reserve the liquid. Strain the liquid if any grit has settled. Chop the porcini coarsely.

Meanwhile, bring the vegetable stock to a simmer in a saucepan.

Melt the butter in a large, heavy-based pan over a medium heat. Add the onion and fry until translucent, then add the rice. Fry briskly until the rice makes a crackling noise and looks slightly translucent. Add the porcini and fresh mushrooms and garlic and fry briefly until the mushrooms start to collapse and the garlic is fragrant. Add the vermouth or wine and the porcini water all at once and stir. When the liquid has been absorbed, add one ladleful of hot stock. Keep stirring regularly.

When the stock has been absorbed, add another ladleful of stock. Continue in this way until the rice is looking creamy, about 18–20 minutes. Taste for doneness – the rice should be *al dente* – somewhere between chalky and mushy. If it's still chalky, add more stock, letting it be absorbed until perfectly cooked.

Stir in the Parmesan cheese. Cover and leave to stand for about 3–5 minutes. Serve the risotto on warmed plates with extra Parmesan cheese passed around, and plenty of freshly ground black pepper.

50 g/2 oz/½ cup dried porcini
125 ml/4 fl oz/½ cup boiling water
1.2 litres/2 pints/5 cups well-flavoured vegetable stock
50 g/2 oz/4 tbsp butter
1 large onion, finely chopped
350 g/12 oz/1¼ cups risotto rice, such as Arborio or Carnaroli
250 g/9 oz fresh wild mushrooms, cleaned and coarsely chopped
3 garlic cloves, de-germed, chopped
125 ml/4 fl oz/½ cup dry vermouth or white wine
50 g/2 oz/½ cup freshly grated Parmesan cheese, plus extra to serve
Freshly ground black pepper

**Serves 4–6**

*Panzanella* can be as rustic as just bread and tomatoes with a little garlic and oil, or it can be slightly more elaborate like this one. In any case, there are a few tricks to making the best *Panzanella*. First, choose the very best ripe tomatoes in season. Second, use a good coarse-textured bread like a ciabatta, which is a day or so old. You can cheat the ageing by cutting the loaf in half and leaving in a warm oven for a few minutes to dry out. Trick three: by carefully saving all the juices from the grilled peppers and tomatoes, you preserve the essence of flavour, forming the base of the dressing, which impregnates the bread with a wonderfully juicy song of summer. Finally, if you pound the garlic with salt in a mortar, you get a glorious undertone of garlic, with no harshness.

# Panzanella
# Bread Salad Tuscany, Italy

Preheat the grill (broiler) to its highest setting. Grill the peppers until blackened all over, place in a plastic bag and leave to sweat until cool. Once cool enough to handle, peel the peppers and cut into strips, reserving any juice.

Halve the tomatoes and scoop out the core over a sieve (strainer) placed over a bowl. Cut the tomatoes into strips. Place the cores in a blender and purée. Push the purée through the sieve into the bowl of juice.

Pound the garlic with a large pinch of coarse salt in a mortar until smooth. Alternatively, use a garlic press. Combine the tomato juice, pepper juice, vinegar, pepper and garlic paste then whisk in the olive oil. Taste for seasoning.

Combine the peppers, tomatoes, capers, olives, ciabatta and basil. Mix well with the dressing. Leave to marinate for about 1 hour at room temperature. Serve drizzled with more olive oil if liked.

2 red (bell) peppers, halved, stem removed and de-seeded

2 yellow (bell) peppers, halved, stem removed and de-seeded

500 g/1 lb 2 oz ripe vine or Italian plum tomatoes

2 garlic cloves, de-germed

Coarse sea salt

4 tbsp red wine vinegar

Freshly ground black pepper

125 ml/4 fl oz/½ cup finest extra virgin olive oil, plus a little extra for drizzling

2 tbsp capers, drained

24 high quality black olives, stoned (pitted)

1 small or ½ large loaf day-old ciabatta, cut into coarse cubes

1 bunch/1 cup loosely packed fresh basil, leaves torn

**Serves 4–6**

Originating in the less affluent region of Puglia in the south, the other name for this dish in the local dialect is *Alla Molica*. This peasant-style recipe no doubt evolved from rustling something out of nothing when the cupboards were bare, and with typical Italian effect, the result is absolutely gorgeous. In poorer regions of southern Italy, breadcrumbs would often be used as a substitute for the more expensive grated cheese. Fresh egg pasta like pappardelle or tagliatelle works best, but you could use spaghetti or any pasta you like.

# Pappardelle alla Pangrattato e Noci
# Pasta with Crumbs and Walnuts Italy

For the pasta, bring a large saucepan of water to the boil and salt it well (as with all pasta water, it should be as salty as the Mediterranean sea).

Rip the bread into pieces and place in a food processor. Process to light crumbs – you should end up with about 500 ml/16 fl oz/2 cups in volume.

Heat a large frying pan over a low heat and add 4 tbsp olive oil. Add the crumbs, increase the heat and stir frequently until all the crumbs are very crisp and golden. Push the toasted crumbs to one side of the pan. Add the remaining olive oil and the chopped garlic and walnuts. Cook for 1–2 minutes until the garlic is fragrant, then stir through the crumbs. Remove the pan from the heat and set aside.

Cook the pasta in the boiling water until *al dente*. Drain very thoroughly, so that when the crumb mixture goes in it will stay crisp. Return the pasta to the pan. Toss the crumb mixture and parsley through the pasta and serve immediately with a drizzle of olive oil and plenty of grated Parmesan cheese and black pepper.

Fresh pasta, about 500 g/1 lb 2 oz (enough for 4–6 people)

Sea salt

150 g/5 oz fresh or slightly stale country bread such as ciabatta or pain de campagne

5 tbsp olive oil, plus extra for drizzling

3 garlic cloves, chopped

75 g/3 oz/¾ cup walnuts, crushed or chopped

Generous handful of fresh flat-leaf parsley, chopped

Freshly grated Parmesan cheese

Freshly ground black pepper

**Serves 4-6**

This is definitely not one for the low-fat repertoire. The whole point of this dish is that it is unctuous, wicked, delectable. Again, salting the aubergines is a step I usually include only when frying. Here the aubergines are cooked in the traditional manner for the dish – dipped in flour and fried in quite deep sunflower oil at a high temperature, which in addition to salting, gives a crisper, less oil-laden result. Combined with all that cheese, a very judicious slick of rich tomato sauce, fused together in the oven, then eaten at room temperature – it's a wonderfully indulgent and classic treat.

# Parmigiana di Melanzane
# Aubergine (Eggplant) Parmesan

Naples, Italy

Arrange the aubergine slices in a colander and sprinkle with a light but even coating of salt, in between layers if necessary. Leave to drain in the sink for at least 30 minutes–1 hour. Pat the aubergine slices dry with kitchen paper (paper towels). Spread some flour on a large plate and coat each aubergine slice, then shake off the excess flour.

Have ready a wire rack set over a large tray, for draining the aubergines. Alternatively, line a tray with kitchen paper. In a large frying pan over a high heat, heat a 1 cm/½ inch depth of oil for frying until very hot. Using tongs, fry the aubergines in batches, turning once, until golden on both sides. Drain and cool.

Preheat the oven to 200°C/400°F/Gas Mark 6.

To make the sauce, combine the tomatoes with the olive oil and salt to taste in a small saucepan. Reduce by half over a medium heat, stirring occasionally. It will look like very little sauce, but don't worry, that's all you need.

To assemble, place one layer of aubergine slices in the base of the lightly oiled casserole or gratin dish. Smear a little tomato sauce over the surface. Top with a few mozzarella slices, a light layer of Parmesan cheese, some torn basil then start another layer. Finish with a layer of aubergines and a little Parmesan cheese. Bake in the oven for 30 minutes, or until deep golden and bubbly. Leave to cool to just warm or ideally to room temperature. Cut into portions and serve with a light leafy salad.

1 kg/2 lb 4 oz aubergines (eggplants), sliced lengthways into 5 mm/ ¼ inch slices

Salt

Plain (all-purpose) flour for dredging

Sunflower or vegetable oil, for frying and greasing

300 g/11 oz Italian mozzarella, ideally buffalo milk, drained, dried and thinly sliced

50 g/2 oz/½ cup freshly grated Parmesan cheese

10–12 large fresh basil leaves, torn

**For the tomato sauce:**

1 x 400 g/14 oz can Italian plum whole peeled tomatoes, drained and coarsely chopped

1 tbsp olive oil

Salt

Leafy salad, to serve

20 x 30 cm/8 x 12 inch casserole or gratin dish

**Serves 4–6**

"*Norma*" refers to the opera by Sicily's native son, Bellini, from Catania. The word is also used to describe anything or anyone *ne plus ultra* – the ultimate, the zenith, in Catanian dialect. This dish is, indeed, a triumph of simplicity. The ingredient which will make it fully authentic is *ricotta salata*, salted, matured ricotta, which is a local speciality, and can be found in true Italian delis or specialty cheese stores. Failing that, I've offered an alternative – fresh ricotta and Parmesan, two other common ingredients in Sicilian cooking, which still work beautifully.

# Pasta Alla Norma
# Pasta with Aubergines (Eggplants) and Ricotta Sicily, Italy

Arrange the aubergine slices in a colander and sprinkle with a light but even coating of salt, in between layers if necessary. Leave to drain in the sink for at least 30 minutes–1 hour. Pat the aubergine slices dry with kitchen paper (paper towels).

Bring a large saucepan of water to the boil for the spaghetti and salt it well.

To make the sauce, drain the tomatoes of excess liquid in a sieve (strainer), leaving chunks. Heat a frying pan or saucepan over a medium heat and add 3 tbsp olive oil. Add the onion and fry until translucent, then add the garlic and fry until fragrant, about 1 minute. Add the tomatoes and cook until reduced slightly, about 5 minutes. Stir in the basil and season with salt and pepper to taste. Remove the pan from the heat and set aside.

Heat a large frying pan over a medium heat and add a shallow pool of oil. Fry the aubergine slices, in batches if necessary, until light golden on both sides. If the aubergines seem to drink up all the oil, remember that as they cook, their sponge-like cells will collapse and release the oil as they soften, so don't pour in lots more oil unless they are still very dry towards the end of cooking.

Cook the spaghetti until *al dente*, then drain, returning to the pan quickly so as not to lose all of the moisture. Toss through the tomato sauce, fried aubergines (it's fine if they break up slightly) and the salted ricotta or ordinary ricotta. Serve in warmed bowls with more crumbled salted ricotta, or with freshly grated Parmesan cheese.

1 large or 2 medium aubergines (eggplants), about 500 g/1 lb 2 oz, cut into 1 cm/½ inch circles

Sea salt and freshly ground black pepper

2 x 400 g/14 oz cans chopped tomatoes

Olive oil

1 large onion, halved and sliced

3 garlic cloves, chopped

Generous handful of fresh basil, torn or shredded

300–400 g/11–14 oz dried spaghetti

150 g/5 oz/⅔ cup salted ricotta, crumbled, plus more to taste

OR 125 g/4 oz/½ cup fresh ricotta, plus freshly grated Parmesan cheese to taste

**Serves 4–6**

True infant artichokes are edible throughout, as they haven't yet developed a hairy choke (see page 92). Often slightly more mature artichokes – adolescents, really – are sold as babies, but they can still be used in this recipe. If they are closer to the size of your fist than the size of a golf ball, then you should really remove the choke. Simply slice in half from the stem to the top and use a teaspoon to scrape out the hairy bits. Leave in a bowl of water with lemon juice or vinegar to stop discoloration, then proceed as below. It is difficult to give quantities for this recipe, as I don't know what size artichokes you'll find, but it's not the kind of recipe that requires exact measurements anyway, in true rustic French country style.

# Poivrade aux Fines Herbes et a L'huile Baby Artichokes in Herb Oil Provence, France

Place the prepared artichokes in a large saucepan with a lid and tuck in the herb sprigs and garlic. Add the peppercorns and a generous sprinkling of salt. Pour in enough oil to come halfway up the artichokes then add enough water to cover them. Cover the saucepan and bring to the boil. Once boiling, take the lid off but leave the heat on high. Let it boil vigorously – it will splutter and crackle as the water and oil fight each other. Eventually all the water evaporates and the oil wins. By this time the artichokes should be tender throughout, about 15–20 minutes, depending on their size.

Leave to cool, then serve with fresh crusty bread.

Enough baby artichokes to fill a large
  saucepan halfway, stem trimmed to
  1 cm/½ inch, and tops trimmed
  to about 1 cm/½ inch
Large fresh woody herb sprigs,
  including bay leaves, thyme,
  rosemary and lavender
1 whole bulb of garlic, sliced through
  the middle
Several peppercorns
Salt
Lots of olive oil
Fresh crusty bread, to serve

**Serves 4–6**

It's the *pistou* – a basil and garlic paste – which makes this otherwise fairly ordinary vegetable soup unique. *Pistou* is a sister of pesto, though the Italians never thought of putting it in their minestrone. The components of the soup are entirely season-led, and while sometimes the *pistou* is as simple as just basil, garlic and olive oil, in summer a sun-ripened tomato is pounded in with the basil. Notice how no stock is used, just water, as the vegetables make their own stock as they cook with the *bouquet garni*, resulting in a clean, fresh flavour. Traditionally dried beans are used, but I've used canned for convenience.

# La Soupe au Pistou
# Vegetable Soup with Crushed Basil

Provence, France

Heat the oil in a saucepan and stir in the leek, celery, onion and garlic. Stew slowly, stirring frequently, until tender, about 10 minutes. Add the salt and pepper, the seasonal vegetables, beans and *bouquet garni* and cook for 5 minutes, then add the water. Bring to the boil and leave to simmer for 30 minutes.

To make the *pistou*, pound the garlic and coarse salt in a mortar until smooth. Add the tomato, basil, Parmesan cheese and oil and work to a smooth paste. Alternatively, whiz in a spice grinder or blender.

Ladle the soup into serving bowls and garnish with a generous spoonful of *pistou*.

1 leek, white only, finely sliced

4 celery sticks (stalks), diced

1 onion, finely sliced

2 garlic cloves, finely chopped

4 tbsp olive oil

Salt and freshly ground black pepper

About 1 kg/2 lb 4 oz seasonal vegetables, diced or sliced, such as carrots, green beans, courgettes (zucchini), turnips, fresh artichoke hearts – whatever is available

1 x 400 g/14 oz can haricot or cannellini beans, drained and rinsed

*Provençal bouquet garni* (thyme and rosemary sprigs, a bay leaf and a strip of orange rind tied with cotton)

1 litre/1¾ pints/4 cups water

**For the *pistou*:**

2 garlic cloves, de-germed and chopped

Coarse salt

1 very ripe tomato, chopped

20 fresh basil leaves

4 tbsp finely grated Parmesan cheese

8 tbsp olive oil

**Serves 4–6**

I make this recipe over and over again at any time of year. It's inspired by Patricia Wells' recipe for "Celeriac Lasagne" in her book *At Home in Provence*. The thin-sliced celeriac almost resembles sheets of pasta layered with rich tomato sauce and cheese, similar to lasagne. I have a tendency to flaunt this dish with almost evangelical fervour – I believe it's the greatest celeriac dish ever. Better than *Remoulade* and certainly my favourite of all gratins. It has been argued that if you cook anything in that much cream and cheese, it is bound to be good, but once you taste it you'll understand – the tomato sauce transforms the celeriac into something absolutely celestial. Serve with a simple leaf salad.

# Celeri au Gratin
# Celeriac (Celery Root) Gratin Provence, France

Preheat the oven to 200°C/400°F/Gas Mark 6.

To make the sauce, heat a very large saucepan with a lid over a medium heat and add the oil. Add the onion and cook until soft and translucent then add garlic and cook until fragrant. Add the tomatoes, salt and pepper, vinegar and sugar and simmer for about 5 minutes, or until slightly thickened. Taste for seasoning.

Peel the celeriac, cut into quarters and slice finely (this can be very easily done with the slicing blade of a food processor or mandolin). Stir the celeriac into the tomato sauce. Cover the pan and simmer for about 10 minutes, or until tender but still a little firm. Stir in the cream and taste and adjust the seasoning if necessary.

Spoon half of the mixture into a well-greased large gratin dish, sprinkle over half the grated cheese, then finish with remaining mixture, smoothing down the top. Top with the remaining cheese. Bake in the oven until golden and bubbling around the edges, about 30–40 minutes.

**For the sauce:**
2 tbsp olive oil
1 medium onion, finely chopped
3 garlic cloves, finely chopped
2 x 400 g/14 oz can chopped Italian plum tomatoes
Sea salt and freshly ground black pepper
1 tsp wine vinegar
½ tsp dark brown sugar

**For the gratin:**
1.5 kg/3 lb 5 oz celeriac (celery root), untrimmed weight
180 ml/6½ fl oz/generous ¾ cup double (heavy) cream
Butter, for greasing
180 g/6½ oz/generous 1 cup Parmesan cheese, grated

**Serves 6**

*Aïoli*, the famous uber-mayonnaise with a serious garlic burn, provides the dressing for this collection of typical Provençal vegetables. Chickpeas don't make much of an appearance in northern French cooking, but in the south they are much loved. Making the real *aïoli* requires the patience of a saint and the freshest, unadulterated organic eggs you can get, as they remain raw. If you lack either, I've offered an alternative quick dressing, inspired by Rose Elliot in her *Bean Book*. This luxurious salad doesn't take well to refrigeration and should be enjoyed promptly at room temperature.

# Aïgroissade Chickpea Salad with Garlic Mayonnaise Provence, France

Steam the potatoes and carrots until just tender, then add the French and broad beans and steam for a further 2–3 minutes. Alternatively, place the potatoes and carrots in a saucepan, cover with water, add salt and bring to the boil. Cook until nearly tender, then add the beans and cook for about 2–3 minutes, or until all the vegetables are tender. Drain and cool.

*To make the* aïoli, place the egg yolks, garlic and salt in a food processor. Start the motor and use a teaspoon to add the oil one drop at a time until the mixture starts to thicken and turn pale. This requires the utmost patience, but the result is worth it! Eventually you can start adding the oil in a very slow and steady stream until it's all incorporated. Beat in the lemon juice. (If the mixture splits, you can try adding another yolk.)

*To make the alternative quick dressing*, beat the mayonnaise, yogurt, garlic paste and lemon juice together in a bowl until smooth.

Mix together the cooked, cooled vegetables with the chickpeas and artichokes. Stir through the *aïoli* or alternative dressing and serve immediately.

225 g/8 oz baby new potatoes
125 g/4 oz baby carrots
125 g/4 oz French (green) beans
125 g/4 oz fresh or frozen broad (fava) beans
Salt (optional)
1 x 400 g/14 oz can chickpeas, drained and rinsed
1 x 400 g/14 oz can artichoke hearts, drained, quartered

**For the classic *aïoli*:**
2 organic egg yolks
2 plump garlic cloves, de-germed
½ tsp salt
125 ml/4 fl oz/½ cup light olive oil, or half and half extra virgin and sunflower oil
1 tbsp lemon juice

**For an alternative quick dressing:**
3 tbsp mayonnaise
4 tbsp natural (plain) yogurt
2 garlic cloves pounded with ½ tsp coarse sea salt until smooth
1 tbsp lemon juice

**Serves 4–6**

As Central Mediterranean islands, Malta and Gozo have been subjected to invasion after invasion throughout history and, of course, the cuisine reflects this. With the closest neighbour Sicily being only 112 km/70 miles away, the Italian influence is profound. The Maltese name of this dish suggests it is authentically Maltese – the language is Semitic, with many French and Italian words. A soft goat's cheese from Gozo called *gbejniet* would be traditional, but ricotta works beautifully.

This dish is a real celebration of the artichoke, with complex layers of beans, eggs and cheese suspended in thick tomato-onion sauce.

# Stuffat tal-Qaqocc
# Artichoke Stew with Eggs and Ricotta  Malta

Prepare the artichokes by tearing off the tough outer leaves near the base. Cut off about halfway down, completely removing the tough and spiky parts of leaves, just above the choke. Cut in half through the stem and scoop out the hairy choke with the aid of a teaspoon. Place in a bowl of water acidulated with the lemon juice to stop them oxidizing.

Heat a large saucepan with a lid over a medium heat and add the oil. Add the onions and fry gently until soft and translucent. Add the garlic and as soon as it is fragrant, add the tomatoes. Bring to the boil, then add the sugar, vinegar, parsley and salt and pepper to taste.

Add the prepared artichokes and reduce the heat. Cover and simmer, stirring occasionally, until the artichokes are soft and cooked through, about 30 minutes. The stew will be very thick.

Add the broad beans and peas and stir through. Make 4 hollows with a wooden spoon and break the eggs into them. Spoon the ricotta in between the eggs. Cover while the eggs, beans and peas cook. As soon as the eggs are poached to your liking, serve the stew hot.

4 large fresh artichokes
Lemon juice
3 tbsp olive oil
3 medium onions, finely chopped
2 garlic cloves, crushed
2 x 400 g/14 oz cans chopped tomatoes
Pinch of sugar
Dash of balsamic vinegar
2 tbsp chopped fresh flat-leaf parsley
Salt and freshly ground black pepper
125 g/4 oz/1 cup fresh or frozen broad (fava) beans
125 g/4 oz/1 cup fresh or frozen peas
4 organic eggs
4 heaped tbsp ricotta cheese

**Serves 4–6**

*Fassoulia* is the Greek name for beans in general, and any beans at all love the company of tomatoes – no accident as they are both plucked from the vine around late summer. *Gigandes Plaki* is another name for this dish, this time referring to the specific gigandes beans or elephant beans from Macedonia, in *plaki* or sauce. Butter beans are their closest cousins. You can, of course, use dried beans – see tips in recipe for *Caraotas Negras* on page 54.

This dish is an absolute fixture of the Greek table, but traditionally, not as part of *mezedes* or "little dishes", which are appetizers. *Fassoulia* would fall under the category of *fagakia*, which refers to small courses, as part of a multi-course feast, or substantial enough to make a meal in themselves. *Fassoulia* with warm, toasted pitta bread and a light salad makes a lovely, simple, summery lunch.

# Fassoulia
# Giant Beans in Tomato Sauce Greece

Heat a wide pan over a low heat and add the olive oil. Add the onions and cook until soft and translucent.

Add the garlic, beans, tomatoes, herbs, honey, vinegar and salt and pepper to taste, bring to a simmer and cook very gently for about 1 hour. Some of the beans will break up and thicken the mixture towards the end of cooking. If it seems to be catching on the base, you can add a tiny bit of water, but the final texture should not be soupy – it should be so thick that it stands up when pushed to the side of the pan.

Serve warm or cold with toasted pitta bread. If left overnight, the flavour improves.

4 tbsp olive oil

2 medium onions, sliced

4 plump garlic cloves, chopped

2 x 400 g/14 oz cans elephant beans, butter beans or other white beans, drained and rinsed

2 x 400 g/14 oz cans chopped Italian plum tomatoes

1 tsp dried oregano or 2 tsp fresh, chopped

1 tsp dried dill weed or 2 tsp fresh, chopped

2 tsp dried thyme or a cluster of fresh thyme sprigs

1 tbsp honey

2 tsp red wine vinegar

Sea salt and freshly ground black pepper

Toasted pitta (pita) bread, to serve

**Serves 4**

This is a magnificent spinach and feta affair, with an intense aroma of dill and the delicate crunch of buttery filo pastry. Using part cottage cheese and part feta makes it lighter and not too salty, and though the raw rice might seem a little peculiar, it is a clever trick – it absorbs excess liquid and keeps the pastry crisp. The pie can also be made in a springform cake tin for a slightly more elegant presentation – perfect for the vegetarian centrepiece of a celebration dinner. Serve with boiled potatoes and a tomato and olive salad.

# Spanakopita
# Spinach Filo (Phyllo) Pie Greece

Preheat the oven to 180°C/350°F/Gas Mark 4.

To make the filling, heat the oil in a large saucepan over a low–medium heat. Add the spring onions and cook until soft. Stir in the spinach and cook until just wilted. Drain in a colander and press out as much moisture as possible. Leave to cool, then place on a clean cloth, gather up the sides and squeeze the excess moisture out of the spinach. Chop coarsely.

In a bowl, combine the spinach with the cheeses and herbs and mix thoroughly. Taste for seasoning – you may only need to add pepper, as the feta is salty enough. Add rice and mix thoroughly.

Unwrap the filo (phyllo) pastry, and if necessary, cut to fit the base of the baking dish. Cover the pastry with a barely damp cloth to prevent it drying out and becoming brittle. Combine the olive oil and melted butter. Brush the butter mixture all over the casserole or gratin dish. Place one layer of filo pastry on the base, brush with the butter mixture, top with another layer, brush with the butter mixture, and so on, forming 7 layers. Spoon all of the filling on top, spreading out evenly.

Continue layering the filo pastry on top of the filling, again forming 7 layers. Brush the top with butter and then, using a very sharp knife, cut the pastry before baking – cut all the way through into serving-sized diamond shapes or squares.

Bake the pie in the oven for 45 minutes–1 hour, until sizzling, deep golden and crisp right through each of the filo pastry layers. Cut again along the original slits before serving.

**For the filling:**
1 tbsp olive oil
3 spring onions (scallions), white and green parts, cleaned and chopped
350 g/12 oz/7½ cups fresh spinach, washed and trimmed, or frozen leaf spinach, defrosted
175 g/6 oz/generous ¾ cup cottage cheese, drained of any excess whey
250 g/9 oz/1 cup feta cheese, crumbled
2 tbsp chopped fresh dill
2 tbsp chopped fresh parsley
2 tsp raw long-grain rice
Salt and freshly ground black pepper

**For the pastry:**
7 large leaves of filo (phyllo) pastry, cut in half, or 14 medium leaves
3 tbsp olive oil
50 g/1¾ oz/4 tbsp butter, melted

20 x 30 cm/8 x 12 inch casserole or gratin dish

**Serves 4–6**

The gastronomy of Tenerife is, as with so many islands, a real mish-mash of global influences, but it also has a cuisine all its own. The Conquistadores, returning from the New World, brought the potato to the Canary Islands first, before they made it back to mainland Europe. This resulted in an extensive legacy of three dozen varieties known as "coloured potatoes", which came directly from the Andes and are still grown today. The *negra* or black variety is the proper one for this classic dish – it is not actually black but has a deep yellow flesh, often called *yema huevo* or egg yolk. It's easy to be alarmed by the amount of salt used here, but don't be. The potatoes are limited as to how much they can absorb, and the salt gives the skins a delectably chewy texture and a fluffy interior. The two sauces here are also delicious dribbled over a slab of bubbling grilled (broiled) goat's cheese, another island speciality, or halloumi (see *Saganaki*, page 111).

# Papas Antiguas con Dos Mojos
# Ancient Potatoes with Two Sauces

Tenerife, Canary Islands

Wash the potatoes and place in a large saucepan with a lid. Add enough water just to barely cover the potatoes. Stir in 200 g/7 oz salt. Bring to the boil and cook until tender, about 15–20 minutes.

Drain and return the potatoes to the pan over a high heat. Add another handful of salt. Cook, uncovered, shaking the pan frequently, until a sparkly white coating appears on the potatoes and they become wrinkled and completely dry.

To make the Red *Mojo*, microwave the red pepper with the 1 tbsp of water for 2 minutes, or until soft, then cool and peel. Alternatively, boil or steam until soft. In a mortar, pound the garlic with the salt and cumin seeds until smooth. Work in the red pepper, chilli, paprika and vinegar. Whisk in the oil. Alternatively, whiz until smooth with a hand-held blender – easier than an upright blender because of the small quantity. However, mechanical blending is considered unorthodox and some flavour will be compromised.

To make the Green *Mojo*, pound the garlic with the salt and cumin seeds in a mortar until smooth. Add the coriander and pound to a paste, then work in the chilli and vinegar. Whisk in the oil. Alternatively, use the blender method as described above.

Serve the potatoes warm or cold with the *mojos*, as a snack or appetizer.

1 kg/2 lb 4 oz baby new potatoes
200 g/7 oz sea salt, plus another handful

**For the** *Mojo Rojo* **(Red):**
1 red (bell) pepper, de-seeded and quartered
1 tbsp water
6 medium garlic cloves, de-germed
½ tsp coarse sea salt
½ tsp cumin seeds
1 large fresh red chilli (chili), de-seeded and coarsely chopped
1 tsp paprika
1 tsp red wine vinegar
2 tbsp olive oil

**For the** *Mojo Verde* **(Green):**
1 garlic clove, de-germed
½ tsp coarse sea salt
½ tsp cumin seeds
Small bunch of fresh coriander (cilantro), about 80 g/2¾ oz, leaves and some stems, finely chopped
1 large fresh green chilli (chili), de-seeded and coarsely chopped
1 tsp white wine vinegar
2 tbsp olive oil

**Serves 4–6**

*Saganaki* is a very loose term, seeming to encompass numerous types of and methods for frying cheese. Halloumi is my personal favourite for this simple first course. Halloumi is made in Cyprus and is usually a combination of goat's, sheep's and cow's milk, with a mild, salty flavour and slightly rubbery texture, which becomes sensuous when heat is applied. Although I often see it described as a "good melter", in fact its most unique quality is that it doesn't melt when cooked, but develops a scrumptious crispy crust and luscious interior. In terms of what to add to it, less is more – it can be served simply with a wedge of lemon, and it's also wonderful with the two *Mojo* sauces on page 109. The combination below, devised by food stylist Jane Suthering for the photograph, turned out to be not only a beautiful presentation, but also the perfect harmony of flavour and texture. The most important thing to remember is this: serve right away, piping hot, otherwise it loses those wonderful qualities.

# Saganaki Fried Cheese Cyprus

Slice the cheese into 5 mm/¼ inch pieces across the narrower end of the cheese. Heat a large non-stick frying pan over a medium–high heat and add the oil. Arrange the cheese in the pan, not touching, and fry until golden underneath. Use tongs to turn the cheese over and cook until golden.

Squeeze the lemon juice over the cheese while in the pan, removing any escaping seeds. Remove the cheese to warmed serving plates, scatter the oregano, olives, lemon zest over and season with black pepper. Serve immediately.

250 g/9 oz (1 average brick) halloumi cheese
2 tbsp olive oil
Juice of ½ large lemon
Handful of fresh oregano leaves
Handful of black Kalamata olives in oil, drained
Pared zest of ½ lemon, chopped
Freshly ground black pepper

**Serves 4**

This *tortilla* is not the maize (corn) flatbread of Latin America, but the thick eggy *torte* from Spain, where they take their *tortillas* very seriously. On a recent visit to Barcelona, I stumbled across a festival where a *tortilla* contest was in full swing. There were trestle tables lined up end-to-end down the street, where dozens of perfect *tortillas* were being examined by a panel of studious judges. How I wished I could have been one of them!

The potato didn't arrive in Spain until 1570, nearly a hundred years after its discovery by the Spanish in Peru. It then took hundreds of years for it to be accepted in much of Europe, but it didn't take the Spanish long to make potatoes into *tortillas* ("little cakes"). A *tortilla* is mentioned in *Ouverture de Cuisine*, published in Belgium in 1604, using potatoes, eggs, butter, parsley and oregano.

To make a proper *tortilla*, you need an alarming amount of olive oil to cook the potatoes, but rest assured, most of this oil is poured off. This recipe makes a large *tortilla*, which is a little cumbersome to flip over, but feeds a family heartily and keeps up to three days in the refrigerator. The recipe can be halved and made in a small frying pan for a mini version. A slice of *tortilla* can be eaten alone as a snack, and is also great in lunchboxes or on a picnic. A simple salad would be the best accompaniment.

# Tortilla de Patatas
# Potato Omelette Navarra, Spain

Peel the potatoes, then slice quite thinly, though don't worry about them being paper thin – just as thin as you can comfortably manage.

Heat a 30-cm/12-inch non-stick frying pan over a medium heat and add all the oil. Carefully add the potatoes and onion to the pan and cook, stirring frequently and without colouring, for about 20–30 minutes, or until soft and breaking up. Keep moderating the heat so they don't go brown and crisp, but rather soften gently in the hot oil.

Place a large sieve (strainer) over a bowl and drain the potatoes. Break them up slightly and leave them draining until slightly cool. A significant amount of oil will drain off and this may be re-used for another purpose.

In a large bowl, beat the eggs thoroughly and add about 1 tsp salt or to taste. Stir the cooled potatoes into the eggs. Stir very well so that every piece of potato is coated with egg.

(method continues above right)

1.25 kg/2 lb 12 oz potatoes
500 ml/16 fl oz/2 cups olive oil
1 large onion, halved and thinly sliced
6 organic eggs
Sea salt

**Serves 6–8**

Reheat the frying pan over a medium heat. Scoop the mixture back into the pan and cook until golden and set underneath, about 6–8 minutes. Slide the *tortilla* on to a large plate or board (larger than the pan, for safety), cover with another plate or board and flip over. Slide the *tortilla*, uncooked side down, back into the pan. Return the pan to the heat and cook until the underside is golden, the egg is set throughout and it becomes a cohesive mass, which shakes back and forth in the pan.

Slide the *tortilla* on to a large board or serving plate and serve hot, warm or cold.

This sexy little number is served as a *tapa*, snack, or first course. *Miel de Caña*, a light molasses made in Malaga, is the appropriate sweetener, which I was lucky enough to acquire a jar of, but honey works beautifully too. Salting the aubergines before frying will deliver a crisper, less oil-laden result.

# Berenjenas con Miel
# Aubergines (Eggplants) with Honey Andalucia, Spain

Slice the aubergines lengthways into very thin slices. Place in a colander and sprinkle salt over each piece. Leave to drain for 30 minutes, then pat dry thoroughly with kitchen paper (paper towels).

Place the flour in a wide bowl and stir in a generous pinch of salt. Heat enough olive oil in a large frying pan to barely submerge one layer of aubergines. Dredge the aubergines in the seasoned flour, then fry until golden on both sides. Drain on kitchen paper, then arrange on a plate and serve warm, with molasses, black treacle or honey drizzled over them.

2 small aubergines (eggplants), about 300 g/11 oz, top trimmed

Sea salt

50 g/2 oz/⅓ cup plain (all-purpose) flour

Olive oil

2 tbsp molasses, black treacle or runny honey

**Serves 4**

The name means "white garlic" and this is usually referred to as a white *gazpacho*. If you are only familiar with tomato-based *gazpacho*, you have just got to try this. *Gazpacho* existed in Spain well before the tomato came back from the New World, and while we normally associate *gazpacho* with tomatoes, the true elements that link all *gazpachos* are bread, oil, vinegar and garlic, and the fact that they are usually served icy cold. A blender is essential for making this, and you must keep tasting until you achieve the texture that is to your liking. Serve it on its own or with extra crusty bread.

# Ajo Blanco
# Chilled Garlic and Almond Soup with Grapes Andalucia, Spain

Place the bread in a dish that will hold it in a single layer and pour the milk over. Leave until the milk is absorbed.

Place the soaked bread, almonds, garlic, vinegar, oil, salt and half the water in a blender and whiz until smooth. Check the consistency and add more water until you get a consistency you like. Taste for seasoning.

Chill the soup until very cold. Also chill the grapes.

Serve the soup in teacups or bowls, each garnished with 6–7 chilled grapes.

100 g/3½ oz premium quality crusty white bread (2 thick slices), ideally a day old

125 ml/4 fl oz/½ cup milk

100 g/3½ oz/⅔ cup whole blanched almonds

2–3 garlic cloves, halved, de-germed if old

1–2 tbsp white wine vinegar, or to taste

3 tbsp finest extra virgin olive oil

Salt

Up to a 500 ml/16 fl oz/2 cups cold water

Small bunch red or green grapes, halved and de-seeded

This is a surprising, 100 per cent vegetarian *paella,* called "blind" because there are no bones or shells to pick out of it, so you can eat it with your eyes closed. The vegetables are cut to practically microscopic proportions, so they just melt into the rice. Traditionally, a true *paella* is cooked *al fresco* by the man of the house; when it's prepared by a woman indoors, it's called *arroz* (rice). Certainly no one will notice the absence of meat here, especially as the smoky pimentón (see page 92) gives it the same flavour as chorizo. The best thing about this dish is the crust, which forms on the base, which everyone fights over.

# Arroz con Verduras Ciego
# Blind Vegetable Rice Andalucia, Spain

Chop the onion, aubergine, courgette and red pepper as small as you can stand. Heat a large, non-stick frying pan, about 30 cm/12 inches in diameter over a medium–high heat and add the oil. Add the vegetables and fry until they are tinged with gold. Add the garlic and cook until fragrant, about 1 minute, then add the tomatoes, pimentón and rice. Stir-fry briefly, then add half the water, the saffron and some salt and pepper to taste and stir. Cover and increase the heat to high. Cook for 10 minutes, checking from time to time that it is not burning.

Pour in the rest of the water, stir once, then cover and reduce the heat to medium. Cook for 20 minutes, checking that it's not burning, but do not stir as this will encourage a nice crust on the base. In the last 5 minutes of cooking, scatter the French beans and peas over the top, cover and cook until the rice is al dente and making a crackling noise. Taste for seasoning. If the rice dries out too much, add water a little at a time, allowing it to be absorbed until fully cooked. Leave to stand for 5 minutes, then serve.

1 medium onion

1 medium aubergine (eggplant)

1 courgette (zucchini)

1 red (bell) pepper

3 tbsp olive oil

3 garlic cloves, finely chopped

2 ripe but firm vine–ripened tomatoes, chopped

1 tsp pimentón (smoked paprika)

300 g/11 oz/1⅓ cups paella rice or Arborio rice (see page 93)

1.5 litres/2½ pints/ 6 cups boiling water

Large pinch of saffron (about 20 strands)

Salt and freshly ground black pepper

125 g/4 oz French (green) beans, finely chopped

100 g/3½ oz/⅔ cup peas, fresh or frozen

# chapter five The Middle East, Asia Minor and the Caucasus

"The food equals the affection." Arabic proverb

Here in the cradle of civilization, hospitality is of utmost importance. The more you eat, the more appreciation you show for the hospitality you've enjoyed — that is the meaning of this proverb. This is a generous response to a particularly rich culture of hospitality throughout this region, where the host will stretch to offer his guest the most lavish spread he can afford, while depriving himself if necessary. Food is traditionally prepared by the women of the house with great skill and knowledge, which is acquired from their mothers and grandmothers. A massive welcome and twice as much food as one could possibly consume — this is the full grace of Arab hospitality, which extends to non-Arab parts of Turkey and the Caucasus, and notably in the form of the Georgian Feast (see *Meet the Expert*, right).

For millennia, this region has been a rather fluid amoeba where borders have been drawn and redrawn, where ancient cultures have been swallowed into empires and then expelled again. Today there are several proud and independent nations with strong cultural identities, some linked by Islam, but all with a passion for their unique identities, and for their food.

# meet the expert:
# Kevin Gould – Georgian Cuisine

Until recently, I was oblivious to the well-kept secret of Georgia and its food. But as soon as I "discovered it", I began to understand what a remarkable and unique place it is and how passionate Georgians are about food and just about everything else in life. I was suddenly hooked – intoxicated – I had Georgia on my mind. When I set out to learn more, Kevin Gould was my man – he's spent much time there and shares my fascination. We met for lunch in a Turkish restaurant, which was not entirely inappropriate. "Georgia has one foot in the West of the busy shipping lanes of the Black Sea," says Kevin, "the other in the East of the Silk Road." The country has a distinctive West-East divide, geographically cleaved by the Suram Gorge, and in culinary terms, the West has shades of Turkey while the East has more Persian attributes.

Although there are influences, Georgian food remains uniquely Georgian, a reflection of its culture. While its strategic position has meant that it has sustained invasion after invasion, its people maintain an uncompromising dignity and a love of their motherland so deep it is practically incomparable. "Georgians have a very strong sense of identity, which cannot be described as pride," says Kevin. "A powerful solemnity is more like it. But Georgia's heart does beat with pride born from the knowledge that she is the oldest wine-making nation in the world." The Georgians have been making wine since 7000 BC; it was they who taught the ancient Greeks how to make it and the Georgian word *ghvino* entered the universal lexicon through them.

Wine, bread, vegetables and meat form the cornerstones of Georgian cuisine. "Vegetable dishes are an essential part of Georgian life," says Kevin. "In Tbilisi, vegetarianism exists among the travelled, educated middle classes. In the regions of Abkhazia and Adjaria, there are mountain-dwellers who live to be 120 years old and profess a mainly vegetarian diet consisting of lots of fresh veg, pulses, eggs, dairy products and nuts." Throughout Georgia, walnuts are an everyday staple, especially ground into sauces, and hazelnuts are deeply loved. "Georgian hazelnuts are the sweetest and nuttiest you'll ever eat. Wave after wave of Americans travel to Georgia dreaming of making millions farming the world's best hazelnuts."

The immutable ritual of the Georgian table is The Feast. They do not need a special occasion for a Feast – "Georgians feast regularly and seriously," Kevin confirms. "If Georgia's spirit is in her grape, her body is the Feast, where all life is celebrated." Over a table groaning with sumptuous salty cheeses, salads of wild mushrooms, aubergines (eggplants), walnuts, breads, chicken and shish kebab, a toastmaster or *tamada* is elected to oversee proceedings. This person is always admired for his eloquence and ability to perform dozens of poetic toasts devoted to Georgia, while imbibing copious amounts of wine, not sip by sip, but down-in-one, over and over. Kevin explains, "The *tamada* starts with a short toast such as, 'To our brothers who shed blood for Georgia', then '*galmajous*!', which means 'to courage'. Then the toasts get longer and go on for about half an hour. 'To the mountains from which the streams trickle down to the fertile valleys that grow our grapes to make our wine'. The *tamada's* skill is drawing from the ancient well of Georgian emotion and casting it over the diners. There are always tears, singing, and afterwards, dancing on the table!"

*Kevin Gould is a chef, consultant, photographer and intrepid traveller. He is the author of* Loving and Cooking with Reckless Abandon *and* Dishy.

# focus on ingredients

**Pomegranates** – These hard-skinned fruits full of seeds inextricably encased in blushing, juicy pulp, are important all over the eastern Mediterranean, the Middle East and the Caucasus as well as India and China. They are best tackled by slicing in half, then turning inside-out, producing a gush of jewel-like seeds separated by inedible membranes. The pulp has a sweet-sour floral taste, and the seed within is indisputably hard and can be chewed and swallowed or spat out. The beautiful juice is easy to extract by rubbing seeds through a sieve (strainer). Pomegranate molasses is pure concentrated pomegranate juice. It's an intense sweet-sour condiment, and wonderful drizzled over salty white cheese. Grenadine is also made from pomegranate juice but contains added sugar.

**Sumak** (*sumaq, sumac, somagh*) – The dried, ground berries of a type of sumak tree, this spice has a pronounced acid flavour. It really tastes like lemon juice in powdered form, though it has a very noticeable and attractive red-auburn colour. It is often offered as a tabletop condiment in Turkey and the Middle East, for liberal sprinkling on kebabs and salads (see *Fattoush*, page 136). It's quite vulnerable to spoilage and should be kept in an airtight container in a cool, dark place, but even then might not last more than a couple of months.

**Baldo rice** – This short-grain rice is related and similar to Arborio rice but has a quicker cooking time. It is appreciated for its qualities of both stickiness and creaminess with a delicate flavour, making it perfect for pilafs, flavoured rice dishes such as risotto, and rice stuffings especially, as it moulds well into shapes (see *Biber Dolmasi* on page 133). It is grown in Italy and the USA as well as Turkey, where it is especially in demand.

**Aubergines** (eggplant, *berenjena, berenhein, melanzane, brinjal*) – These wonderfully versatile vegetables, originally from India but in prolific use the world over, range hugely in size, shape and colour. The "eggplant" moniker is descriptive of the small, white egg-shaped variety pictured below, which is quite rare. The shiny purple-black skinned aubergine is the most common, and they should be selected for freshness, with a very shiny skin and a taut, bouncy feel – never dull, wrinkled or soft. The act of salting to draw out liquid used to be applied to all aubergines before cooking, but any bitter juices which they used to contain have been bred out of the contemporary aubergine. Salting does, however, collapse the sponge-like cells, so if frying, they will absorb less oil. Salting is usually otherwise unnecessary if baking, grilling (broiling) or steaming.

**Pomegrates and Pomegranate Molasses**

**Aubergines**

**Baldo Rice**

**Sumak**

Walnuts – The word for these widely celebrated tree nuts comes from an Afghan word meaning "four brains", which refers to the knobbly lobe-like appearance of the nut meats. Walnuts are used widely in both sweet and savoury cooking and the strong-flavoured oil is perfect for salad dressing. Georgians are unique in the world in their use of walnuts as an integral part of their daily cooking – a wise thing too, as they are a super food, full of protein and omega-3 oils, which are the healthy fats also found in oily fish. These qualities make walnuts a crucial part of a vegetarian diet.

Yogurt – A true super food, yogurt is embraced all over the Middle East and India, as well as the entire English-speaking world where it has become a staple as recently as this century. Yogurt is fermented milk containing micro-organisms which make it highly digestible and extends its shelf-life. They convert the lactose in the milk to lactic acid, making it suitable for those with lactose intolerance, and give yogurt its distinctive tang. It has a long history of being appreciated for its cure-all, health-giving, life-prolonging properties, which are now scientifically proven and documented. In recent times has been shown to help fight colon cancer. The biblical Abraham is supposed to have been visited by an angel who revealed to him the life-enhancing properties of yoghurt; hence his longevity. In cooking, yogurt curdles when it boils – it can be stabilized with flour or egg.

Bulgar wheat (*bulgur, burghul, borghul,* cracked wheat) – This is a staple grain of the entire area covered by this chapter, with the exception of Georgia, though its neighbour Armenia has a particular passion for it (see *Bulgar Pilav,* page 127). Bulgar has gained international popularity as an essential element in the Lebanese dish, *Tabbouleh* (see page 138). It is the whole grain of wheat, which is par-boiled, dried and then ground to a coarse texture. Since it is relatively unrefined, it has a delicious nutty flavour and lots of vitality-enhancing B-vitamins and iron due to the inner layers of bran. As it is partially cooked, it needs only a brief soaking or boiling before it is ready to eat.

Fenugreek – This spice is more often associated with Indian cooking, as the seeds are a crucial component in spice mixes which give a classic flavour to a curry. I have placed it in this chapter however, where it does have the most extraordinary use in the Yemen for making a spicy condiment called *Hilbeh* (see page 141). It is also used in Afghani and Ethiopian cooking. The seeds may be cooked lightly, but they become very bitter if overheated. The just-sprouted seeds are eaten as an addition to salads, especially in the USA, and the leafy plant, sold in bunches of stems with lots of two-fold clover-like leaves, is cooked as a green vegetable, especially in India and the Yemen.

This dazzling, filling and nutritious walnut sauce (*Bazha*) is used with all manner of fish, fowl and vegetables in Georgia, but has a special partnership with fried aubergines. Festooning the dish with pomegranate seeds is traditional and makes it very beautiful. Serve with rice or *Bulgar Pilav* (see page 127) and salad for a well-rounded meal.

# Badrijani Bazhashi
# Walnut-stuffed Aubergines (Eggplants) Georgia

Arrange the aubergine slices in a colander and sprinkle with a light but even coating of salt, in between layers if necessary. Leave to drain in the sink for at least 30 minutes–1 hour.

Heat a large frying pan over a medium heat and add a shallow pool of oil. Pat the aubergines dry with kitchen paper (paper towels) just before slipping them into the hot oil. Fry in batches, turning with tongs, until soft and light golden but not crisp or brittle. Drain on kitchen paper, then leave to cool.

Place the walnuts, garlic, paprika, coriander and vinegar in a food processor or blender. Add salt to taste. Grind together, pouring in water gradually until a thick, smooth, barely pourable paste forms.

Take each aubergine slice and place a heaped teaspoonful of paste at one end. Fold the aubergine over the paste and top with another spoonful. If the aubergine slices are long enough, fold back over the paste again, making an "S-shape", and top again with paste.

Arrange on a platter. Sprinkle with coarsely chopped coriander and pomegranate seeds. Serve as soon as possible, as the walnut sauce splits after a while.

3 smallish or 2 medium aubergines (eggplants), about 450 g/1 lb, sliced lengthways 7 mm/⅓ inch thick
Sea salt
Sunflower oil, for frying
100 g/3½ oz/scant 1 cup whole walnuts
1 garlic clove, quartered
1 tsp paprika
3 tbsp coarsely chopped fresh coriander (cilantro), plus extra to garnish
1 tbsp wine vinegar
125–150 ml/4–5 fl oz/½–⅔ cup tepid water
Fresh pomegranate seeds, to garnish (optional)

**Serves 4**

This is an absolute essential at every Georgian feast. It's fast food Georgian-style, as you can always pick up a *khachapuri* on the run from a café or food stall. It might be round, square or boat-shaped; large or individual size; made from yeasted dough or puff pastry. Another version encloses cheese and a quivering soft egg with butter dribbling over the top. This version is more like what home cooks would make. It is really more of a pie than a bread, and it is easy and fabulous! I've tried to emulate the salty but stringy Georgian cheese used in *khachapuri* with a combination of Gouda and feta and it really works.

# Khachapuri
# Cheese Bread Georgia

To make the dough, place the flour, butter and salt in the food processor and whiz until the mixture resembles fine crumbs. Alternatively, place the flour, butter and salt in a large bowl and work through the mixture with your fingertips until the same crumbly mixture results. Add the eggs and yogurt and process until a dough forms. Do not over-process. Knead the dough briefly to until smooth. Roll the dough into a ball, wrap in clingfilm (plastic wrap) and leave to chill in the refrigerator for 1 hour.

Preheat the oven to 180°C/350°F/Gas Mark 4. Cut the dough in half and roll out on a lightly floured surface into 2 x 28–30 cm/11–12 inch circles.

To make the filling, mix both cheeses and egg together in a bowl. Place one dough circle on an oiled baking sheet and mound the filling on top, leaving a border around the edge. Place the other dough circle on top of the filling and fold the bottom layer's edges over and the top layer's edges and press to seal.

Mix the egg yolk and milk together in a bowl and brush all over the khachapuri with a pastry brush. Bake in the centre of the oven for 45 minutes. If the glaze seems to be turning too dark during cooking, you may need to move it to a lower shelf for the duration. Serve hot.

270 g/9½ oz/2 cups strong white (bread) flour
150 g/5 oz/5/8 cup chilled butter, cubed
½ tsp salt
2 organic eggs
4 tbsp natural (plain) yogurt
200 g/7 oz feta cheese, crumbled
400 g/14 oz Gouda cheese, grated
1 egg, plus 1 egg yolk
1 tbsp milk

**Serves 4–6**

Darra Goldstein in *The Georgian Feast* describes the large mushrooms which appear each year on the trees in the spring near Telavi, in the wine country. Simple and delicious, make sure that you use the most flavourful wild mushrooms you can find.

# Khis Soko Wild Mushrooms with Herbed Eggs Georgia

Clean the mushrooms – if they are truly wild, they will probably need to be washed or soaked to remove any remnants of the forest floor. Larger ones, such as ceps, may only need a wipe. In any case, make sure they are thoroughly dry before cooking. Chop the mushrooms quite finely.

Beat the eggs, herbs and spring onions together in a bowl and season with salt and pepper to taste.

Place a large frying pan over a medium heat and add the butter. When the butter has melted, increase the heat to high and add the mushrooms. Stir-fry just until wilted and glossy but stop before they begin to release much liquid. Pour in the egg mixture and stir. Cook just until it clings to the mushrooms, about 1 minute. Serve with bread or with *Bulgar Pilav* (see page 127).

350 g/12 oz best wild mushrooms, such as ceps (cèpes), girolles, chanterelles, morels
3 organic eggs, beaten
2 tbsp finely chopped fresh coriander (cilantro)
1 tbsp finely chopped fresh mint
2 spring onions (scallions), finely chopped
Sea salt and freshly ground black pepper
30 g/1 oz/2 tbsp butter
Bread, to serve

**Serves 4**

A velvety deep purple purée with chilled cucumbers bursting between your teeth and a faint garlic undertone – this summer soup is an ingenious way of using up a glut of blackberries. Adapted from *The Classic Cuisine of Soviet Georgia* by Julianne Margvelashvili.

# Makvlis Supi Blackberry Soup with Cucumber and Herbs Georgia

Rinse the blackberries. Place in a food processor or blender and whiz to a purée. You may need to add a little water to get the blades moving. Push through a sieve (strainer) into a large bowl. A slightly messy job, but worth it, I assure you. You should end up with just under 1 litre/1¾ pints/4 cups of smooth blackberry purée.

(method continues above right)

1 kg/2 lb 4 oz fresh blackberries
1 garlic clove, peeled
Coarse sea salt
4 tbsp chopped fresh coriander (cilantro)
2 tbsp chopped fresh mint
2 baby cucumbers or 1 English cucumber, peeled and diced

**Serves 4–6**

Pound the garlic with a large pinch of salt in a mortar until smooth. Alternatively, use a garlic press. In a large bowl, combine with the coriander, mint, blackberry purée and half of the diced cucumber, leaving the remaining diced cucumber for the garnish. Keep the cucumber for the garnish chilled in the refrigerator until required. Taste for seasoning. Chill the soup for at least 1 hour. Serve each bowl topped with the reserved diced cucumber.

Georgians love beans and serve them in numerous ways. This unusual dish is a cross between a bean chilli and a warm salad. It is substantial, nutritious, and packed with protein, but best of all, the walnut-herb sauce has a real knockout flavour — a vegetarian classic if there ever was one. Georgians would usually add dried marigold powder (*shaffran*) to this dish, and this spice gives much of Georgian cuisine its unique flavour as well as a yellow hue, though it is nothing like saffron. This one goes without but is still excellent, and the mix of herbs and spices produces a surprising smoky undertone.

# Lobio Nigozit
# Red Beans and Walnuts Georgia

Heat a saucepan over a low heat and add the oil. Add the onion and fry until soft and translucent.

Meanwhile, in a food processor or large mortar, grind together the walnuts, herbs, garlic, spices and salt to taste, until a coarse paste results.

Stir the beans, paste, pomegranate molasses and water (or suggested alternative) into the pan and stir until heated through. Remove the pan from the heat and leave the mixture to cool slightly. Transfer to a serving bowl and serve warm or at room temperature, sprinkled with coriander leaves and pomegranate seeds.

1 tbsp sunflower oil

1 medium onion, chopped

50 g/2 oz/½ cup walnuts

Generous handful of fresh parsley leaves

Generous handful of coriander (cilantro) leaves, plus a few extra to garnish

½ tsp dried thyme

1 small garlic clove

⅛ tsp ground cinnamon

Pinch of ground cloves

½ tsp dried chilli (red pepper) flakes

Sea salt

2 x 400 g/14 oz can kidney beans, drained and rinsed

4 tbsp pomegranate molasses (page 118) plus 4 tbsp water, OR 2 tbsp balsamic vinegar mixed with 1 tsp caster (superfine) sugar and 4 tbsp water

2 tbsp fresh pomegranate seeds (optional)

**Serves 4**

Georgia is famous for her delectable pomegranates (see page 118, for tips on tackling them). A symbol of hope and desire, Georgians prize these legendary fruits and use them in many dishes and in sauces in particular. They love a tart edge to their food, and pomegranates reliably deliver this strong sweet-sour effect. The beautiful jewel-like seeds release a tangy, magenta juice, adding a fruity acidity and pink hue to this sauce. It is said, "With a Georgian sauce, you can swallow nails," so even a hater of aubergines might find this salad palatable.

## Badrijani Salati
# Aubergine (Eggplant) Salad with Pomegranate Georgia

Place the aubergine slices in a large colander and sprinkle salt over all of them. Leave in the sink to drain for 30 minutes, then pat the aubergine slices dry with kitchen paper (paper towels).

Heat a large frying pan over a medium heat and add a shallow pool of oil. Fry the aubergines, in batches if necessary, until golden on both sides, then drain on kitchen paper. Cool. Arrange on a platter.

The following step is optional, but it really will bring out the best flavour. Toss the coriander seeds for the dressing in a small dry frying pan over a high heat until they darken one shade – only about 1 minute.

Place the coriander seeds in a mortar and grind with the garlic and sea salt. (Alternatively, crush with the back of knife.) Add the herbs and pound a bit to release the flavours. Place the pomegranate seeds in a sieve (strainer) and, holding it over the mortar, crush the seeds with a fork to release the juice – you should have about 1–2 tablespoons juice. Stir in the chilli flakes or cayenne pepper, mayonnaise and yogurt and mix well. Taste for seasoning. Spoon the dressing over the aubergines and sprinkle with extra pomegranate seeds and chopped parsley.

8 baby aubergines (eggplants), sliced lengthways, OR 2 medium aubergines, about 400 g/14 oz, sliced into 1 cm/½ inch circles
Sea salt
Sunflower oil for frying

**For the dressing:**
1 tsp coriander seeds
1 garlic clove, degermed
½ tsp coarse sea salt
3 tbsp chopped fresh parsley, plus extra to garnish
3 tbsp chopped fresh purple or ordinary basil
3 tbsp chopped fresh coriander (cilantro)
Handful of pomegranate seeds, (about 4 tbsp) plus extra to garnish
Pinch of dried chilli (red pepper) flakes or cayenne pepper
1 tbsp mayonnaise
2 tbsp yogurt

**Serves 4**

*Falafel* have been around for so long, nobody can be sure of their origin, though many cultures lay claim to them. The Coptic Christians of Egypt declare them theirs, though they call them by a different name, *tamia*, and make them with broad (fava) beans. In Lebanon, Syria and Jordan the recipe changes to half broad, half chickpea; in Israel they add bulgar wheat. This particular recipe is how they are made in Palestine, and while migrant Palestinians may well have taught the whole Middle East how to make *falafel*, what does it really matter?

*Falafel* make superb party food, as a canapé with a dipping sauce. Typically they are formed with a shaping apparatus called '*aleb falafel*', which pops out uniform shapes into hot oil, then they're served in pitta bread with various vegetables and sauces (see below).

# Falafel
# Chickpea Fritters Palestine

Place the chickpeas in a very large bowl and pour lots of cold water over them (at least 3 times the volume of chickpeas). Leave to soak for at least 6 hours or overnight.

Drain the chickpeas thoroughly and place in a food processor. Add the parsley, garlic, onion and spices and start the motor on high. You will probably have to keep scraping down the sides to get it evenly puréed. Add up to 3 tbsp of water if necessary until a smooth but fairly solid mass forms. Finally, whiz in the baking powder.

Leave the mixture to rest in the refrigerator for 30 minutes.

Heat a 2.5–5cm/1–2 inch depth of oil in a heavy-based pan. Unless you own a falafel maker, use your hands to form firmly packed balls. It may help to keep moistening your hands with water. I prefer balls the size of large cherries. Alternatively, you can make them double the size and flatten them slightly. If you like, they can be refrigerated or frozen now for later use.

As with most fried foods, falafel are best eaten straight after frying, so be ready with your accompaniments. Test the oil – a pinch of the mixture should sizzle immediately but not violently. A small cube of bread should brown in 20–30 seconds. Fry several falafel at a time until golden all over, then drain on kitchen paper (paper towels). Serve immediately on their own or stuffed into bread with the suggested accompaniments.

375 g/13 oz/2 cups dried chickpeas
12 long stems of fresh parsley leaves, about 40 g/1½ oz, well washed and dried, then coarsely chopped
3 garlic cloves, de-germed
1 medium onion, coarsely chopped
1 tsp sea salt, or to taste
1 tbsp ground cumin
2 tsp ground coriander
¼ tsp turmeric
½ tsp cayenne pepper
3 tbsp water
½ tsp baking powder
Sunflower or vegetable oil, for deep-frying

**To serve:**
Warm thin pitta (pita) or *khobez* bread
Hummus
Tahini (sesame seed paste)
Chilli (chili) sauce, store-bought or home-made (see recipe for *Pilipili* on page 166), or *Hilbeh* (see page 141)
Mixed salad
Pickled chillies (chilies)

**Makes 60 small or 30 large, serves 6–8**

Armenians are very partial to bulgar wheat (see page 119), and it is certainly a healthier grain than refined white rice, with lots more flavour. If you have a choice of grades, a *Pilav* should always be made with a coarse bulgar wheat. This *Pilav* will make a flavourful base for whatever you eat with it, without dominating. Whatever you have it with, it wouldn't be complete without a dollop of creamy yogurt – *madzoon* in Armenian – as it complements the *Pilav* perfectly.

Serve with *Badrijani Bazhashi* (see page 120), *Khis Soko* (page 122) or *Palava* (page 165) and a dollop of yogurt.

# Bulgar Pilav
# Cracked Wheat Pilaf Armenia

Place the bulgar wheat in a fine sieve (strainer) and rinse it under cold running water until the water runs clear. Leave to drain.

Heat a saucepan with a lid over a medium heat and add the oil. Add the onion and fry until golden. Add the drained bulgar wheat, dried herbs and salt and pepper to taste. Fry for 2 minutes, then stir in the water. Bring to the boil, cover and leave to simmer for 10 minutes, or until the water is absorbed and the grains are tender.

Transfer to a warmed serving dish and either stir through or top with the pine nuts and herbs, if you like. Serve with a dollop of yogurt.

280 g/10½ oz/1¾ cups coarse bulgar (bulgur) wheat
2 tbsp olive oil
1 medium onion, finely chopped
2 tsp dried basil
½ tsp fresh chopped or dried rosemary
1 bay leaf
Sea salt and freshly ground black pepper
500 ml/16 fl oz/2 cups hot water
Natural (plain) yogurt, to serve

**To garnish (optional):**
2 tbsp pine nuts
2 tbsp finely chopped fresh coriander (cilantro)
2 tbsp finely chopped fresh parsley

**Serves 4–6**

Armenia, like its neighbours in the Caucasus Georgia and Azerbaijan, is strategically placed at the gateways of Europe, Asia and the Middle East. Armenians have had to tolerate thousands of years of invasion, occupation and displacement, but have managed to maintain their strong cultural identity, their unique alphabet and their language. This recipe reflects some of their culinary identity: a love of aubergines, nuts, cheese, pasta, liberal use of herbs and most importantly, yogurt (see page 119). This is adapted from Armenian author Arto Der Haroutunian's *The Yogurt Book*, a fascinating look at the importance of yogurt throughout the world. When his family emigrated to Britain, his mother brought her prize possession – a yogurt starter that had been in the family for generations. "Yogurt begets yogurt," he says, "it is eternal."

## Arshda Madznov
# Macaroni Baked in Yogurt Armenia

Preheat the oven to 200°C/400°F/Gas Mark 6. Brush the casserole or gratin dish with oil.

Bring a large saucepan of water to the boil and salt it well. Cook the macaroni or pasta until *al dente*. Drain thoroughly.

Meanwhile, heat a large frying pan over a medium heat and add a shallow pool of oil. Add the aubergine slices and fry until soft and golden. Drain on kitchen paper (paper towels).

Beat together the yogurt, egg yolks, fennel seeds, dill, garlic and salt and pepper to taste in a large bowl. Stir the pasta through this mixture to coat evenly. Scoop into the baking dish and smooth the surface.

Cover the pasta with interleaved rows of sliced cooked aubergine and tomato. Sprinkle the feta and almonds over the top. Cook in the oven until hot, bubbly and golden on top, about 20–25 minutes. Serve with a crisp green salad.

olive oil, for frying and greasing

Sea salt and freshly ground
   black pepper

200 g/7 oz dried macaroni or other
   pasta shapes

2 medium aubergines (eggplants), about
   450 g/1 lb, sliced into thin circles,
   about 5 mm/¼ inch thick

500 ml/16 fl oz/2 cups natural
   (plain) yogurt

2 egg yolks

1 tsp fennel seeds

2 tsp dried dill weed

1 garlic clove, crushed

3 large vine-ripened tomatoes, sliced
   into thin circles

100 g/3½ oz feta cheese, crumbled

30 g/1 oz/⅓ cup flaked or slivered
   almonds (a good handful)

Crisp green salad, to serve

20 x 30 cm/8 x 12 inch casserole or
   gratin dish

**Serves 4–6**

There are two stories about the swooning Priest. One is that he was overwhelmed with pleasure when he tasted this. The other is that, when he saw how much precious olive oil his wife used to cook it, he keeled over.

As this version is baked, the olive oil is used fairly sparingly. Usually I only salt aubergines for frying (see page 118), but it's a good idea in this oven-baked recipe too, as there is time to do it while you prepare the stuffing and it helps season the aubergines.

# Imam Biyaldi
# The Priest Fainted – Stuffed Aubergines (Eggplants) Turkey

Preheat the oven to 200°C/400°F/Gas Mark 6. Leave the stem on the aubergines. Using a potato peeler, remove several strips of peeling from the stem to base around the aubergines to give a striped effect. This is more for aesthetics than anything else – though sometimes aubergine skins can seem a little tough. Leaving the stem intact, cut the aubergine in half from top to bottom, then again into quarters. Sprinkle about ½ tsp of salt inside each and leave in a colander in the sink.

To prepare the stuffing, heat the olive oil in a medium saucepan over a medium heat and add the onions. Fry until thoroughly soft, then add the garlic. Fry for a minute or so until fragrant. Remove the pan from the heat and stir in the tomatoes, parsley, salt, pepper and sugar.

Select a large casserole dish with a lid or use foil for covering. Wipe the inside of the aubergines with kitchen paper (paper towels). Fill the aubergines with the onion mixture and lay them in the casserole.

Mix the tomatoes, oil, water, vinegar, brown sugar and salt and pepper to taste together in a large bowl and pour over the aubergines. Cover and bake in the oven for about 1 hour. Uncover and bake for a further 30 minutes, or until thoroughly cooked. The aubergines should be as soft as butter, so that a knife pricked in them meets no resistance. Serve warm with rice, or to be faithful to tradition, serve cold with pitta bread.

3 medium-sized long aubergines (eggplants), about 750 g/1 lb 10 oz
Salt

**For the stuffing:**
3 tbsp olive oil
3 medium onions, halved and sliced
6 garlic cloves, chopped
1 x 400 g/14 oz can chopped tomatoes
Generous handful of fresh parsley, chopped
Salt and freshly ground black pepper
1 tsp dark brown sugar

**For the cooking liquid:**
1 x 400 g/14 oz can chopped tomatoes
2 tbsp olive oil
125 ml/4 fl oz/½ cup water
1 tbsp red wine vinegar
1 tsp dark brown sugar
Salt and freshly ground black pepper

Cooked rice or pitta (pita) bread, to serve

**Serves 6**

I am extremely fortunate to live a few minutes walk from Green Lanes in North London. This area could be called "Little Turkey" as it is heavily populated by Turkish exiles, many of who have set up food stores and restaurants. We frequently pop down to Green Lanes for a bite and it's always a tough choice; there are literally dozens of *ocakbasi* or barbecue restaurants to choose from, all equally good and with similar formats: open charcoal barbecues in the middle of the restaurant, overseen by a skilled cook who whizzes back and forth in an office chair on wheels, tending his various kebabs. These restaurants also invariably have pizza ovens and serve *pide* and *lahmacun*, always described as Turkish pizza. This is my interpretation of one of my favourite *pides* in Green Lanes.

# Peynirli Pide
# Cheese Pizza with Yogurt Turkey

To make the dough, place the flour in a bowl and mix in the salt and yeast. Make a well in the centre and add 2 tbsp of the olive oil. Start stirring in the water to form a dough. When most of the flour has been incorporated and the dough is still quite sticky, knead in the bowl with one hand to incorporate the rest of the flour, but stop before the dough feels dry.

Turn the dough out on to a clean, dry surface and knead lovingly for 8 minutes until smooth and elastic. Pour some oil into the bowl and pop the dough back into it, turning the dough so that it gets a coating of oil. Cover the bowl with a damp cloth and leave to prove, preferably in a warm spot, for 30 minutes–1 hour, or until doubled in size. Once proved, you can punch the dough down and store in a sealed bag the refrigerator for up to 3 days – just remember to keep punching it down every once in a while.

Preheat the oven to 220°C/425°F/Gas Mark 7. Oil 2 baking trays with olive oil. Punch down the proven dough and divide into 4 portions. Roll out the pieces into 4 thin ovals and place on the trays. Spoon the yogurt over the middle of each oval, leaving a 2.5 cm/1 inch border all around. Top with a row of sliced peppers and onion and sprinkle with sultanas and dill. Season lightly with salt and pepper, then top with cheese. Fold the long sides over the filling, not to cover completely but just to enclose the edges. Pull the ends of the dough together and seal, forming a boat-shaped enclosure around the filling.

Bake the *pide* in the oven for 20–30 minutes, or until golden and stiff. Cool briefly, then devour while still warm.

500 g/1 lb 2 oz/3⅓ cups strong white (bread) flour

1 tsp salt

1 x 7 g/¼ oz packet (package) easy-blend dried (bread machine) yeast

300ml/10 fl oz/1 cup plus 3 tbsp hand-hot water

Olive oil

6 tbsp thick and creamy yogurt

1 yellow or red (bell) pepper, cored and thinly sliced

1 medium onion, halved and thinly sliced

3 tbsp sultanas (golden raisins)

4 tbsp chopped fresh dill

Salt and freshly ground black pepper

125 g/4 oz Gruyère, Gouda or other melting cheese

Turkish cooks are adamant about their traditional recipes: this dish must be served cold, (though I think it's just as delicious served freshly cooked), and it is preferable served alone as its own course. Turkish vegetable dishes have their own honour and are usually served separate from the meat course. Irfan Orga, in his book *Turkish Cooking*, plainly states, "The judicious use of herbs and spices is most important in the intelligent preparation of food." This dish is a good example of this. The rice, infused with the flavour of the pepper, has a subtle and sublime character, which I have tried to enhance – rather than extinguish – with the use of dill and cinnamon.

# Biber Dolmasi
# Stuffed (Bell) Peppers Turkey

To make the stuffing, heat a saucepan over a medium heat and add the oil. Add the spring onions and pine nuts and fry until the nuts are slightly golden, then add the rice. Fry until slightly translucent and tinged with gold. Add the water, tomato, dill, cinnamon, currants or sultanas and salt and pepper to taste. Stir, cover and bring to the boil. Reduce the heat to a simmer and cook for about 15–20 minutes, or until all the liquid has been absorbed and the rice is tender.

Meanwhile, prepare the peppers. Slice the tops off about 1 cm/½ inch below the stem to form a lid. Remove and discard all the seeds and membranes.

Choose a large saucepan with a lid that will accommodate all the peppers standing upright with the stem-lids on, ideally quite snugly together. Alternatively, use 2 saucepans. (If you don't have the requisite pan(s), use the alternative cooking method below.)

Fill the peppers with the rice mixture, fairly solidly but not too packed. Place in the cooking vessel and put the stem-lids on. Pour the vegetable stock or water into the base of the saucepan. Place the pan over a medium heat and cover. Cook until the peppers are soft, about 20–30 minutes. Make sure that the saucepan does not boil dry. Discard or reserve the stock for another use.

To oven cook, preheat the oven to 200°C/400°F/Gas Mark 6.

Stand the stuffed peppers with stem-lids on in a roasting dish, ideally snugly together so they can't fall over. Pour the stock or water into the dish. Drape foil carefully over the peppers and seal around the edges of the dish. Bake in the oven until tender, about 40–50 minutes. Serve warm, or to be faithful to tradition, cool in the liquid, then chill in the refrigerator and serve.

6 green (bell) peppers
250 ml/8 fl oz/1 cup vegetable stock or water

**For the stuffing:**
2 tbsp olive oil
4 spring onions (scallions), sliced
4 tbsp pine kernels (pine nuts)
300 g/11 oz/1½ cups short-grain rice, such as baldo (page 118), sushi, risotto or pudding rice
600 ml/1 pint/2½ cups water
1 vine-ripened tomato, chopped
4–5 tbsp chopped fresh dill
1 tsp ground cinnamon
4 tbsp currants or sultanas (golden raisins)
Sea salt and freshly ground black pepper

**Serves 6**

Soothing and comforting, perfect for when you're feeling a bit delicate, this soup is a noted hangover cure. The tranquillity it imparts is reflected by the name – *yayla* refers to the cool and peaceful highland plateaus all over Turkey. Before the onset of summer, villagers who keep herds maintain old nomadic ways and migrate with their cattle, sheep and goats to the cool heights of the *yayla*. Here they escape the heat and provide new food sources for their animals, and lots of milking and yogurt-making goes on.

The soup can be made porridge-like or broth-like, as you prefer. The rice will continue to expand and thicken in the stock as it stands. Some like it with a dribble of garlic-chilli oil on top.

# Yayla Corbasi
# Yogurt Soup with Rice and Mint Turkey

Heat a heavy-based saucepan over a low heat and add the butter. When the butter has melted, add the onion and cook until soft and translucent. Add the rice, 600 ml/1 pint/2½ cups water, mint and salt to taste. Bring to the boil, stirring, then reduce to a simmer, cover and cook until the rice is soft, about 15–20 minutes depending on what type of rice is used. Keep stirring and tasting from time to time.

Whisk the yogurt and 100 ml/3½ fl oz/generous ⅓ cup water together in a bowl, then whisk into the soup. Reheat to just below boiling point and cook for 5 minutes, whisking periodically. Serve immediately.

30 g/12 oz/2 tbsp butter

1 medium onion, finely chopped

100 g/3½ oz/½ cup short-grain rice, ideally Baldo (see page 118)

600 ml/1 pint/2½ cups hot water

1 tbsp dried mint

Sea salt

250 ml/8 fl oz/1 cup thick natural (plain) yogurt

100 ml/3½ fl oz/generous ⅓ cup hot water

**Serves 4**

Coriander, butter and lemon juice give this pasta dish a gorgeous fragrance. This is a Thursday night dish in Syrian Jewish households. Split red lentils are often used instead for more of a smooth sauce, or sometimes it is served as a soup – this is made by retaining the lentils in their cooking water and combining everything at the end.

# Rishta bi Ats
# Noodles with Lentils Syria

Rinse the lentils and place in a saucepan with a lid. Cover with plenty of water, then cover with the lid and bring to the boil. Boil rapidly for at least 10 minutes, then reduce the heat to a simmer. Add salt to taste halfway through cooking. Cook until tender – this could take anywhere from 30 minutes–1 hour, depending on the age of the lentils. Add more boiling water if they seem to be drying out. Drain, return to the pan, cover and set aside until required.

Meanwhile, heat a frying pan over a medium heat and add the oil. Add the onion and fry until nicely browned. Add the garlic and fry until fragrant. Remove the pan from the heat and set aside.

Bring a large saucepan of water to the boil and salt it well. Add the pasta and cook until al dente (only about 2 minutes if fresh). Drain, then return to the pan. Add the lentils, onion and garlic, coriander and butter and place over a low heat. Reheat while tossing with tongs to combine everything evenly. Taste for seasoning and add lemon juice and black pepper to taste. Serve in warmed bowls with yogurt and lemon wedges.

250 g/9 oz/1¼ cups brown lentils
Salt and freshly ground black pepper
2 tbsp olive oil
1 medium onion, coarsely chopped
3 garlic cloves, finely chopped
250 g/9 oz fresh tagliatelle or other noodles
Generous handful of fresh coriander (cilantro) sprigs, about 10–12 sprigs, chopped
50 g/2 oz/4 tbsp butter, cubed
1–2 tbsp lemon juice, or to taste, plus lemon wedges, to serve
Natural (plain) yogurt, to serve

**Serves 4–6**

Amongst the oodles of versions of *Fattoush* that exist, two main elements are consistent: one, the bread element. This should always be a flatbread, and the thinner the better, as it's crispy and delicate when toasted. Two: the sour element, which might just be lemon juice, but is usually complemented by *sumak* (see page 118) or pomegranate molasses (see page 118), two distinctly Middle Eastern ingredients that pack a punch of citrus zing. A very simple version of *Fattoush* is sometimes made with just onions, tomatoes, parsley and bread, with olive oil and pomegranate. This slightly more elaborate version is a classic hit of zest and crunch.

# Fattoush Bread Salad Lebanon

Preheat the oven to 200°C/400°F/Gas Mark 6. Separate the bread as best you can into thin layers. Lay them on a baking sheet and drizzle oil over them. Toast in the oven until crisp and golden, then cool.

For the dressing, place the garlic and salt in a mortar and crush to a paste with a pestle. Alternatively, use a garlic press. Beat together with the lemon juice, pomegranate molasses and oil, directly in the mortar or in a screw-top jar.

Mix the tomatoes, spring onions, cucumbers, green pepper, radishes, herbs and lettuce together in a large bowl. Toss the dressing through the salad. Finally, crush the toasted bread into bite-sized pieces, toss into the salad and mix well. Serve immediately.

2 large pieces Arabic flatbread such as khobez, or 4 pitta (pita) breads

Extra virgin olive oil

3 large ripe tomatoes, about 300 g/ 11 oz, cut into chunks

1 bunch of spring onions (scallions), thinly sliced

2 small Lebanese cucumbers or ½ English cucumber, quartered and cut into chunks

1 small green (bell) pepper, chopped

6 radishes, sliced

Generous handful of fresh flat-leaf parsley leaves

Generous handful of fresh mint leaves

1 cos (romaine) lettuce heart, shredded

**For the dressing:**

1 small garlic clove

1 tsp coarse salt

4 tbsp fresh lemon juice

2 tbsp *sumak* or pomegranate molasses (see page 118)

4 tbsp extra virgin olive oil

**Serves 4**

Of all the recipes in this book, few have evoked more adamant opinions in different directions than this dish. Some add mint; others insist it must never be used. Some use a food processor; others declare it is sacrilege to do so. Some like it with lots of wheat and just a few herbs, others, like me, believe that the wheat should be significantly outnumbered by the other ingredients. I set out to try and create the best *tabbouleh* ever – an amalgam of dozens of different conversations, ingredients and methods, refined into one ultimate recipe. For me, this is it. I hope you approve.

# Tabbouleh
# Cracked Wheat Salad Lebanon

First boil the kettle. Place the bulgar wheat in a medium-sized bowl and pour boiling water over it. Leave to swell for at least 30 minutes until soft. Taste a bit and if it is unpleasantly chalky, leave a little longer.

If your knife is blunt, time to sharpen it. Wash the parsley very thoroughly and dry as much as possible with a clean cloth. Chop very finely. In my experience, chopping in the food processor can result in a bitter mush. Once coarsely chopped, it helps to carefully grasp the pointed end of the knife with the non-chopping hand – then you can use the knife like a guillotine, to finely chop the parsley.

Once the bulgar wheat is soft, drain and press out as much moisture as possible.

Now these 2 extra steps are not absolutely essential, but will make this tabbouleh that much better. After draining the bulgar wheat, squeeze with your hands, pressing out more moisture, then lay out on a clean tea (dish) towel to dry further for about 5 minutes.

Return the bulgar wheat to the dry bowl and add the spring onions. Squeeze the onion and bulgar wheat together – the onion juice will penetrate the grain. Season well with salt and pepper. A bit of bulgar wheat will be lost in all of this, but not enough to matter.

Combine everything in a large bowl, adding lemon juice and olive oil last. Taste and season as you see fit with more salt, pepper, lemon juice and oil, if necessary.

100 g/3½ oz/scant ⅔ cup coarse bulgar (bulgur) wheat (see page 119)

1 large bunch fresh parsley, stems and leaves, about 100 g/3½ oz

6 spring onions (scallions), finely sliced

Sea salt and freshly ground black pepper

3 ripe vine-ripened tomatoes, about 350 g/12 oz, cut into small dice

2 baby Lebanese cucumbers, or ½ English cucumber, cut into small dice

4 tbsp fresh lemon juice

4 tbsp finest extra virgin olive oil

**Serves 4–6**

"Meatless Soup" is another name for this, a rarity in true Persian cooking. There are many variations, sometimes with pomegranate juice and eggs. Yogurt and walnuts have been used for both culinary and medicinal purposes since ancient times in Persia, and their health-giving properties are still appreciated today. It is well proven that yogurt is essential for digestion among other benefits, and walnuts are an important source of omega-3 oils and protein. One ancient Persian health tip encourages substituting walnuts for red meat to "make a man gentle and kind". Worthiness aside, this soup is quick, refreshing, and light yet substantial, with an alluring element of the exotic.

# Eshkaneh
# Walnut Soup with Yogurt and Apricots Iran

Heat a saucepan over a medium heat and add the oil. Add the onion and cook until tinged with gold. Reduce the heat to low. Add the flour and walnuts and cook, stirring, for about 3 minutes. Add the apricots, dried mint, fenugreek, if using, and salt and pour in the hot water gradually, stirring all the time. Leave to simmer for 15 minutes, or until the soup thickens slightly.

Place the yogurt in a measuring jug or bowl and stir well. Stir a ladleful of soup into the yogurt, then pour the yogurt into the soup pan. Reheat for 1–2 minutes to just below boiling point, then serve immediately.

2 tbsp olive oil
1 large onion, finely chopped
2 tbsp plain (all-purpose) flour
50 g/2 oz/⅓ cup chopped walnuts
6 ready-to-eat dried apricots,
    coarsely chopped
1 tbsp dried mint
1 tsp fenugreek seeds (optional)
1 tsp salt
750 ml/1¼ pints/3 cups boiling water
500 ml/16 fl oz/2 cups natural
    (plain) yogurt

**Serves 4**

*Kichri, khichari, kedgeree* – they are all Indian inventions: rice and lentils cooked together and often served for breakfast (in *kedgeree*, lentils are replaced by smoked haddock, an Anglicization). This version was a staple for Jewish families in Iraq and comes from culinary historian Sami Zubaida. It was a favourite dish of his boyhood in a Jewish household in Baghdad. Iraqi food is generally heavy on the meat and dairy, usually served together, which is not permitted in strict Jewish diets. This dish was a compromise – if the meat wasn't there, they could be lavish with the dairy, hence this unusual cheese topping, and they'd probably have melted butter and yogurt too.

# Kichree
# Spiced Lentils and Rice with Melting Cheese Iraq

Heat a large, heavy-based saucepan over a medium heat and add 3 tbsp of the oil. Add the garlic and fry until just starting to turn golden. Add the tomato purée, cumin, rice and lentils and stir. Stir in the boiling water and add salt and pepper to taste. Cover, reduce the heat to the lowest possible simmer and cook for 20 minutes. By this time most of the water may have been absorbed, so add little more if it seems dry. Cook for a further 20–25 minutes, or until the lentils are collapsed and the rice is very soft.

Meanwhile, heat the remaining olive oil in a frying pan over a low heat. Add the onion and fry slowly until very soft and golden. When the lentils and rice are nearly cooked but could still take a further 5 minutes or so (check they are not burning on the bottom), scatter the onions over the top. Cover with cheese slices. Cover the pan and let the cheese melt. Alternatively, melt the cheese in the frying pan on top of the onions. Serve immediately.

5 tbsp olive oil
4 garlic cloves, finely chopped
2 tbsp tomato purée (paste)
2 tsp ground cumin
200 g/7 oz/1 cup basmati rice
200 g/7 oz/1 cup split red lentils
1 litre/1¾ pints/4 cups boiling water
Salt and freshly ground black pepper
1 large onion, sliced
200 g/7 oz halloumi cheese or pizza
    mozzarella, thinly sliced

**Serves 6–8**

A friend married to a Yemeni had told me about a strangely wonderful foamy spiced jelly much loved in Yemen, and my curiosity launched me on a search for a recipe. I guess I was not surprised to find it in the first place I looked, Claudia Roden's exhaustive *The Book of Jewish Food.*

Making *Hilbeh* is like playing with a culinary chemistry set. Just pour boiling water over the fenugreek powder, and watch it grow and transform into a weird alien jelly! On a molecular level, the fenugreek "surrounds" the water, making millions of springy bubbles. This extraordinary property makes fenugreek very useful in the food industry as a stabilizer and it also has many health-giving properties such as lowering cholesterol and as a supplement for diabetics.

The jelly is blended with tomatoes and spices to make a unique dip for bread. Yemeni Jews transported *Hilbeh* to Israel, where they eat it with *Falafel* (see page 126).

# Hilbeh
# Spiced Fenugreek Jelly Yemen

Place the fenugreek powder in a large bowl. Pour plenty of boiling water over the powder and stir. (Using lots of water helps take away some of the bitterness of the fenugreek.) Leave to stand for several hours or overnight.

Carefully pour the water off, revealing a surprising mound of fenugreek jelly.

Place the garlic, tomato, tomato purée, caraway seeds, cardamom seeds, chilli flakes and salt in a blender and process until very smooth. Taste for seasoning. Add the fenugreek jelly and pulse to mix.

Serve as a dip for warm pitta bread.

1 tbsp finely ground fenugreek
  powder
At least 1 litre/1¾ pints/4 cups boiling
  water
2 garlic cloves, de-germed
1 large vine-ripened tomato, quartered
2 tsp tomato purée (paste)
Pinch of caraway seeds
½ tsp cardamom seeds, from about
  3–4 pods
½ tsp chilli (dried red pepper) flakes
Sea salt
Warm pitta (pita) bread, to serve

**Serves 4–6**

# chapter six
# The Maghreb, Northern and West Africa

The regions in this chapter are linked more geographically than gastronomically. The Maghreb, which includes Morocco, Algeria and Tunisia, is more often classified as part of the Middle East, due to the invasion of the Arabs in the 7th century AD, and the indigenous Berber population mostly absorbed the Arab influence into their cooking. The full effect of the "Arabization" of the culture lives on today, characterized by complex Eastern spices and a love of sweet and sour flavour, an idea imported from Persia. Egypt, with its proximity to the Middle East, has also been absorbed into Arab culture.

South of the Sahara, the picture is very different. This is the developing world, where a starch plus a stew forms the backbone of the diet, and often meat would simply not be an option. While there may not be the same developed complexity in the cuisine, there is ingenuity born out of necessity, with imaginative use of ground nuts, seeds, beans, roots and leaves, and a healthy dose of hot chilli to excite the palate when no other spice is available.

"The art (of cookery) reflects the degree of a nation's civilization. Dishes cleverly and carefully prepared, as pleasing to the eye as to the taste, contribute not only to our physical well-being but...the blackest depression vanishes at the sight of a really good meal." Ahmed Sefrioui, Moroccan author

# meet the expert:
# Anissa Helou – Moroccan Cuisine

Anissa Helou is an enthusiast and expert on cooking throughout the Mediterranean, but Morocco awakens a special intrigue for her. "The cooking of Morocco is subtle and mysterious," she says. "The atmosphere and spectacle of the Souk (market) and the wonderful dining experiences to be had within are intoxicating."

Listening to Anissa's description evokes fascination, but also the desire for clarity within the mystery. It seems that certain ideas we have of salads and couscous, for example, are not the same as Moroccans'. "Moroccan salads are quite different from what we understand as salads here," Anissa explains. "When they are raw, they are often dressed not in oil but with fragrant orange blossom or rose water, vinegar, lemon juice or fruit juice. Of course, spices and herbs are added, and sometimes sugar." The taste is a refreshing and subtle combination of sweet and sour. There are also cooked salads like *Zaalouk* (see page 152) and *Khezzu M'Chermal* (see page 150), and as for the presentation, "the salads are laid on the table in pairs, or more, so that all diners have easy access to them. They remain on the table throughout the meal for diners to refresh their palate between every few mouthfuls."

The use of couscous, the Maghreb's world-famous native staple, is another concept which is often misunderstood. "Couscous is never served as an accompaniment to tagines, as people tend to serve it in the West. Instead, it is served with its own accompaniments," she says. The couscous is seen as the core of the meal, and everything else on the table is there to enhance it. "A seven-vegetable broth, often without meat; chicken cooked with onions and raisins; fish in tomato sauce; these are among the 'side dishes' served with steamed couscous. Every Friday, the whole nation sits down to a lunch like this. A sweetened couscous is also served as an *entremet*, after the main course and before fruit or dessert. When it is prepared this way, it is called *S'ffa* (see page 148)."

Though lamb, chicken and fish are sought at nearly every meal, clearly vegetables play a key role and are used in profusion, as a trip to the Souk will demonstrate. "One of my favourite past-times in Morocco is visiting the weekly markets around Marrakesh," says Anissa. "Here you see vegetables piled high on straw mats right on the floor. These will have been picked by the farmers that morning or the day before and brought to

market on the backs of donkeys (all parked like cars at the entrance to the market place). Within hours, the mounds of vegetables will have dwindled to nothing as shoppers from nearby villages stock up for the week."

Once the freshest and best supplies have been hand-picked, it's off back home to cook, or, how about a rest while someone cooks for you? Now there's a novel idea, as Anissa explains. "You can buy whatever ingredients you like, and then take them to one of the ambulant cooks, set up in their own corner under tents, to have him prepare your lunch." Recently, Anissa took a group of students to the Souk, where they brought the day's shopping to such a cook. "We sat under the tent, gathered in a circle on a large straw mat and had a succession of tagines served to us, with farm-made barley bread, all eaten with our hand. We finished the meal with fruit and mint tea. Needless to say, it was not only exquisite but perfectly fresh and none of us had anything but fabulous memories of that day." It seems the Moroccans really appreciate that the experience of a meal can be so much more than just eating.

*Anissa is the author of several cookbooks, including* Street Café Morocco *and* Lebanese Cuisine. *She is a frequent guest on British radio and television, writes regularly for the* Weekend Financial Times, *and has her own cookery school.*

**Harissa**

**Daikon radish (*mooli*, *turp*)**

# focus on ingredients

Ras-el-hanout – This North African spice
mixture, meaning "head of the shop" or "top shelf",
is so called because literally dozens of spices,
perhaps all of the spices for sale in the *souk* or
market might go into the mix. It could be compared
to curry powder in that it is an all-purpose seasoning
for tagines and stews. It seems the mixture and its
uses differs quite a lot between Morocco and
Algeria/Tunisia; in the latter it is quite a mild mix,
usually containing ground rosebuds, which is used
quite freely (see *Taam Legume* on page 146). In
Morocco, ras-el-hanout is used sparingly and only
in sweet or game tagines. It is a fabulously aromatic
and expensive spice mixture, which is highly valued
in Morocco and used mostly in celebratory dishes.
It is also used for certain winter dishes, which "heat
the blood".

Harissa – This is a generic name for a pungent hot
chilli (chili) paste, which is served separately at the
table to add heat to the meal in the Maghreb. For
convenience, harissa is sold in small cans or metal
tubes – the dark orange contents are searingly hot

and "a dab'll do ya". Other types of harissa are
available – as a thick red sauce like salsa, or as a dry
mix with a few herbs, which can be mixed with water
and oil. Less often, it is used as an ingredient to be
blended into a recipe.

Radish (*daikon*, *mooli*, *turp*) – Radishes are adored
in North Africa, the Mediterranean and Asia. The
common pink globe radishes are made into salads
with oranges and carrots in Morocco, and in Algeria,
the long, white daikon radish (pictured above) is used
as a vegetable for cooking (see *Taam Legume* on
page 146). They are related to turnips and behave
much the same in cooking, in that they retain a firm,
juicy texture and a peppery bite. This huge radish
which grows up to 46 cm/18 inches long, though a
native of Asia, is also adored in Turkey, where it is
served in raw slices at the start of a meal as a sort of
palate cleanser, along with black olives, lemon wedges
and fresh green chillies (chilies).

Argan oil – A remarkably delicious nutty tasting
oil from Morocco, the flavour of which resembles
sesame oil. It is produced in a most unusual way with

**Ras-el-Hanout**

**Ful Medames**

the help of goats or camels, who eat the fruit of the argan tree, then expel the stone (pit) "au natural". The stones are gathered by women and shepherds, and they are cracked open to reveal the nuts, which are then pressed to produce this precious oil. Argan oil is not a cooking oil but is used exclusively for flavouring; it is used in some sweets and drizzled over salads. It is also eaten for breakfast, simply with bread.

Couscous – Couscous is a staple food across the whole of North Africa and into parts of the eastern Arab countries as well. It is often mistaken for a grain of itself, but in fact it is a grain product, made from wheat semolina, and can best be described as tiny pellets of pasta. Unlike pasta, however, it is not made from kneaded dough, but rather by sprinkling salted water over wheat flour to form tiny individual pieces. Often couscous is made from barley or other grains. Commercial couscous is par-cooked, so it only needs about 5 minutes soaking time, making it a superb convenience food. Mix dry couscous with a little salt and a few small knobs of butter; cover in boiling water and leave to swell, fluff with a fork and serve, or reheat in a microwave. It's that simple!

Orange flower water (orange blossom water, *zharr*) – Exactly as its name suggests, this is obtained by distilling the blossom of the bitter Seville orange. An essential oil called neroli precipitates in the process, and the scented water remains. It has a delicate perfume, which can be added to sweet and savoury dishes, especially grains like couscous (see *S'ffa* on page 148) and drinks. It is absolutely beautiful added to warm milk sweetened with honey.

Ful medames (*ful mudammes*, *foul medames*) – These beans are the foundation of the daily Egyptian staple by the same name. In the UK, the beans are known as broad beans, in the US as fava beans, having been dried and sold as such, or dried, cooked and canned. They are a fabulously buxom bean with a satisfying creamy texture (see recipe for *Ful Medames* on page 159).

Egusi (*agushi*, *mbika*) – These are a type of melon seed used mainly in West African cooking. They are ground into a high-protein meal, which is used to thicken and flavour stews, soups and sauces. Pumpkin seeds, being if the same family, are the best substitute (see *Palava* on page 165).

Friday is "couscous day" in the Maghreb, and most people sit down to a lunch with a seven-vegetable couscous such as this one. This recipe calls for the North African "curry powder", *ras-el-hanout* (see page 144), but I have made it optional in case you can't find it – doing without it shouldn't stop you making this cinnamon-scented stew. *Mooli* (daikon), the giant white radish (see page 144) is also used, but you could substitute turnip, swede or at a push, potato. I love a dollop of yogurt with this, but that might be considered an unorthodox Arab addition. Yogurt would be unthinkable to the Berber Algerian who described to me the proper way to make this recipe – but have it your way.

# Ta'am Legume
# Mixed Vegetable Couscous Algeria

First prepare the vegetables. Cut the mooli (daikon) or turnip, carrot, courgettes and sweet potato into 6-cm/2½-inch cylinder-shaped pieces, then cut once diagonally, then holding the piece together, cut diagonally across the previous cut, making 4 chunks. Cut the celery heart, with leaves, into chunks.

Heat a large saucepan over a low–medium heat and add the oil. Add the onion and cook until soft and translucent. Add the spices and salt. Stir briefly, then add the vegetables and stir to coat with the spices.

Add the chickpeas, tomatoes, tomato purée and honey. Pour in just enough water to barely cover the vegetables and stir. Cover, bring to the boil, then leave to simmer for about 30 minutes, stirring occasionally, until the carrots are soft.

Meanwhile, prepare the couscous. Boil the kettle. Place the couscous in a bowl (200 g/7 oz/1 cup for 4 and 300 g/11 oz/1½ cups for 6), mix in a pinch of salt and dot with butter, if using. Pour over just enough water to cover the couscous. Cover the bowl and leave to stand for 5 minutes. Fluff with a fork. Taste a grain and if it is still hard, cover the bowl and microwave on High power for 1–2 minutes.

Serve the stew ladled over the couscous in soup bowls. Pass the harissa around the table.

½ mooli (daikon) or turnip,
about 250 g/9 oz, peeled

1 large, fat carrot,
about 200 g/7 oz, peeled

2 courgettes (zucchini), about 200 g/7 oz

1 small or ½ large orange-fleshed sweet
potato, about 200 g/7 oz, peeled

1 celery heart

2 tbsp olive oil

1 large onion, sliced

2 tsp ras-el-hanout (optional)

1 tsp ground cumin

1 cinnamon stick, broken in half if longer
than your index finger

1 tsp salt

1 x 400 g/14 oz can chickpeas,
drained and rinsed

1 x 400 g/14 oz can chopped tomatoes

2 tbsp tomato purée (paste)

1 tbsp honey

200–300 g/7–11 oz/1–1½ cups couscous
Salt
30 g/1 oz/2 tbsp butter, cubed (optional)
Harissa (see page 144), to serve

**Serves 4–6**

This aromatic dish is not actually a dessert, but is served in between the main course and the dessert with a glass of buttermilk, usually at celebration feasts in the Maghreb. *S'ffa* is the name of the couscous itself which is a particularly fine grade, almost as fine as semolina. As a Londoner, I'm lucky enough to have found the proper *S'ffa* in my local Moroccan store, but you might struggle to find it. I tried grinding ordinary couscous but it didn't work – the result was sticky and not fluffy. Just use ordinary instant couscous instead. Though not traditional, this is wonderful for breakfast with tea and yogurt.

# S'ffa
# Sweet Couscous with Fruit Maghreb

In a large saucepan, place the boiling water, sultanas, apricots, butter and salt. Simmer until the sultanas are plump, about 5 minutes. Remove the pan from the heat and stir in the couscous and orange flower water, if using. Cover and leave to stand for 3–5 minutes, or until the water is absorbed and the couscous is tender. Immediately fluff with a fork, separating every grain – if left too long, the couscous will clump together irrevocably.

Stir through the sugar and cinnamon and mix thoroughly.

For a traditional presentation, spoon the couscous on to a warmed serving platter and quickly form with your hands into a cone shape. Use your thumb and index finger to sprinkle alternating stripes of cinnamon and icing sugar down the sides of the cone. Serve immediately, or cover and reheat in a microwave before serving.

500 ml/16 fl oz/2 cups boiling water

75 g/3 oz/½ cup sultanas (golden raisins) or raisins

8 dried apricots, coarsely chopped

4 tbsp butter

Large pinch of salt

350 g/12 oz/2 cups fine or ordinary couscous

1 tbsp orange flower water (optional; see page 145)

2 tbsp icing (confectioners') sugar plus extra for dusting

1 tsp ground cinnamon plus extra for dusting

**Serves 6–8**

The holiest month of the Muslim lunar calendar is Ramadan. During daylight hours throughout the month, practising Muslims go on a strict fast – not even a drop of water may pass the lips. This is a demonstration of one's devotion to Allah, as well an exercise in self-control and a cleansing of the body and mind. *Suhoor* is an early breakfast before sunrise, then when the sun sets, it's time for *iftar*, the breaking of the fast. This is when everyone enjoys a restorative bowl of *harira*, along with a few dates for instant energy. The *harira* might contain lamb or chicken or might indeed be a vegetarian version such as this one. Part of the practice of the fast discourages gorging oneself before and after the fast, to further strengthen the piety of the soul. This filling and nourishing soup is pure health-in-a-bowl.

# Harira
# Thick Vegetable Soup
# for Ramadan Morocco

Heat the oil in a saucepan with a lid. Add the onions and fry until translucent, then add the garlic, ginger, paprika and cumin seeds. Fry briefly until fragrant, then add the whole tomatoes and boiling water. Cover and simmer for about 10 minutes, or until the tomato skins loosen. Pluck off the tomato skins, taking care not to burn your fingers. Break up the tomatoes slightly, then purée the mixture using a hand-held blender. Alternatively, use a potato masher to crush the tomatoes. Add salt and pepper and taste for seasoning.

Add the chickpeas, herbs, lemon juice and tomato purée. Bring to the boil and simmer for 5 minutes. Stir in the flour mixture to thicken the soup. Simmer for a further 5 minutes. Serve each bowl with a drizzle of extra virgin olive oil over the surface.

2 tbsp olive oil

2 onions, about 200 g/7 oz, chopped

2 garlic cloves, chopped

1 tsp freshly grated fresh root ginger

1 tbsp paprika

1 tsp cumin seeds

600 g/1 lb 5 oz whole tomatoes (about 5 plump vine-ripened tomatoes)

500 ml/16 fl oz/2 cups boiling water

Sea salt and freshly ground black pepper

1 x 400 g/14 oz can chickpeas, drained and rinsed

3 tbsp chopped fresh parsley

3 tbsp chopped fresh coriander (cilantro)

3 tbsp chopped celery leaves

1 tbsp fresh lemon juice

1 tbsp tomato purée

2 tbsp plain (all-purpose) flour, slackened with 3 tbsp cold water

Extra virgin olive oil, to serve

**Serves 4–6**

This meatless tagine appears in *La Cuisine Marocaine de Rabat* by Hayat Dinia, in the chapter for "*les Repas des Jours Maigres*" or meals for meagre days. I suspect it may have been cooked when a family couldn't afford a chicken, so they told the children, "there was a chicken, but it flew away". The addition of sweet potato makes it particularly satisfying, with a potent fragrance from lots of fresh coriander and spice.

# Djaja Tarat The Chicken That Flew (Chickpea Stew) Morocco

Heat a large saucepan over a medium heat and add the oil. Add the onion and fry until translucent, then add the sweet potato, chickpeas, spices, coriander and salt and pepper to taste. Pour in just enough water to cover the vegetables. Bring to the boil and simmer, uncovered, for 20 minutes, or until the sweet potato is tender. There should be a small amount of deliciously fragrant broth left, but it should be significantly reduced. Serve in bowls as a soup, or with plain couscous.

2 tbsp olive oil

1 medium onion, finely chopped

1 large, orange-fleshed sweet potato, about 375 g/13 oz, peeled and cubed

2 x 400 g/14 oz cans chickpeas, drained

½ tsp ground cinnamon

½ tsp ground cumin

½ tsp ground pimiento (allspice)

Large pinch of saffron (about 20 threads)

200 g/7 oz chopped fresh coriander (cilantro)

Sea salt and freshly ground black pepper

**Serves 4–6**

Carrots make an appearance on the table at just about every meal in the Maghreb. This lovely cooked carrot salad, served warm or cold, is a favourite element of a spread of salads such as *Zaalouk* (see page 152) and *Mechouia* (see page 156).

# Khezzu M'Chermal Sweet Carrot Salad with Garlic Morocco

In a saucepan with a lid place the carrots, garlic, paprika, sugar, vinegar, salt, honey and water. Cover and bring to the boil, then reduce the heat to a low simmer. Cook until the liquid is absorbed and the carrots are tender, about 20 minutes. Keep checking – if the water has disappeared before the carrots are tender, add a little more water, a tablespoon at a time. If there seems to be a lot of liquid and the carrots are already quite tender, finish the cooking uncovered so the water can evaporate.

Serve warm or cold.

500 g/1 lb 2 oz, about 4 large carrots, peeled and cut into thick diagonal slices

2 garlic cloves, grated or finely chopped

½ tsp sweet paprika

1 tsp sugar

1 tsp wine vinegar

½ tsp salt or to taste

1 generous tsp honey

6 tbsp water

**Serves 4–6**

This is one of the easiest and most satisfying preserves to make. In exchange for very little effort you are rewarded with a versatile and exotic condiment. The rind, which is the only part used once the lemons are ready, has a mysterious perfume and adds a subtle tart flavour to tagines, salads or couscous. The best preserved lemons are the small *duqqa* type, which look like a kind of yellow lime and aren't much bigger than a walnut, and these are the type you will usually find imported from Morocco. Ordinary lemons are fine to use for home-made, but you do want the skins to be as thin as possible. As a general rule of thumb, I have found that the rounder the lemon, the thinner the skin.

# Lamoun Makbouss
# Salted Preserved Lemons Morocco

Preheat the oven to 160°C/300°F/Gas Mark 2.

Keeping the rubber seal separate, line a baking tray with a piece of kitchen paper (paper towels) and place a large preserving jar on it. Place in the oven for 10 minutes. Remove the jar and cool. Boil the kettle. Pour boiling water over the rubber seal and leave to dry.

Scrub the lemons under hot running water, without damaging the skin. Cut into quarters, leaving 1 cm/½ inch of the stem-end, so that sections are still attached. Sprinkle 1 tsp of salt inside each lemon. Place 1 tbsp of salt in the base of the sterilized jar. Pack in the lemons, sprinkling a little more salt in between, and squashing them in well.

Seal and leave the jar in a warm place for 3–4 days. The juices will have been drawn out of the lemons. Press the lemons down again and pour in enough lemon juice to completely cover them. Pour a thin layer of olive oil on top to act as a protective film. Seal and leave to ripen for a month in a cool place. Keeps for 2 years.

5 organic thin-skinned lemons
5 tbsp salt
Juice of about 3 additional lemons
1–2 tbsp olive oil

0.75–1 litre/1¼–1¾ pint/3–4 cups
   capacity preserving jar with
   rubber seal

Smoking the aubergine is the key to the flavour here. It's an exciting technique which feels primitive: you really want those fierce flames to torch the aubergine, reducing the resilient skin to ash and creating smoke which is absorbed by spongy flesh inside. If you don't have a gas flame, the same can be achieved on a barbecue. Failing that, pierce the aubergines several times and microwave or roast in an oven preheated to 220°C/425°F/Gas Mark 7 until completely soft, then cool, remove the skin and use in the recipe. It will still taste gorgeous. Serve with flatbread and *Khezzu M'Chermal* (see page 150).

## Zaalouk
# Smoky Aubergine (Eggplant) and Tomato Salad Morocco

Push 2 totally heatproof forks into the stems of the aubergines and place the bodies directly on to a high gas flame. Turn occasionally until completely soft and collapsed; the skin should be blackened to the point of ash in places and steam should be escaping through the fork holes.

Remove to a plate and leave to cool completely. Peel off the charred skin, saving any juice, which oozes on to the plate. Don't worry if a few little charred bits remain as they will add to the flavour. Chop the flesh finely.

Pound the garlic with a large pinch of coarse sea salt in a mortar until smooth. Alternatively, use a garlic press. In a bowl, combine the aubergine flesh with juices, crushed garlic, tomato, spices, preserved lemon rind or lemon zest, salt and pepper and the oil. Taste for seasoning and serve.

2 medium aubergines (eggplants), about 500–600 g/1 lb 2 oz–1 lb 4 oz

1 garlic clove

Coarse sea salt

1 large vine-ripened tomato, coarsely chopped

½ tsp paprika

½ tsp ground cumin

1 tsp finely chopped preserved lemon rind (optional – see page 151) or 1 tsp finely grated lemon zest

Freshly ground black pepper

2–3 tsp argan oil (optional – see page 144) or extra virgin olive oil, to taste

**Serves 4–6**

*Charmoula* is a fantastic all-purpose marinade. It's an excellent blend of dominant flavours, which brings out the best in its vehicle, in this case potatoes. Most often it's used for meat or fish, but also has a great affinity with vegetables – wonderful with fried aubergine slices – and can be slackened with tomato purée to make a brilliant sauce for beans. Serve these intense potatoes as part of a spread of salads such as *Mechouia* (see page 156) and *Khezzu M'Chermal* (see page 150).

# Charmoula Batata
# Potatoes in Spice Marinade Morocco

Cut the potatoes into 1 cm/½ inch thick slices. It is best to steam the potatoes so they retain their shape, which can be done either in a microwave or steamer. To microwave, layer the potato slices in a microwave-safe container and add a dash of water. Microwave on High power for 10 minutes, then leave to stand for 3–4 minutes. Check that they are all cooked through but still holding together. Alternatively, steam the potatoes in a steamer until tender.

Meanwhile, make the *charmoula*. Pound the garlic with 1 tsp of salt in a mortar until smooth. Add the paprika, cayenne, cumin, parsley, coriander and the remaining 1 tsp of salt. Pound until a coarse paste results. Stir in the lemon juice, then gradually stir in the oil – a fork is a good tool for whisking it in. Taste for seasoning – it should have a fairly potent flavour, and remember the so far unsalted potatoes will absorb much of the saltiness.

Make a layer of hot potatoes in the base of a serving dish. Smother with the *charmoula*. Top with another layer of potatoes, then *charmoula*, etc. Leave to cool, then eat, or refrigerate and enjoy over the next 3 days.

1 kg/2 lb 4 oz medium potatoes, scrubbed but not peeled
3 garlic cloves
2 tsp coarse sea salt
2 tbsp paprika
½ tsp cayenne pepper
1 tsp ground cumin
Large handful of fresh parsley leaves, about 35 g/1¼ oz, chopped
Large handful of fresh coriander (cilantro) leaves and stems, about 35 g/1¼ oz, chopped
2 tbsp fresh lemon juice
100 ml/3½ fl oz/generous ⅓ cup extra virgin olive oil

This dish was born in Tunisia, where every cook sports their own version, but peppers and eggs are the principal elements. *Shakshouka* has crossed the Mediterranean eastwards to find firm footing in the culinary repertoire of the Middle East. It has been embraced particularly warmly by the Israelis. In fact, the first time I ate *Shakshouka* was in my local Jewish bakery, Sharon's, where they serve it in a pitta (pita) bread with salad.

This recipe makes rather a lot of *Shakshouka*, but one well-known fact about this dish is that it gets better and better each day, so why not make enough to last a while? It's also a really impressive dish for entertaining. Alternatively, halve the recipe.

# Shakshouka
# Fried (Bell) Peppers with Eggs Tunisia

Heat a large saucepan over a medium heat and add the oil. Add the onions and fry until translucent. Add the peppers and fry for 5 minutes, or until softened slightly. Add the tomatoes, salt and pepper, vinegar, sugar, mint and spices. Simmer, stirring frequently, until reduced and very thick, about 30–40 minutes. A wooden spoon dragged across the bottom should leave a clear canal.

Preheat the oven to 190°C/375°F/Gas Mark 5.

Leave the mixture to cool briefly, then spoon into a large ovenproof dish, big enough to accommodate the mixture to a depth of about 2.5 cm/1 inch. Make 8 separate indentations with the back of a spoon, then crack the eggs into the indentations. Bake in the oven for about 10–15 minutes, or until the egg whites are completely set, and the yolks are set to your liking. Sprinkle with a little parsley and serve hot, warm or cold.

3 tbsp olive oil
2 large onions, sliced
6 red (bell) peppers, cored and sliced
3 x 400 g/14 oz can chopped tomatoes
Salt and freshly ground black pepper
1 tbsp sherry vinegar
1 tbsp dark brown sugar
2 tsp dried mint
½ tsp pimiento (allspice)
½ tsp dried chilli (red pepper) flakes
8 organic eggs
Chopped fresh parsley, for sprinkling

**Serves 8**

*Mechouia* simply means grilled (broiled). It's also seen as *mechwya* or *chlada felfla* in Algeria and Morocco. Many different versions abound, but it always contains grilled pepper, the star of the show, as no vegetable takes better to grilling than the pepper. While this salad makes an appealing element of a spread, it's substantial enough to be enjoyed on its own as a main course, with plenty of bread for mopping up the peppery, lemony juices.

# Mechouia
# Grilled (Bell) Pepper Salad Tunisia

Heat the grill (broiler) to its highest setting. On a tray lined with baking paper (parchment) or foil, place the pepper halves, together with the chillies and tomato halves, all skin-side-up. Place under the grill. The tomato skins loosen first – remove them to a plate and leave to cool, then pluck off the skin, which should come off easily. Slice the tomatoes thickly.

The chillies will be ready to come out soon after the tomatoes, when the skin is blackened and crinkly all over. Place the chillies (tongs are the best tool for the job) in a clean plastic bag, seal and leave to sweat. Continue grilling the peppers until thoroughly black and blistered all over, then remove and place in the bag with the chillies. Leave to cool.

Peel the chillies (protecting yourself with gloves) and the peppers, then slice into thin strips.

To make the dressing, pound the garlic with a large pinch of coarse sea salt and the coriander seeds in a mortar until the garlic is smooth. Beat in the lemon juice, mint and oil. Taste for seasoning, bearing in mind the saltiness of the cheese in the salad.

On a serving platter, arrange the peppers, chillies and tomatoes. Top with onion rings, olives, eggs and cheese. Drizzle the dressing over everything and serve.

1 red (bell) pepper and 1 yellow (bell) pepper, halved, stems removed and de-seeded

4 large fresh green chillies (chilies), stems and de-seeded (wear gloves)

2 large vine-ripened tomatoes, halved

½ medium onion, finely sliced into rings

20 good quality green olives

3 hard-boiled (hard-cooked) eggs, shelled, rinsed and quartered

100 g/3½ oz feta or other white cheese, crumbled

**For the dressing:**
2 garlic cloves, de-germed
Coarse sea salt
1 tsp coriander seeds
3 tbsp fresh lemon juice
½ tsp dried mint
3 tbsp olive oil

**Serves 4–6**

Here's another cousin of the Spanish *Tortilla* (see page 112) and the Afghani *Khagina* (see page 245) – a sort of crustless quiche, which could contain just about any vegetable, but the potato and artichoke here are particularly gorgeous together. The recipe is a Sephardic hand-me-down adapted from *The Vegetarian Table: North Africa* by Kitty Morse. Preserved lemon really brings out the flavour of the artichoke; use it if you have it to hand (see page 151), or use the finely grated zest of a lemon.

# Markode Aux Pommes de Terre
# Potato and Artichoke Torte Algeria

Preheat the oven to 200°C/400°F/Gas Mark 6.

Heat a large frying pan with a lid over a medium heat and add the oil. Add the potatoes and onion and cook, stirring frequently, until the potatoes are tender, about 10–12 minutes. Add the garlic, paprika, artichoke hearts and preserved lemon, if using, and cook for a further 2 minutes to marry all the flavours. Set aside and cool briefly.

In a large bowl, beat together the eggs with the parsley and a generous amount of seasoning. Pour the contents of the pan into the bowl and stir well until everything is coated with egg. Pour the mixture into the well-greased cake tin (pan) or baking dish. Bake in the oven for 35–40 minutes, or until golden and cooked through – check that the egg has set in the middle by piercing with a sharp knife or skewer – it should come out clean.

Cool briefly, then remove from the tin or dish and cut into wedges while still warm.

3 tbsp olive oil

500 g/1 lb 2 oz waxy potatoes, peeled and cut into small dice

1 medium onion, finely chopped

4 garlic cloves, finely chopped

2 tsp sweet paprika

6 canned artichoke hearts, coarsely chopped

1 tbsp finely chopped preserved lemon rind (optional – see *Lamoun Makbouss* on page 151) or the finely grated zest of 1 lemon

8 organic eggs

4 tbsp finely chopped fresh parsley

Sea salt and freshly ground black pepper

20-cm/8-inch springform cake tin (pan) or baking dish

**Serves 4–6**

In Tunisia, *briks* are made with a special paper-thin pastry called *warka*, which requires a huge amount of skill and patience to make. It's not unlike filo pastry, which my recipe here calls for as a compromise. *Briks* might contain anything, and they are usually deep-fried. The most common filling contains whole egg, which will invariably dribble down your chin as you bite into the crisp pastry. This version omits the difficult task of getting the raw egg into the pastries and allows you to cook the *briks* in the oven, which is far simpler and has no bearing on the flavour or texture. If you do want to deep-fry them, you can use Chinese wheat pastry for wontons or spring (egg) rolls instead.

# Briks
# Potato and Olive Pastries Tunisia

Preheat the oven to 200°C/400°F/Gas Mark 6.

Place the potatoes in a saucepan with a small amount of water and add salt. Bring to the boil and simmer until tender, about 15 minutes. Drain and leave to cool.

Pound the garlic with a large pinch of coarse sea salt in a mortar until smooth. Alternatively, use a garlic press. Mash the potatoes with the garlic, spring onions, olives, preserved lemon or lemon zest, parsley, and salt and pepper to taste.

Mix the melted butter and oil together. Lay out a sheet of filo pastry, brush with the butter mixture and lay another sheet on top. Brush again, top with another layer and finally brush again. Cut into squares: the amount of filling is enough to fill 10 square pieces, about 10 cm/4 inches square. If using small sheets, you will probably need to make another 3 layers. The important thing is to have square pieces, not rectangular, so trim accordingly.

Line a baking sheet with baking paper (parchment). Place a heaped tbsp of filling on each piece of the pastry squares and fold over into a triangular parcel (package), pressing the edges firmly together to seal. Place on the baking sheet and brush the top with butter mixture. Bake in the oven for 8–10 minutes, or until golden and crisp. Eat right away.

450 g/1 lb floury (mealy) potatoes, peeled and cut into chunks

Salt and freshly ground black pepper

1 garlic clove, peeled

Coarse sea salt

2 spring onions (scallions), finely chopped

15 good quality black olives, stoned (pitted) and coarsely chopped

1 tsp finely chopped preserved lemon rind (optional – see *Lamoun Makbouss* on page 151) or 1 tsp finely grated lemon zest

2 tbsp finely chopped fresh parsley

30 g/1 oz/2 tbsp butter, melted

1 tbsp olive oil

3 large sheets or 6 small sheets filo (phyllo) pastry

**Makes 10, serves 4–6**

This is a very ancient dish, traced all the way back to the Pharoahs, and to this day is considered Egypt's national dish, eaten for breakfast, lunch or dinner. The particularly buxom and buttery brown beans are actually broad beans (fava) beans, more commonly eaten fresh and green in the West. If you find the ful beans dried, cook them in the usual manner by soaking overnight, then boiling up in fresh water until tender, which might take 2–7 hours. Alternatively, canned beans are widely available and a big time-saver.

The traditional accompaniment is *Hamine* eggs – boiled in their shells in water with lots of brown onion skins. The onion skins impart their remarkably potent copper-coloured pigment – the shells turn a deep mahogany brown, the whites turn beige and go beyond rubbery to soft again, and the yolks become very creamy. I make these every Easter for fun, as I know no better egg dye (see recipe below). My own embellishment is to lift them out of the water after about 30 minutes and tap them all over with the back of a spoon - the dye seeps into the cracks, creating a beautiful "marble" effect once peeled.

# Ful Medames Brown Beans Egypt

Place the beans, with their liquid, in a saucepan and heat gently over a medium heat. Drain. Stir through the garlic, a pinch of salt and pepper and oil.

Ladle into soup bowls and sprinkle with the chopped parsley. Serve with side dishes of lemon wedges, *Hamine* eggs, olives and olive oil.

**For the beans:**
2 x 400 g/14 oz cans ful beans (brown broad (fava) beans)
2 garlic cloves, crushed
Sea salt and freshly ground black pepper
1 tbsp extra virgin olive oil
2–3 tbsp finely chopped fresh parsley
**To garnish:**
Lemon wedges
*Hamine* eggs (see below), or whole hard-boiled (hard-cooked) eggs
Good quality black olives
Olive oil

**Serves 4**

# Hamine Eggs

First peel the onions, reserving every bit of the papery skin. In a small saucepan, make a layer of onion skins and place the eggs on top. Cover with more onion skins, tucking them in between the eggs. Fill the saucepan with water to cover the eggs by at least 2.5 cm/1 inch depth. Add the oil. Bring to the boil, then reduce to a simmer. Simmer very gently for 5–6 hours, topping up with water as necessary, although the oil will go some way towards preventing evaporation. Leave the eggs to cool in the liquid. Leave to chill in the refrigerator until ready to serve.

6 large brown skinned onions
6 organic eggs
2 tbsp sunflower or vegetable oil

**Serves 6**

A luxurious rice dish festooned with fruit, nuts and spices, fit for a Pharaoh. Egyptians, like the rest of North Africa, are very partial to couscous as a staple starch, but rice is even more popular, and it is usually cooked with butter, as in this recipe. The rice and vermicelli combination is an influence from Egypt's Arab neighbours to the East, where similar, plainer versions are a regular staple known as *riz bi sh'areh*, *roz bil shaghria* or *riz mfalfal*.

This spectacular dish is the star of the meal and can be enjoyed with some fairly plainly cooked lentils or beans, or any of the legume recipes in this book.

# Pacha Rice
# Studded Rice and Vermicelli Egypt

Place a large saucepan with a lid over a medium heat and add the 45 g/ 1½ oz/3 tbsp butter. When the butter has melted, add the onion and cook until golden. Add the garlic, herbs, spices and seasoning. Stir for 1–2 minutes until fragrant, then add the sultanas and rice. Fry until the rice is tinged with gold, then pour in the water. Stir, cover and bring to the boil. Reduce the heat to a simmer and cook until the rice has absorbed all the water and is tender, about 15–20 minutes, depending on the type of rice you are using.

Meanwhile, bring a small saucepan of salted water to the boil. Cook the pasta until tender, only about 3 minutes. Drain thoroughly.

Melt the remaining 30 g/1 oz/1 tbsp butter in a frying pan over a low–medium heat and add the almonds. When they begin to colour add the cooked pasta. Fry until the pasta becomes a little bit crunchy and golden in places. Stir into the cooked rice mixture, spoon into a warmed serving dish and sprinkle with coriander leaves.

45 g/1½ oz/3 tbsp butter
1 medium onion, finely chopped
2 garlic cloves, chopped
½ tsp dried thyme
2 tbsp chopped fresh coriander (cilantro), plus a few leaves to garnish
½ tsp dried basil (optional)
½ tsp turmeric
1 tsp coriander seeds, crushed
Salt and freshly ground black pepper
50 g/2 oz/½ cup sultanas (golden raisins)
250 g/9 oz/1¼ cups long-grain rice
500 ml/16 fl oz/2 cups water
125 g/4 oz vermicelli or angel hair pasta, broken into about 2.5 cm/1 inch pieces
30 g/1 oz/1 tbsp butter
50 g/2 oz/⅓ cup blanched almonds, coarsely chopped

**Serves 4–6**

As old as the hills and with as many variations as there are Egyptian families, *dukkah* could be relied upon for sustenance when there wasn't much else around, provided there was bread, and olive oil. It's a tasty and moreish mix, which makes a fantastic, up-to-date appetizer despite its humble origins.

Toasting the ingredients separately may appear tedious, but it really is necessary to achieve the right flavour, as each component toasts at a different rate, and it really isn't a bother.

Most recipes say that *dukkah* "keeps indefinitely if stored in an airtight container", but in my experience, any nut or seed which has been toasted becomes rancid before too long. Best stored in the freezer.

# Dukkah
# Nut and Spice Mix Egypt

Toast the sesame seeds in a large, dry frying pan over a medium–high heat, shaking the pan, until golden and popping. Remove to a ceramic bowl to cool.

Add the hazelnuts to the pan. Toast, shaking the pan, until the oils come to the surface of the nuts and they appear shiny and patched with gold. Remove to the bowl with the sesame seeds.

Finally, add the coriander and cumin seeds. Toast for about 1 minute, or until fragrant and turned a slightly darker shade, but take care not to burn. Add to the bowl. Leave to cool completely.

When cool, place the nuts and seeds in a food processor with the salt and pepper. Process on high speed for a short time, so that the mixture is crushed to a coarse powder. Over-processing will result in a paste, which should be avoided – the *dukkah* should be a crushed dry mixture.

To serve, place the *dukkah* in a bowl alongside a small bowl of olive oil. Serve with strips of bread, to be dipped first in oil, then in the *dukkah*.

70 g/2¾ oz/⅓ cup sesame seeds
70 g/2¾ oz/½ cup blanched hazelnuts
3 tbsp coriander seeds
2 tbsp cumin seeds
½ tsp sea salt
Freshly ground black pepper

**To serve:**
Warm pitta (pita) bread or flatbread,
  sliced into strips
Extra virgin olive oil

**Serves 8**

This decidedly Anglo–Egyptian recipe, adapted from Claudia Roden's *Middle Eastern Food*, was a favourite in her family growing up in Cairo and has worked its way into my regular repertoire – I love the way her English connections come into play with the piccalilli. This very Middle Eastern style "salad" is more of an intensely flavoured purée, which disappears in no time accompanied by warm pitta bread.

# Salad Rachèle
## Aubergine (Eggplant) and Tomato Pickle Salad Egypt

Choose a large saucepan with a lid which will accommodate all the ingredients. Drizzle a little olive oil over the base of the pan, then make layers of aubergines and tomatoes, sprinkling a little salt and oil in between each layer. Cover and place over the lowest possible heat. Cook gently for 30 minutes without stirring, until the aubergines are as soft as butter and offer no resistance when prodded with a fork.

Transfer to a bowl and, while still hot, stir the piccalilli gently through the mixture. Leave to cool. It improves overnight. Serve with pitta bread or flatbread.

Olive oil

3 medium or 2 large aubergines (eggplants), about 1 kg/2 lb 4 oz, sliced into 1 cm/½ inch circles

4 ripe, plump vine-ripened tomatoes, about 500 g/1 lb 2 oz, medium sliced

Salt

1 medium jar piccalilli, 200 g/7 oz, chopped if in large pieces

Pitta (pita) bread or other flatbread, to serve

**Serves 4–6**

The Coptic Christians of Egypt traditionally eat this dish during fasts, but it's become a popular street food. Sometimes macaroni or spaghetti goes into it as well as rice, which is layered with spiced lentils and topped with fried onions and tomato sauce. The sauce should be assertively tangy and hot. Restaurants and street stalls in Cairo specialize in *kosheri* (also seen as *kushari* or *kochary*) and here you will be offered extra garlicky vinegar and chilli sauce to maximize the flavour.

# Kosheri Lentils and Rice with Sweet Onions Egypt

Preheat the oven to 110°C/225°F/Gas Mark ¼ for keeping warm.

Rinse the lentils and place in a saucepan with a lid. Add enough water to cover the lentils, then cover with the lid and bring to the boil. Boil rapidly for at least 10 minutes, then reduce the heat to a simmer. Check and stir frequently, and keep adding hot water as the lentils expand. Add salt to taste halfway through cooking. Cook until the lentils are thick and collapsed – this could take anywhere from 30 minutes–1 hour, depending on the age of the lentils. You want to achieve a porridge-like consistency, which is smooth and not watery. Finally, stir in the cumin, cayenne and black pepper to taste. Cover and keep warm.

Cook the rice according to the packet (package) instructions. Keep warm.

To make the sauce, heat a saucepan over a medium heat and add the oil. Add the garlic and fry briefly until fragrant, then add the tomatoes. Cook for about 10 minutes until thickened slightly. Add the water, vinegar, cayenne and salt and pepper. Stir and bring to the boil, then turn off the heat. Taste for seasoning. It will taste very tart, but this is as it should be. Keep warm.

Meanwhile, heat a large frying pan over a medium heat and add the oil and onion rings. Cook, turning with tongs, until golden, sprinkle with a little sugar, and cook until crispy. Drain on kitchen paper (paper towels).

The *Kosheri* can be assembled in individual bowls or one large, warmed serving dish. Make a layer of lentils, a layer of rice, another of lentils and another of rice, then pour the sauce over the surface. Scatter the sweet onions over the top.

250 g/9 oz/1¼ cups red or yellow split lentils
Salt and freshly ground black pepper
1 tsp ground cumin
½ tsp cayenne pepper, or to taste
200 g/7 oz/1 cup rice of your choice

**For the sauce:**
2 tsp sunflower oil
3 garlic cloves, finely chopped
1 x 400 g/14 oz can chopped tomatoes
60 ml/2¼ fl oz/generous ¼ cup water
2 tbsp wine vinegar
Cayenne pepper to taste

**For the sweet onions:**
2 tbsp sunflower oil
1 large onion, sliced into rings
Few pinches of sugar

**Serves 4–6**

If you've adopted the word "palaver" into your vocabulary to mean a mess or some complicated business, you'll be interested to know that the word came from the Portuguese word *palavra* or talk, which came to refer to the chatter of an argumentative committee. This dish is far from complicated, so I'm not sure why it has that tag. Ghanaians translate this as "Spinach Sauce" – sauce is the name for many African stews, to be served with mashed vegetables, grain porridge or rice.

*Palava* is traditonally made using *egusi*, a type of melon seed (see page 145). I've used hulled, toasted pumpkin seeds here, which provide protein, a host of other nutrients and a delicious, rich flavour. Serve with plain rice, *Bulgar Pilav* (see page 127) or *Irio* (see page 187).

# Palava

# Spinach, Tomato and Pumpkin Seed Stew Ghana

Place the pumpkin seeds in a large frying pan and toast over a medium–high heat, shaking frequently while the pop and crackle, until golden and puffed. Remove to a tray or flat dish and leave to cool.

When cool, place in a blender or food processor with the 4 tbsp water. Process to a coarse purée.

Meanwhile, heat a large saucepan over a medium heat and add the oil. Add the onion and fry until golden, then add the tomato, tomato purée, spinach, salt, cayenne, 250 ml/8 fl oz/1 cup water and the pumpkin paste. Stir and bring to the boil, then reduce to a low simmer. Cover the pan and cook for about 30 minutes, stirring frequently. The stew will be very thick. Serve with plain rice.

150 g/5 oz1 cup hulled pumpkin seeds
4 tbsp water
4 tbsp sunflower oil
1 large onion, coarsely chopped
1 large tomato, coarsely chopped
125 ml/4 fl oz/½ cup tomato purée (paste)
450 g/1 lb frozen spinach, thawed, drained and squeezed
1 tsp salt
½ tsp cayenne pepper, or to taste
250 ml/8 fl oz/1 cup water
Freshly cooked plain rice, to serve

**Serves 4–6**

These original bean cakes, made from West Africa's indigenous black-eyed beans, go back a long way. African slaves transported this recipe to the Americas where they became *akkra* or *akrats* in the Caribbean and *acaraje* in Brazil. The traditional method is a rather fiddly operation using dried beans, which must have the skins rubbed off – I assure you, you lose nothing but tedium by using canned beans here. *Pilipili* is a generic term for chilli sauce in Africa, referring to the small but mighty periperi, Africa's favourite chilli. This word is also the origin of the name of the *Berbere* spice mix from Ethiopia (see page 172). *Akara* can be served as an appetizer or as part of a main meal with grains and vegetables.

# Akara with Pilipili
# Bean Cakes with Chilli Sauce Nigeria

Place the beans in a food processor and, with the blade turning, add warm water a tablespoon at a time, until reduced to a smooth paste, which drops off a spoon, about the consistency of a thick cake mixture (batter). Add the onion, dried chilli flakes, salt, egg, flour and baking powder and pulse to mix thoroughly.

Heat a shallow pool of oil in a large frying pan over a medium heat. Fry heaped teaspoons of bean batter until golden on each side. Drain on kitchen paper (paper towels). Set aside.

To make the *pilipili*, bring a saucepan of water to the boil. Add the peppers and boil until soft, about 8–10 minutes. Drain and place in a blender or food processor with the chillies, salt, garlic, lemon juice and process until smooth. Serve the warm sauce with hot *akara*.

**For the *akara*:**

2 x 400 g/14 oz cans black-eyed beans (black-eye peas), drained and rinsed

1 small onion, very finely chopped

½ tsp dried chilli (red pepper) flakes or cayenne pepper, to taste

Salt

1 egg

4 tbsp plain (all-purpose) flour

1 tsp baking powder

Sunflower or vegetable oil for frying

**For the *pilipili*:**

2 red (bell) peppers, stem removed and de-seeded

1–2 hot fresh green chillies (chilies), or to taste, stem removed

½ tsp salt

1 garlic clove, coarsely chopped

Juice of ½ lemon

**Makes 24, serves 4–6**

# chapter seven Central, East and Southern Africa

This part of Africa has been neglected in world-themed cookbooks. As many of the rich cultural traditions of the region were eclipsed by colonialism, Africa suffered, and is only now beginning to truly assert its identity. In the Western world, tourism is one of the main instruments for enabling our culinary understanding, and though tourism is a growing industry in this region, it is still fairly nascent. While we are accustomed to the funky flavours of a Moroccan couscous for instance, we might never have even heard of, let alone tasted, an Ethiopian *we't* or a Kenyan *ugali*. Here the food available to tourists is more likely to be cheese omelette from a safe, hygenic hotel, as the real eating is going on behind closed doors at home.

The perception of Africa south of the Sahara as a land of famine is, of course, directly contradictory to the concept of gastronomy. But from the Mountains of the Moon to the Cape of Good Hope, in the face of deprivation ingenuity has prevailed, and with the blessing of a host of flavourful ingredients from Asian immigrants, a vegetarian cuisine of global significance has evolved.

"Hunger makes the best sauce." African proverb

# meet the expert:
# Rita Pankhurst – Ethiopian Cuisine

Rita Pankhurst was born in Romania, was educated at Oxford, then settled in Addis Ababa, the Ethiopian capital. There she married Prof. Richard Pankhurst, son of noted women's rights campaigner Sylvia Pankhurst, and had two children. She has worked as a librarian, bibliographer and editor, and for pleasure, as a student of Ethiopian culture and officer of several voluntary organisations.

After first hearing Rita Pankhurst talking engagingly about Ethiopia on BBC Radio 4's Food Programme, I thought she'd be the perfect candidate to relate an insider's understanding of Ethiopian food, at the same time having the objective view of a European. I was thrilled to discover I had a link through my family to hers. I tracked her down in Addis, where she lives for most of the year, over a crackly phone line. I've always been intensely curious, how did the food of Ethiopia, with its colourful veggie tradition, its deft spicing techniques and uncommon dining rituals, come to be so unique in all the world?

"Ethiopian food culture is shaped primarily by its geographical location and its physical characteristics", said Rita. "Centuries of hazardous contact with the outside world, due to its proximity to the Middle East and India, meant that it has always been subject to influence. Its climate and topography, unlike much of the rest of Africa, is conducive to the development of a great variety of crops – this has shaped its culinary complexity." Indeed it is a land of staggering physical extremes – deep river valleys such as the Great Rift Valley carve through massive volcanic mountains and fertile plateaus, in addition to hostile desert landscapes.

Though it was occupied by the Italians from 1936–41, Ethiopia was never colonised, due to the shrewd diplomacy of its royal family. However, it has not been immune to strife – in the latter quarter of the 20th century, the royal family was ousted by a brutal regime leading to bloody wars and famine compounded by drought. Unfortunately, the image of a desperate Ethiopia spread throughout the world, eclipsing the notion of its true sophisticated culture. Happier days precipitated with a democratic election in 1995 and a peace treaty with its long-time enemy Eritrea in 2000.

While vegetarianism in the rest of Africa has been mostly an involuntary existence due to deprivation, Ethiopia's Orthodox Christians, which make up around half the 66.5 million population, deliberately avoid meat and dairy products for around 208 days a year. Naturally, this has forged a rich and varied cuisine based on grains, pulses and spices.

As Rita explained, "There is an age-old Indian influence on Ethiopian cuisine, coming through traders who used the Monsoon winds that blew the sailing vessels from India to the African coast for six months of the year, and then blew in the opposite direction for the other six months. Cardamom, cumin, fenugreek, cinnamon, turmeric, cloves and nutmeg probably came via India. Ethiopians and Indians, as well as many Middle Easterners, share the custom of eating directly with their hands and many pick up the main dish with some pancake-like bread." This bread, called *Injera* (see page 173), is the foundation of the Ethiopian diet, eaten everyday with every meal, just as rice is in Asia. During celebration feasts, a large, colourful mushroom-shaped basket called a *mesob* is lined with huge, round blankets of *Injera*, onto which a selection of stews are arranged, most laced with a searingly hot *Berbere* spice mix (see page 172). The diners gather round the *mesob* and share in the feast, using torn pieces of the *Injera* to scoop up the food, with plenty of wine or beer brewed from local honey. The meal concludes with coffee, a gift to the world, native to the region of Kefa.

Rita remembers an amusing incident involving *Injera*. "A shy young man who had just arrived in Addis was taken to a restaurant. He saw the *Injera* in front of him, neatly folded. Thinking it was his napkin, he put it on his lap, and being too shy to replace it when he realized his mistake, he sat through the meal with the damp *Injera* still on his lap."

"Cuisine…is just another by-product of a high-rising society with lots of hard cash as the yeast."

Harva Hachten, *Best of Regional African Cooking*

# focus on ingredients

**Groundnuts** – peanuts, goobers, monkey nuts – are so-called because their pods grow underground. They were introduced to Africa by Portuguese settlers after Columbus discovered them in South America. They are not actually nuts, but qualify botanically as a legume, which makes sense, if you consider the name "peanut", and the shape of the pod – some varieties yield up to seven nuts in one pod. As they thrive in tropical climates and are easy to grow, they are heavily relied upon as a protein source in the African diet, as meat is often scarce. They are also extremely high in antioxidants, which protect cells in the body from damage linked to heart disease and cancer, and they have a high ratio of monounsaturated or "good" fats. Groundnuts are used mainly finely crushed in African cooking, making their way into numerous stews and soups (several in this chapter), and are also formed into deep-fried dough balls and made into delicious sweet biscuits (cookies) with coconut.

**Chickpea flour** – gram flour, besan, pea flour, powdered peas – This flour is made from lightly toasted chickpeas, ground to a fine powder. It appears light

yellow and turns a deep, mustard yellow when wet. It's the Indians who use chickpea flour the most, in batters for deep-frying and doughs for bread and noodles. However, it is used in Africa as well, as it is a cheap, nutritious and long-lasting thickener for the ever-present stews. It is usually sold in stores selling Indian foods and or health foods, but it is also easy to make yourself, if you have a powerful blender. However, do be prepared for an almighty racket and possibly a scratched blender jar: put dried chickpeas in a single layer in a roasting tray and cook in an oven preheated to 200°C/400°F/Gas Mark 6 for about 6–8 minutes, or until lightly toasted and smelling quite nutty. Cool completely, then grind to a fine powder and store in an airtight container.

**Nigella** – *kalonji*, *ajown*, *netch azmud*, love-in-the-mist, *habba sauda*, black cumin, black onion seed – These tiny, tear-drop shaped, jet-black seeds are no relation to the onion and are not the same as cumin. Their distinctive and quite potent taste is reminiscent of oregano with a whisper of aniseed (anise). Used extensively in Ethiopian and Indian cooking, both whole and ground, they are often scattered over

**Groundnuts**

**Chickpea Flour**

Turkish and Arabic flatbreads and are also used in sweet pastries in the Middle East (it is native to the Levant).

Ugali – *putu*, mealie pap, *nsima*, *oshifima*, *bidia* – Ugali is the Swahili word for a thick porridge, which deserves a special mention. Throughout Africa south of the Sahara, this is a daily staple, which is an essential stomach-filler and meal-stretcher. It is eaten as an accompaniment to stews, but rather than sitting on the plate with the stew spooned over it, it is usually used as a utensil: a piece of it is taken with fingers from the communal bowl and the thumb is used to make an indentation, thus creating an edible spoon of sorts, for scooping up the stew. Ugali is usually made from white cornmeal, but is also made with millet, sorghum or coarse cassava flour. To make cornmeal ugali, use a proportion of 1:1½

**Ironbark Pumpkin**

white cornmeal to water. Combine in a saucepan with salt, bring to the boil and cook, stirring regularly, for 20–30 minutes until creamy but stiff; add butter and serve with stew.

Spinach – Spinach originated in Persia and the word comes from its old Persian name. Though unknown before around the 5th century AD, its popularity soon spread across the world, not least in Africa, where it is called *Mchicha* in Swahili (see *Mchicha Wanazi* on page 185). In African cooking, spinach – or one of hundreds of other types of greens such as sweet potato leaves – will often serve as the base of a stew, which is then nutritionally enhanced with ground nuts or seeds (see also *Palava* on page 165). It has many nutritional virtues (antioxidants, vitamins), and did wonders for Popeye, but not because of its iron content, a common misconception.

Though it does have a high iron content, this is negated by its content of oxalic acid, which makes the iron, as well as calcium, unavailable to the body.

Pumpkin – The word evokes an image of a plump, round, orange vegetable, but it can be used to describe any member of the squash family of which it is a part. In fact, the orange-skinned variety is one of the least appealing in flavour and texture, especially once they get large. Squashes such as butternut and ironbark, with beige skin, and acorn and kabocha, with green skin, have a dense orange flesh, which is sweet and velvety. The seed of the pumpkin is delicious (see *Palava* on page 165, and *Papadzules* on page 46) and highly nutritious. Africans adore the leaves of all sorts of pumpkin and squashes as a base for stews, or added at the end of cooking. The blossom of the plant is a delicacy, either stuffed or battered and fried.

This richly spiced butter forms the foundation of many Ethiopian stews, lending an inimitable extra dimension. It can be used in place of the cooking fat in any spicy dish, from Indian curry to Mexican chili, and tastes rather fine simply spread on toast.

# Niter Kibbeh
# Spiced Clarified Butter Ethiopia

In a small saucepan, gradually melt the butter and bring it to the boil. When the top is foamy, add the onion, garlic, ginger, cardamom, cinnamon, cloves, nutmeg, fenugreek, turmeric and basil and reduce the heat to a simmer. Simmer over a very low heat, making sure there is no sign of burning, for about 20 minutes, or until the solids fall to the bottom.

Pour the liquid through a clean cloth, such as a j-cloth or muslin (cheesecloth) into a heatproof container. Discard the solids. Leave to cool briefly, then pour into a container with a tight-fitting lid. Leave to cool completely and store in the refrigerator for up to 2 months.

250 g/9 oz/1⅛ cups unsalted butter
1 small onion, finely chopped
1 garlic clove, finely chopped
1-cm/½-inch piece fresh root ginger, peeled and grated
½ tsp cardamom seeds removed from the pod, crushed
1 cinnamon stick, about 7.5 cm/ 3 inches long
2 cloves
¼ tsp freshly grated nutmeg
¼ tsp fenugreek seeds
¼ tsp turmeric
½ tsp dried basil

**Makes 250 g/9 oz/1⅛ cups**

This essential spice mix, the Ethiopian "curry powder," is the foundation of all the distinctive spicy stews of Ethiopia and Eritrea, and the mix will vary greatly from cook to cook. I've experimented with many mixes and this is my favourite, adapted from *Sundays at Moosewood.* How hot you make it is up to you – Ethiopian curries are notoriously hot, and even children share the heat of the *Berbere*-laced meals.

# Berbere Hot Spice Powder Ethiopia

Toast the cumin seeds, cloves, cardamom, peppercorns, fenugreek, coriander seeds and chilies in a dry frying pan over a medium heat, shaking the pan frequently, until lightly coloured. Leave to cool, then grind in a spice grinder with the ginger, allspice, turmeric, salt, cinnamon and paprika until a fine powder forms. Store in an airtight container.

2 tsp cumin seeds
8 cloves
1 tsp cardamom seeds (removed from pod)
½ tsp whole black peppercorns
1 tsp fenugreek seeds
1 tsp coriander seeds
8 small red dried chilies (chilies)
½ tsp ground ginger

¼ tsp ground allspice
¼ tsp turmeric
1 tsp salt
¼ tsp ground cinnamon
3 tbsp paprika

**Makes about 80 g/3 oz/½ cup**

*Injera* is absolutely essential with every Ethiopian spread, and its sour flavour marries perfectly with the spicy stews. In Ethiopia it is made with *teff*, the world's tiniest grain, which thrives in the mountains there. I've made the recipe more accessible by using wheat flour and it takes about 2 minutes to make – but there the shortcuts stop. You must then wait 3 days, while it develops a wonderful sourdough flavour and a light and springy texture. A little forward planning is all that's necessary for this very authentic replica. You will need a large, reliable non-stick pan for cooking these; if you find they are sticking, you may need to add a very light slick of oil to your pan before adding the batter.

# Injera
# Sourdough Flatbread Ethiopia

Select a large ceramic, glass or plastic bowl, which will allow the batter enough room to rise. Combine the flours and yeast in the bowl. Stir in the warm water and mix to a fairly thin, smooth batter. Cover with a clean damp cloth and let the mixture sit for a full 3 days at room temperature, stirring once a day – it will bubble and rise.

When ready to cook the injera, stir the bicarbonate of soda and salt into the mixture and leave to stand for 15 minutes.

Heat a large non-stick frying pan over a medium heat until a drop of water bounces on the surface. Use a 125 ml/4 fl oz/½ cup measure (or about ⅔ teacup) to scoop the batter and pour into the hot pan, swirling quickly to coat the surface from the centre outwards – lots of little holes will form immediately. Cook until the surface of the pancake is dry; do not flip or allow to brown underneath – it should be soft and pliable. Remove to a warmed plate and cook the remaining *injera*.

300 g/11 oz/2⅓ cups strong white (bread) flour
100 g/3½ oz/⅔ cup wholemeal (whole wheat) self-raising (self-rising) flour
1 x 7 g/¼ oz packet easy-blend dried (bread machine) yeast
625 ml/1 pint/2½ cups warm water
½ tsp bicarbonate of soda (baking soda)
1 tsp salt

**Makes about 8–10, serves 4–6**

## variations

*Fitfit* is a common snack or breakfast food – a delicious and clever way of using leftover *injera*:

**For Temateem Fitfit or Injera Salad** (not far off the Italian *Panzanella* (see page 95) or Lebanese *Fattoush* (see page 136), mix 1–2 *injera*, torn into small pieces, with chopped fresh tomato, chopped onion, chopped green chilli, a little salt and lemon juice.

**For Yesalit Fitfit**, toast a few tbsp of sesame seeds in a dry pan. Cool and crush to a paste, then mix with *injera* torn into small pieces, and a little salt.

This chunky stew will provide a textural contrast in a spread of Ethiopian stews such as *Yeshiro We't* (see page 176) and *Yedifin Miser* (see opposite), mopped up with a pile of *Injera* (see page 173), naturally. If you are not planning an Ethiopian extravaganza, however, this is a quick, easy and nutritious supper, which can be enjoyed as a winter warmer, as a substantial stew or spooned over rice. Notice the unusual technique of cooking the onion first without oil. This seems to be fairly universal as the first step in all Ethiopian stew-making, unlike anywhere else in the world. As the onion effectively steams in its own juice, the resulting texture will always be meltingly soft and never tough (which can sometimes result from frying the onion at too high a temperature).

# Ye'atakilt W'et
# Spicy Mixed Vegetable Stew Ethiopia

Heat a large saucepan with a lid over a medium heat and add the onion (without any oil). Cook, stirring, in the dry pan until soft. Add the *Niter Kibbeh* or oil, garlic, *Berbere* and paprika and fry for 2 minutes. Add the green beans, carrots and potatoes and cook, covered and stirring occasionally for 5 minutes.

Add the tomatoes, tomato purée, stock or water and salt and pepper, bring to the boil and simmer, uncovered, until the vegetables are tender. Taste for seasoning and stir in the parsley. Serve with *Injera* (see page 173) and yogurt or cottage cheese.

1 large red onion, finely chopped

4 tbsp *Niter Kibbeh* (see page 172), or sunflower oil

2 garlic cloves, chopped

1 tbsp *Berbere* (see page 172)

1 tbsp paprika

125 g/4 oz green beans, cut into small pieces

1 large carrot, about 200 g/7 oz, medium chopped

1 medium potato, about 200 g/7 oz, medium chopped

2 vine-ripened tomatoes, about 250 g/9 oz, medium chopped

4 tbsp tomato purée (paste)

500 ml/16 fl oz/2 cups vegetable stock or water

Salt and freshly ground black pepper

Generous handful of fresh parsley, finely chopped

**To serve:**
*Injera* (see page 173)
Yogurt or cottage cheese

**Serves 4–6**

Among the unique herb and spice blends of the Ethiopian spice cupboard is a mix called *alicha we't kemem*, or "mild stew seasoning", which is ground dried ginger, garlic and basil. Here I've used fresh ginger and garlic and a double dose of basil in both dried and fresh form. This gently seasoned stew is served as a contrast to the fiery *berbere*-laden stews such as *Ye'takilt We't* (see opposite) and *Yeshiro We't* (see page 176). Curiously, a handful of chopped fresh chillies would still be scattered over the top for good measure, as the Ethiopians have an extraordinary chilli-heat threshold. This can also be enjoyed simply as a soup, with a spoonful of yogurt on top.

# Yedifin Miser Alicha We't
# Mild Lentil Stew with Basil Ethiopia

Heat a saucepan with a lid over a medium heat. Add the onion (without any oil) and stir-fry until wilted and tinged with gold, about 2 minutes. Reduce the heat and add the oil, ginger, garlic, turmeric and dried basil. Stir constantly over a low heat until very fragrant and the garlic is golden, about 2 minutes.

Add the lentils, stir for 1 minute, then add the boiling water, cover and bring to the boil. Reduce the heat to a simmer and cook, covered, for 15 minutes, then stir in the salt. Cover and simmer until lentils are tender, adding more water if necessary, though the stew should be thick and not watery. When the lentils are thoroughly tender, stir in the fresh basil. Taste for seasoning and serve with *Injera* (see page 173) and yogurt.

1 large red onion, finely chopped
2 tbsp sunflower oil
4-cm/1½-inch thumb fresh root ginger, very finely chopped or grated
2 plump garlic cloves, finely chopped
½ tsp turmeric
1 tbsp dried basil
250 g/9 oz/1¼ cups brown lentils
750 ml/1¼ pints/3 cups boiling water
1 tsp sea salt, or to taste
Generous handful of fresh basil, chopped or torn

**To serve:**
*Injera* (see page 173)
Yogurt

**Serves 4–6**

The use of powdered chickpeas or chickpea flour (see page 170) here is quite remarkable. In India it is widely used for batters and dough, but with typical Ethiopian cleverness here, just 4 tbsp transforms a seasoned stock into a nutritious, thick and filling stew. In fact, many Ethiopian cooks grind their own dried legumes with a host of spices, then store it in jars for an instant stew of "hot powdered peas" – this mixture is called *mit'in shiro*. This tasty stew is quite wonderful for a quick and simple lunch or supper with rice and a few steamed vegetables, though traditionally it makes up part of a multitude of *we't* (spicy stews) and *alicha we't* (mild stews), and is always eaten with *Injera* (see page 173). *Niter Kibbeh* (see page 172), the clarified spiced butter, is quite fundamental to the flavour here.

# Yeshiro We't
# Stew of Spiced Powdered Chickpeas

Ethiopia

Heat a large non-stick pan over a medium heat. Add the onion (without any oil) and stir-fry until soft and brown. Reduce the heat and add the *Niter Kibbeh*, ginger, garlic, *Berbere* and nigella seeds. Cook, stirring constantly, until the garlic is golden. Pour in the stock and bring to the boil, then reduce to a simmer.

Mix the chickpea flour with enough cold water to make a pourable paste. Gradually pour the chickpea paste into the simmering mixture, while stirring constantly to avoid lumps. Simmer for about 30 minutes, or until very thick. Taste for seasoning and add salt and pepper as necessary. Serve with *Injera* and *Ye'atakilt We't*.

1 red onion, finely chopped
4 tbsp *Niter Kibbeh* (see page 172)
4-cm/1½-inch thumb fresh root ginger, very finely chopped or grated
2 plump garlic cloves, finely chopped
2 tbsp *Berbere* (see page 172)
2 tsp nigella seeds (see page 170)
500 ml/16 fl oz/2 cups well-flavoured vegetable stock
4 tbsp chickpea flour (see page 170)
Sea salt and freshly ground black pepper

**To serve:**
*Injera* (see page 173)
*Ye'atakilt We't* (see page 174)

**Serves 4–6**

Mussolini didn't do Eritrea any favours when his fascist regime invaded in 1936, ruling until 1941. However, the Italians had been in the region many years before, in the mid to late 19th century, and were responsible for building roads, railroads and schools there. Of course they also brought their culinary traditions, which, over time, fused with Eritrean ones. Spaghetti Napoli is certainly a vegetarian classic, but I thought it much more interesting to include this Eritrean adaptation of that dish, which spices up the sauce with *Berbere* (see page 172). This super-quick sauce cooks in the time it takes to cook the spaghetti.

# Spaghetti Zigni
# Noodles with Hot Sauce Eritrea

Bring a large saucepan of water to the boil and salt it very well. Cook the spaghetti until *al dente*, about 9–11 minutes, or follow the packet (package) instructions.

Meanwhile, heat a large frying pan over a medium heat and add the oil. Add the garlic and cook until fragrant, about 1 minute. Add the green pepper, tomatoes, salt and pepper, *Berbere* and oregano. Cook, stirring, until the tomatoes begin to collapse, about 3–4 minutes. Stir in the tomato purée and simmer for 1 minute.

Drain the spaghetti and serve with the sauce and freshly grated Parmesan.

500 g/1lb 2 oz spaghetti

**For the Zigni sauce:**
2 tbsp olive oil
4 garlic cloves, finely chopped
1 green (bell) pepper, cored and chopped
2 large vine-ripened tomatoes, chopped
Sea salt and freshly ground black pepper
2 tsp *Berbere* (see page 172)
1 tsp dried oregano
2 tbsp tomato purée (paste)

Freshly grated Parmesan cheese, to serve

**Serves 4**

This is a lovely, simple treatment of pumpkin or squash, but it is only as good as the pumpkin you use. Avoid insipid jack-o-lantern style pumpkins and seek out a sweet-fleshed variety such as acorn, iron bark or kaboucha (see pumpkin, page 171). Traditionally this is eaten with *Injera* (see page 173), though it makes a good vegetable side dish and can be served with *Pacha Rice* (see page 161) or any rice or bean dish, or on its own as a chunky soup with a dollop of yogurt.

# D'ba Zigni
# Spiced Pumpkin in Broth Eritrea

Heat a saucepan over a medium heat and add the oil. Add the onion and cook until tinged with gold. Add the ginger and *Berbere* and cook until the *Berbere* turns a shade darker. Add pumpkin and stir to coat with spices. Add the tomato purée, salt and water. Stir, cover and bring to the boil. Simmer for 15–20 minutes, or until the pumpkin is soft.

If you prefer it thicker and less brothy, remove a few pieces of pumpkin and mash until smooth. Return to the pan and stir through.

2 tbsp sunflower oil

1 large onion, finely chopped

5-cm/2-inch thumb fresh root ginger, finely chopped

2 tsp *Berbere* (see page 172)

750 g/1 lb 10 oz pumpkin, peeled, de-seeded and cut into cubes or wedges

3 tbsp tomato purée (paste)

1 tsp salt

500 ml/16 fl oz/2 cups water

**Serves 4**

Zigni sauce (see page 177) also makes a mighty fine pizza – an Eritrean Pizza Margarita. Please don't be daunted by the home-made dough – it only takes 10 minutes to make, it's easier than you might think and the flavour makes it really worth the effort. Be sure to use mozzarella which is suitable for pizzas. The superlative buffalo mozzarella would be wasted here, as it is too wet and not meant for grating. Naturally, you could add whatever other toppings you like on ordinary pizza.

# Pizza Zigni
# Spicy Pizza Eritrea

To make the dough, place the flour in a large bowl and mix in the salt and yeast. Make a well in the centre and add the 2 tbsp olive oil. Start stirring in the water to form a dough. When most of the flour has been incorporated and the dough is still quite sticky, knead in the bowl with one hand to incorporate the rest of the flour, but stop before the dough feels dry.

Turn the dough out on to a clean, dry work surface and knead lovingly for 8 minutes until smooth and elastic. Pour some oil into the bowl and pop the dough back into it, turning the dough so that it gets a coating of oil. Cover the bowl with a damp tea (dish) towel and leave to prove, preferably in a warm place for 30 minutes–1 hour, or until doubled in size. (Once proved, you can punch the dough down and store in a sealed bag the refrigerator for up to 3 days – just remember to keep punching it down every once in a while.)

Preheat the oven to 220°C/425°F/Gas Mark 7. Sprinkle the polenta evenly over 2 baking trays. This will prevent the pizza sticking and give the crust a toothsome crunch. Punch down the proven dough and divide into 2 pieces. Roll out the pieces into 2 thin pizza bases, either round, square or rectangular – whatever your trays will accommodate. Spread Zigni sauce over both pizzas, then top with cheese.

Bake the pizzas in the oven for 20–30 minutes, or until golden and stiff. Leave to cool briefly, cut into wedges and devour while still warm.

500 g/1 lb 2 oz/3½ cups strong white (bread) flour
1 tsp sea salt
1 x 7 g (¼ oz) packet easy-blend dried yeast (active dry yeast)
2 tbsp olive oil, plus extra for oiling
300 ml/10 fl oz/1¼ cups hand-hot water
3 tbsp polenta (cornmeal)
1 quantity Zigni Sauce (see page 177)
250 g/9 oz pizza mozzarella (see note on page 7), grated

**Serves 4–6**

This quick, simple, brilliant yellow curry is one of thousands of dishes which demonstrates the profound influence of the Indians in East Africa. As it's just over the expanse of the Indian Ocean, Indians have come to Africa since ancient times, and migrant railroad workers were also brought over by the British during colonial rule. *Garam masala* is a regular feature of the Kenyan spice shelf, and I've given a recipe below should you like to make your own, based on a description from Kenyan chef and proprietor Kurshid Khan of Simba's Grill in Vancouver, Canada. Otherwise, use a store-bought mix or a Madras-style curry powder. This curry is best accompanied by a mash such as *Ugali* (see page 171) and an extra protein source such as lentils or dal.

# Mais de Mombasa
# Coconut Sweetcorn (Corn) Curry Kenya

If you are making the *garam masala*, here's how it's done. Place all the spices in a dry pan over a medium heat and toast, shaking the pan frequently, until the spices turn a shade darker, only about 2 minutes. Be careful not to burn or the mix will be bitter. Cool, then grind to a fine powder in a spice grinder. Store in an airtight container in a cool, dark, dry place.

To make the curry, heat a large saucepan over a medium heat and add the oil. Add the onion and red pepper and fry until tinged with gold. Add the garlic and fry until fragrant, then add 1–2 tsp garam masala and turmeric and stir to incorporate. Add the sweetcorn, tomato and salt and stir. Cook until heated through.

Beat the cornflour into the coconut milk and add to the saucepan. Bring to the boil and stir while the mixture thickens. Stir in the lemon juice and taste for seasoning. Garnish with a sprinkling of chopped parsley and serve.

1 tbsp sunflower oil
1 medium onion, finely chopped
1 red (bell) pepper, coarsely chopped
2 garlic cloves, finely chopped
1–2 tsp Kenyan *garam masala*, or to taste (see below)
¼ tsp turmeric
450 g/1 lb/3¼ cups fresh or frozen sweetcorn (corn)
1 plump vine-ripened tomato, chopped
1 tsp salt, or to taste
2 tsp cornflour (cornstarch)
250 ml/8 fl oz/1 cup coconut milk
1 tbsp fresh lemon juice
Chopped fresh parsley, to garnish

**For the Kenyan *garam masala*:**
2 tbsp cardamom seeds (removed from the pod)
2 tbsp cumin seeds
1 tbsp coriander seeds
1 cinnamon stick, 7.5 cm/3 inches long, broken
2 tsp cloves

**Serves 4–6**

"Groundnut Stew" (groundnuts are peanuts) is the staple stew of Sub-Saharan Africa: right now, somebody, somewhere, is cooking or eating groundnut stew. Of course, every version will be slightly different – some very basic, some more elaborate, sometimes with meat and more often not. Groundnuts, a cheap and abundant source of protein and energy, are a blessing for Africans (see page 170). Despite using no spices whatsoever except fresh green chilli pepper, this stew has a remarkably complex flavour. Okra, added halfway through cooking, serves to make the stew extra thick. Serve with plain rice, *Irio* (see page 187) or a plain mash like *Ugali* (see page 171), or for a rather extravagant and rich combo, with *Mseto* (see opposite).

# Huku ne Dovi
# Peanut Stew with Sweet Potato and Greens Zimbabwe

Heat a large saucepan with a lid over a medium heat and add the oil. Add the onion and fry until tinged with gold. Add the carrot, sweet potato, chillies, salt, tomatoes and water. Stir, cover and bring to the boil, then uncover and simmer for about 15 minutes until the vegetables are softening.

Meanwhile, grind the peanuts in a food processor or blender until finely ground, but stop before you end up with peanut butter. Add the okra and peanuts to the stew, stir and taste for seasoning. Cover and simmer for a further 15 minutes, stirring frequently, as the peanuts love to stick to the bottom of the pan.

Finally, stir in the spinach. Cook until it is just done, about 3 minutes. Serve piping hot seasoned with freshly ground black pepper.

1 tbsp sunflower oil

1 medium onion, finely chopped

1 large carrot, about 200 g/7 oz, peeled and cut into medium chunks

1 large sweet potato, about 400 g/14 oz, peeled and cut into medium chunks

1–2 fresh green chillies (chilies), or to taste, sliced

1 tsp salt, or to taste (if using salted peanuts, reduce the salt here)

1 x 400 g/14 oz can chopped tomatoes

750 ml/1¼ pints/3 cups water

150 g/5 oz/1 cup roasted peanuts, ideally unsalted

120 g/3¼ oz/1¼ cups fresh young okra, top trimmed, medium sliced

100 g/3½ oz/generous 2 cups fresh spinach (trimmed weight), well-washed and coarsely chopped

Freshly ground black pepper

**Serves 4–6**

Another Indian-inspired dish, this is a close cousin of *khichari* or *Kichree* (see page 140) – this time it's green lentils, which, being a larger lentil, take longer to cook than the red ones. For this reason, I have cooked them with brown basmati rice, which also takes longer to cook than white basmati, and makes it an altogether more wholesome dish. Bear in mind that the age of the lentils will determine their cooking time, and there is no way of knowing this. It is most important that the lentils are fully cooked – if the rice overcooks slightly, then it really doesn't matter, as the whole thing is fused together with the rich coconut and spices. It's nutritionally complete on its own, but becomes more exciting when served with *Huku ne Dovi* (see opposite) or *Palava* (see page 165).

# Mseto
# Rice and Green Lentils in Coconut milk Tanzania

Heat a large saucepan with a lid over a medium heat and add the oil. Add the onion and fry until tinged with gold. Add the garlic and ginger and fry until fragrant, about 1 minute. Add the lentils, rice, spice powder, if using, and turmeric. Stir until everything is evenly coated, then add the coconut milk, water and salt. Stir, cover, bring to the boil and simmer for about 40–50 minutes, without stirring. Do check often to make sure it is not drying out; if it is, add water a little at a time. Cook until all the liquid is absorbed and the lentils are thoroughly tender. Serve hot.

1 tbsp sunflower oil

1 large onion, coarsely chopped

3 garlic cloves, finely chopped

2.5-cm/1-inch thumb fresh root ginger, peeled and finely chopped

190 g/6¾ oz/scant 1 cup green lentils

175 g/6 oz/scant 1 cup brown basmati rice

1½ tsp Kenyan Garam Masala (see page 181), or Madras-style curry powder (optional)

¼ tsp turmeric

1 x 400 ml/14 fl oz/1¾ cups can coconut milk

600 ml/1 pint/2½ cups water

1 tsp salt, or to taste

**Serves 4–6 as a main course, 6–8 as an accompaniment**

Africans have ingenious ways of getting a lot out of very little – here a bunch of leaves are turned into a hearty meal with this filling and nutritious peanut-coconut sauce. This should be eaten with some sort of African mash such as *Matoke* (see page 186), *Ugali* (page 171) and *Irio* (page 187). *Irio* contains mashed kidney beans and would boost the protein content of the meal.

# M'chicha Wa'nazi
# Spinach in Peanut Coconut Sauce

Tanzania

Place the spinach and salt in a large saucepan with a lid. Cover and place over a medium heat. Use tongs to turn the spinach over from time to time, until it is fully collapsed and wilted (or thawed, if using frozen). Drain thoroughly in a colander, then use a potato masher to push out as much moisture as possible. Cool slightly, then chop coarsely.

Return the pan to a low-medium heat and add the butter. When the butter has melted, add the onion and chillies and cook until the onion is soft and translucent.

Purée the peanuts with the coconut cream in a blender until fairly smooth. Pour into the saucepan, add a good pinch of salt and cook, stirring, until slightly thickened, about 2 minutes. Stir the spinach through the sauce until piping hot, then serve. Alternatively, reheat the spinach in a microwave or pan and serve with the sauce poured over.

700 g/1½ lb fresh spinach, trimmed and thoroughly washed, or 700 g/ 1½ lb frozen spinach

1 tsp salt

30 g/1 oz/2 tbsp butter

1 large onion, chopped

1–2 fresh red chillies or to taste, de-seeded if large, finely chopped

70 g/2¾ oz/½ cup roasted peanuts

250 ml/8 fl oz/1 cup coconut cream

**Serves 4**

*left M'chicha Wa'nazi* served with *Irio* (see page 187).

In Tanzania, Kenya, Mozambique and other parts of East Africa, cold soups are made from fresh local ingredients like avocados and tomatoes to beat the heat. This recipe is a sort of composite of several I've tried, and most of them do not contain any representative from the allium family – ie. onions, garlic, etc., making it one of the only recipes in this book without! This soup capitalizes on the wonderful flavour of the best ripe and juicy tomatoes and perfectly ripe, butter-fleshed avocado – a black-skinned Hass avocado would be my choice.

# Cold Tomato and Avocado Soup East Africa

Place the tomatoes in a blender and whiz until completely smooth, about 1–2 minutes. (You can now strain the liquid if you wish to get rid of the seeds; I don't bother with this step, unless I'm serving guests.)

Add the yogurt, milk, lemon juice, tomato purée, parsley, salt and pepper to the blender. Whiz until smooth, then leave to chill in the refrigerator for at least 2 hours until very well chilled.

Just before serving, cut the avocado in half, remove the stone (pit), scoop out the flesh and mash until smooth. Stir into the chilled soup. Taste for seasoning. Peel and deseed the cucumber and cut in small dice. Serve the soup in bowls or wide glasses, topped with cucumber.

5 plump vine-ripened tomatoes, about 600 g/1 lb 5 oz, quartered
150 ml/5 fl oz/⅔ cup yogurt
125 ml/4 fl oz/½ cup milk
3 tbsp fresh lemon juice
2 tbsp tomato purée (paste)
3 tbsp chopped fresh parsley
1 tsp salt
Plenty of freshly ground black pepper
1 large ripe avocado
1 baby cucumber, or ⅓ ordinary cucumber, chilled

**Serves 4–6**

*Matoke* refers to a specific type of dense-fleshed and rich dwarf banana. When unripe they make a savoury, not sweet, mash – a surprising accompaniment to any of the stews in this chapter. Ordinary green bananas or plantains can be used instead – if you can find matoke, use 10–12 for the recipe.

# Matoke Banana Mash Uganda

Place the bananas, tomato, onion, water and salt in a saucepan. Cover and bring to the boil. Simmer, uncovered, until most of the liquid has evaporated and the bananas are very soft. Remove from the heat, add the butter and mash until smooth.

4 large unripe bananas, peeled and broken into pieces
1 large tomato, finely chopped
1 medium onion, finely chopped
150 ml/5 fl oz/⅔ cup water
½ tsp salt
15 g/½ oz/1 tbsp butter

**Serves 4–6**

I grew up green with envy towards my two older sisters, who shortly before I was born, got to live in Kenya for a year with my parents. As a child, I pored over dozens of huge black and white photographs that my father had taken of leopards sleeping draped over tree branches and lion families sunbathing in tall grass. "I was there," I used to tell them, "you just didn't know it." When I recently asked them for recollections of Kenyan food, my sister Beth's enthusiastic, response was "I LOVE *Irio*!", a child-like, nostalgic flutter in her voice.

*Irio* is a typical of the Kikuyu tribe, Kenya's largest ethnic group. It makes mashed potato more interesting and nutritious by adding beans, greens and corn; often green peas are added as well. Serve with *Mchicha Wa'nazi* (see page 185), *Huku ne Dovi* (see page 182) or any stew or curry.

# Irio Bean, Sweetcorn and Potato Mash Kenya

Place the potatoes in a large saucepan and cover with cold water. Add a generous pinch of salt, cover and bring to the boil. Simmer until just soft, about 10–15 minutes. Add the red kidney beans and sweetcorn and simmer for a further 5 minutes. Drain, then mash with parsley and butter and serve.

4 floury (mealy) potatoes, about 1 kg/2¼ lb, peeled and cut into chunks

Salt

1 x 400 g/14 oz can red kidney beans, drained and rinsed

200 g/7 oz/1½ cups frozen sweetcorn (corn)

2 tbsp chopped fresh parsley or watercress

30 g/1 oz/2 tbsp butter

**Serves 4–6**

Zubeinisa is a London-based home cook from Mauritius, the mother of a friend. She invited me over to teach me how to make *dal roti*, a flatbread filled with a spiced bean paste – a vegetarian classic in itself. I spent all day with Zubeinisa trying to get the technique right and only succeeded on the 32nd roti! However, to accompany our towering stack of breads (mostly imperfect except for the ones she made), she had made this curry dish, which we ate for lunch. It was so delicious, I asked for the recipe, so she dictated it to me and I made some modifications. Here is the result – toothsome green pea cakes in a creamy, brilliant yellow sauce. The Indian influence on this island cuisine sings loud and clear.

# Curry Burry
# Coriander (Cilantro) Pea Cakes in Coconut Curry Mauritius

To make the pea cakes, first soak the chana dal or yellow split peas for at least 4 hours or overnight.

Preheat the oven to 110°C/225°F/Gas Mark ¼ for keeping warm. Drain the beans and place in a blender. Add the garlic, ginger and chilli. Add just enough water to get the blades moving – not more than 3 tablespoons. Blend for 5 minutes. A smooth paste should result. Add the flour, baking powder, salt, and coriander and blend until smooth and green.

Heat a shallow pool of oil in a wide frying pan until a drop of batter sizzles immediately. Fry heaped teaspoons of the batter – you should have 12 – until golden underneath, then turn over with tongs and fry until golden all over. Drain on kitchen paper (paper towels). Keep warm in the oven. (Alternatively, fry them while the curry is cooking.)

To make the curry, rinse out the blender. Place the cumin and coriander seeds in a dry frying pan and cook over a medium heat until one shade darker, about 1 minute. Place in the blender with the remaining ingredients, except the coconut milk, peas and rice. Blend for 3–4 minutes, or until smooth. Pour into a saucepan and bring to the boil. Reduce the heat to a simmer and cook until thickened slightly, about 2 minutes. Add the coconut milk, cover and bring to the boil, then simmer for 15 minutes. (Now is a good time to cook the rice.) Add the peas and cook for a further 2 minutes. Float the warm pea cakes on top and serve ladled over rice.

**For the pea cakes:**

70 g/2¾ oz/generous ⅓ cup chana dal or yellow split peas

1 garlic clove, coarsely chopped

2.5-cm/1-inch piece fresh root ginger, coarsely chopped

1 fresh green chilli (chili)

4 tbsp plain (all-purpose) flour

¼ tsp baking powder

½ tsp sea salt

5–6 fresh coriander (cilantro) sprigs, roughly chopped

Sunflower oil, for frying

**For the curry:**

2 tsp cumin seeds

2 tsp coriander seeds

4 garlic cloves

2-cm/1-inch piece fresh root ginger, coarsely chopped

2 fresh red chillies (chilies)

1 tsp turmeric

Seeds from 4 cardamom pods

½ tsp sea salt

1 tsp sugar

250 ml/8 fl oz/1 cup natural (plain) yogurt

2 x 400 ml/14 fl oz cans coconut milk

75 g/3 oz/⅔ cup frozen peas

Boiled rice, to serve

**Serves 4**

This wonderfully sweet curry fills the house with intoxicating aromas. Here again we see the influence of Asia – South Africa has long been a major stop on the traders' routes, especially the Cape of Good Hope at its southernmost tip. The Dutch settlers brought in slave labour from Malaysia and Indonesia in the 17th and 18th centuries – these people, known collectively as Cape Malay, greatly influenced the cuisine of the region.

# Dried Fruit Curry South Africa

Place the dried fruit in a small saucepan with the boiling water, cover and bring to the boil. Reduce the heat to a simmer and cook for about 20 minutes, or until plump. Do not drain.

Meanwhile, heat a large saucepan over a medium heat and add the oil. Add the onions and fry until tinged with gold. Add the garlic, chillies, ginger, green pepper and all the spices. Cook, stirring, until fragrant, about 1–2 minutes, then add the salt, chopped tomatoes and kidney beans. Pour in the fruit with the cooking water. Stir and bring to the boil, then simmer for about 30 minutes, stirring frequently. Taste for seasoning.

Serve the curry on top of plain rice, sprinkled with peanuts, a few slices of banana and lemon wedges for squeezing over.

6 dried apricots

12 prunes, pitted

75 g/3 oz/½ cup sultanas (golden raisins) or raisins

375 ml/13 fl oz/1½ cups boiling water

2 tbsp sunflower oil

2 medium onions, finely chopped

4 garlic cloves, finely chopped

1–2 fresh green chillies (chilis), or to taste, finely chopped

2.5-cm/1-inch thumb of fresh root ginger, peeled and finely chopped

1 small green (bell) pepper, coarsely chopped

1 tsp ground cumin

1 tsp ground coriander

1 tsp fennel seeds

1 cinnamon stick (about 7.5cm/ 3 inches)

1 tsp sea salt, or to taste

2 plump vine-ripened tomatoes, about 250 g/9 oz, coarsely chopped

2 x 400 g/14 oz cans red kidney beans, drained

**To serve:**

Plain boiled rice

30 g/1 oz/scant ¼ cup toasted peanuts, chopped

1 ripe banana, thinly sliced

Lemon wedges

**Serves 4–6**

Pineapples are big business in South Africa, host of the annual International Pineapple Symposium. Introduced by the Dutch, this region has the perfect climate for growing the rather difficult crop, and beetroot is a staple here too. This salad is a riot of colour, flavour and texture, and its success is dependent on the use of good fresh ingredients – canned pineapple or beetroot will merely deliver something out of a 1970s party manual.

Fresh pineapple can be a little intimidating to the uninitiated. A lively tuft of green leaves is a sign of freshness, and if you can pull one off quite easily, it is ripe – it should also smell fruity. Slice off and discard the top, then make thick slices; then it is easy to cut off the spiky skin. The core may be tough and will probably need to be cut out.

# Beet en Pynappleslai
# Beetroot (Beet) and Pineapple Salad South Africa

If using raw beetroot, bring a saucepan of water to the boil. Scrub the beetroot and boil until tender, about 30–40 minutes. Drain, cool and slip off the stems, roots and skins.

Slice the cooked beetroot thinly. Cut the pineapple into 2.5-cm/1-inch thick round slices, then cut away the skin. Cut the tender flesh away from the core and into bite-sized pieces.

In a ceramic bowl, combine the beetroot, pineapple and onion rings. Mix the vinegar, salt and sugar together, then toss through the salad. Leave to stand for 30 minutes, stirring occasionally.

250g/9 oz raw or cooked beetroot (beet)
½ large fresh pineapple
1 small onion, sliced into thin rings
2 tbsp white wine vinegar
½ tsp salt
½ tsp sugar

**Serves 4**

Nothing green or mealie about this dish – just pure, sweet, brilliant yellow. Make this once and you will be amazed. Not only is it dead simple to do, but it has endless possibilities within a menu. As the starchy accompaniment to a stew or curry, it does not disappear shyly into the background, but makes a starring appearance, and everybody asks for more. Because it has a solid form, it makes an ideal platform for attractive presentation. On its own, it makes the most comforting breakfast or teatime snack, served hot or – dare I suggest – fried, with a little honey or maple syrup. It fills the house with sweet baking smells as it cooks. All those qualities, to me, make it a perfect recipe.

# Green Mealie Bread
# Steamed Sweetcorn (Corn) Loaf South Africa

Grease a 500 g/1 lb 2 oz loaf tin (pan) with the 1 tablespoon soft butter. Set aside. Preheat the oven to 190°C/375°F/Gas Mark 5.

Place the frozen sweetcorn in a heatproof bowl and pour over enough boiling water to cover. Stir and drain.

Place the thawed sweetcorn in a food processor and process for about 30 seconds, to a coarse purée. Add all remaining ingredients and pulse until well mixed.

Pour into the tin, smooth the top and cover securely with foil. Place in a deep roasting tin and pour enough boiling water in the tin to come halfway up the loaf tin, forming a bain-marie. Place carefully in the oven and bake for 1 hour. A skewer punched through the foil into the centre of the loaf should come out clean.

Remove the loaf from the bain-marie and remove the foil. Rest at room temperature for about 10 minutes, then invert onto a plate or board. Whack the top of the tin with a wooden spoon and the loaf should slide out easily.

Serve warm. Alternatively, leave to chill in the refrigerator, slice and reheat in a hot frying pan, then serve with honey or maple syrup.

1 tbsp soft butter
450 g/1 lb/3⅓ cups frozen sweetcorn (corn)
2 tbsp melted butter
3 organic eggs
2 tbsp sugar
2 tbsp plain (all-purpose) flour
2 tsp baking powder
1 tsp salt

**Serves 4–6**

# chapter eight
# Japan and China

"Let little seem like much, as long as it is fresh, natural and beautiful."

China is the birthplace of many important vegetarian traditions and foods, which proliferated through Japan and Korea. Buddhism and its doctrine of vegetarianism sculpted the template of a modern diet, based on a solemn respect for ingredients, appreciation for the healthy aspects of food, as well as harmony and balance on the plate and palate. The mighty soya bean (soybean), thought to have been cultivated first in China as early as 3,000 BC, is the paramount food, ranking with rice and wheat in global importance, but far outperforming them nutritionally, being a far more valuable protein source. Not only that, but its versatility in its many guises, especially in the form of tofu and soy sauce, form the very cornerstones of pan-Asian cuisine. A world without soy would be unthinkable, and it has evolved through the ingenuity of these ancient cultures.

"Flavour and aroma…they are to food what soul is to man. Cooking is essentially the capturing of these qualities, gastronomy the appreciation of them."

Hsiang Ju Lin and Tsuifeng Lin, *Chinese Gastronomy*

# meet the expert:
# Kimiko Barber – Japanese Cuisine

Kimiko Barber came from Japan to England in the 1970s and pursued a career in investment banking before giving it up to follow her true passion – teaching and writing about food and cooking. She is the author of *The Japanese Kitchen*, *Sushi: Taste and Technique* and *Easy Noodles*.

Kim explained how Buddhism came to Japan from China in the 6th century, and soon became established among the ruling upper class. With it, vegetarianism took hold in the seat of power. "This was one of the most important events in the history of Japan," says Kimiko. As Buddhists believe that the killing of animals for food is sinful, numerous decrees were passed banning animal slaughter. Dairy products were produced at this time within the imperial courts, but curiously never became accepted into the mainstream diet, which remains true to this day.

Later, in the 12th century, came a new wave of austerity, Zen Buddhism, and with it, a strict vegan diet, the introduction of tofu and a style of cooking called *shojin ryori*. "It was a simple meal of rice, soup and vegetables," says Kimiko, "and sums up the structure of the Japanese meal that still exists. The three tenets of *shojin ryori* are that cooking must be done with sincerity, cleanliness and good presentation – these are still the fundamental principles of Japanese cuisine." Today, the Buddhist vegan cuisine is experiencing a bit of a revival. Kimiko explains, "Japanese people aren't becoming more religious, but they see *shojin ryori* as a healthy way of cooking. Vegetarianism itself is seen as a Western concept, regarded with slight scepticism and suspicion."

While Buddhism continues to have an influence on the Japanese diet, the single most enduring event in Japan's culinary history was the introduction of rice, some time around the 13th century BC. "The most important ingredient of Japanese cuisine is rice and everything else is to accompany it," says Kimiko. "It is bound up with history, politics, economy, culture and national identity – rice is the soul of Japan." For centuries, rice has been synonymous with power in Japan and its eminence was shaped by the fact that it is difficult to grow. "Japan is a mountainous country with very few plains suitable for rice cultivation, so rice has always been in short supply," says Kimiko. "This long history of scarcity explains why it was

regarded as a sacred food for the rich and powerful." This rice "elitism" gave rise to noodles becoming the major alternative food. Buckwheat and wheat, being much easier to grow, were developed into soba, somen and udon noodles in the 17th century.

Japan underwent a remarkably speedy modernisation at the end of the 19th century, driving this relatively small country to become a major economic power. Today, despite being cutting-edge competitors in a world increasingly dominated by cheap and trashy food, the Japanese are one of the healthiest races. They have the highest life expectancy in the world (over 81 for both men and women) and a low rate of heart disease and obesity – this can be mainly attributed to their low-fat, vegetable-rich diet. "Although our overall protein consumption is on the increase and we are eating more meat and dairy products, vegetable protein is still the major source of protein in our diet, and vegetable dishes are an essential part of every meal."

So you are what you eat, but in Japan, it's not just about what you eat, but how it's prepared. Kimiko recalls, "I have a vivid memory of my grandmother telling me, 'Treat vegetables as if you are touching someone's eye.' In other words, treat the ingredient with respect and handle it gently." This is evidence that the ancient *shojin* way, rooted in Zen Buddhist philosophy, still very much guides the culinary ethos – the process of creating the food is just as important as the eating.

**Tofu**

# focus on
# ingredients

Tofu – bean curd, *dou-fu* – This essential protein source was invented by the Chinese and spread throughout Southeast Asia as the culinary emblem of Buddhism. It is one of the most important products made from soya beans (soybeans), another being soy sauce (see page 274). Tofu has much in common with cheese: the beans are processed into a milk which is then curdled and pressed into cakes, then eaten fresh, or sometimes fermented or flavoured. It is valued by vegetarians because it is one of the only plant-based sources containing all the amino acids that form a complete protein, mimicking meat, while being low in fat. Through the centuries, it has been of particular value to the rice-based cuisines of Japan, China and Korea, providing essential nutrition that rice alone lacks. It has to be said, however, that tofu divides people in the West. It is a great receptor of flavour and texture and must be cooked with a moderate amount of skill to be palatable to some Western palates. It can be found sold fresh, dried, fried, canned, marinated and frozen.

Udon noodles – These thick, white wheat flour noodles are an ancient staple, originating in China but adopted most prolifically into Japanese culture, being a speciality of the south-west of Japan. They are often sold fresh or frozen and are round and glossy; when dried, they are flatter. Udon are beginning to enter the mainstream in Western culture, where the ubiquitous Ramen noodle is still king. Ready-to-cook, long-life udon are convenient and can be heated in a flavoured broth, thrown straight into a wok, or mixed into a salad.

Seaweed – The Japanese incorporate over 50 types of seaweed regularly into their diet. It is very valuable to vegetarians as it contains high levels of iron, calcium and B vitamins, and is the only plant food containing B12, an essential nutrient. Japanese seaweeds are used in a number of ways. *Nori* is a greenish-black, shiny, flat square, most commonly used for sushi rolls. It can also be crumbled to a shimmering powder and used as a garnish. *Konbu* or kelp is sold unprocessed, dried in long black leathery strips which curl at the edges and have a slightly powdery appearance from sea salt. Soon after making contact with hot water it becomes a slippery green sea vegetable again. It is used for making *dashi* stock (see page 198) and imparts an intense taste of the sea. Many other types such as *hijiki* and *wakame* are used as vegetables.

**Udon noodles**

**Miso** – This delicious savoury paste is used to flavour soups and sauces in Japan, but is beginning to penetrate the Western diet by virtue of its immense nutritional properties. It's a fermented paste made from soya beans (soybeans) and salt with a culture derived from rice, wheat or barley. There are many types, ranging from a very light colour to almost black – the darker types have a more intense, salty flavour. It is available in health food stores and Asian food stores, usually sold fresh in the refrigerated section.

**Mirin** – This essential Japanese ingredient is a sweet sake or rice wine for cooking. It is a syrupy, lager-coloured liquid with a complex floral aroma, which adds a unique depth of flavour to food. Mirin also adds an attractive gloss and it is an essential ingredient in teriyaki sauce, which literally means "glossy grill". It is best stored in the refrigerator after opening, and is wonderful to have handy for pouring into stir-fries and marinades.

**Hoisin sauce** – This thick, dark, glossy sauce is made from soy, sugar, salt, chilli (chili), vinegar and sesame oil, forming one classic Chinese flavour that can be spooned conveniently from a jar. It could be called "Chinese ketchup", though it is far more versatile and flavourful than tomato sauce, ideal

Kimchi

**Hon-shimeji Mushrooms**

for adding an instant flavour injection to plain grains, tofu or vegetables.

**Shiitake mushrooms** – There are thousands of varieties of mushrooms (see page 66), and in Japan and China shiitake is king – when you see "Chinese mushroom" in a recipe it means shiitake. Shiitake are mistakenly referred to as "wild" mushrooms – actually they are cultivated, though they are grown on oak branches. Shiitake are often used dried. As with all mushrooms, its smoky-nutty flavour intensifies in the drying. The water used to reconstitute dried mushrooms is also used in the cooking, as it becomes a deeply flavoured stock. Shiitake have astonishing heath benefits – scientists have discovered that they stimulate the immune system and help to fight cancer, as well as lowering cholesterol. Hon-shimeji mushrooms (see picture) are very similar in flavour to shiitake.

**Kimchi** – An intensely flavoured pickled cabbage product, which is an essential ingredient and accompaniment in Korean food. Not all kimchi is vegetarian – sometimes it contains some dried fish, so it's important to read the label if decipherable. It is sold in packets and cans, but can also be made easily at home by soaking spiced cabbage in salted water for 5–7 days – much like sauerkraut with Asian flavourings.

This is a basic, distinctively flavoured stock, which forms the foundation of many of the Japanese recipes in this book, both soups and sauces.

# Shiitake Dashi
# Basic Mushroom Broth Japan

Pour the water into a large saucepan with a lid. If using the seaweed, add to the water now, before boiling. Bring to the boil, then remove the seaweed. Add the mushrooms, spring onions and salt and simmer, covered, for 20–30 minutes. Strain the *dashi*, reserving the mushrooms. Discard the onions. When the mushrooms are cool, they can be squeezed into the stock for a last bit of flavour. Save the mushrooms for use in recipes – they can be kept in the refrigerator for up to 3 days or can be frozen. The *dashi* should be used within 3 days, or can be cooled and frozen in small zip-lock bags for convenient use.

2 litres/3½ pints/8½ cups water
6-cm/2½-inch piece konbu seaweed or kelp (optional)
100 g/3½ oz dried shiitake mushrooms
4 spring onions (scallions), trimmed but left whole
1 tsp salt

**Makes 2 litres/3¼ pints/8 cups**

These 1-hour pickles are an essential accompaniment to any Japanese main meal. Japanese cucumbers are naturally sweet, and like baby Mediterranean or Lebanese cucumbers, they taste like their cousin the watermelon. Try to use a small cucumber (English is fine), but do peel and de-seed if the skin and seeds are tough.

# Kyuri no Shio Zuke
# Salt-pickled Cucumbers Japan

Select a shallow bowl, a saucer which fits inside it and a heavy weight which will sit on top of the saucer, such as a heavy mortar or a container-ful of water.

Mix the cucumbers with the salt in the bowl, using your hands to rub the salt into them. Place the saucer on top of the cucumbers, then place the weight on the saucer. Leave for at least 1 hour.

Drain the liquid from the cucumbers. Add the sugar and toss well with your hand until the sugar dissolves. Squeeze the cucumbers, without wringing them, place in a small bowl and serve as an accompaniment.

13-cm/5-inch baby cucumber, or piece of cucumber, trimmed and finely sliced
½ tsp salt
½ tsp sugar

**Serves 4**

The key to a good *tempura* is, of course, the batter. It is all about texture – the flavour is really quite innocuous. The more delicate the batter, the better – "like gauze" is the translation of one of the Japanese characters that represents it. The origin of the word *tempura* is, oddly, from the Portuguese *tempuras*, "Ember Days" or meatless days – it is thought that Portuguese missionaries in Japan about 400 years ago feasted on deep-fried vegetables on these days, and it caught on. Since then the Japanese have developed *tempura* into an art form. Using ice-cold water prevents the batter from being sticky or elastic, which keeps it light. Always make up the batter immediately before frying, keep it cold, and don't worry about lumps – lumps are good.

# Tempura
# Fried Battered Vegetables Japan

To make the dipping sauce, combine the soup stock, mirin and soy sauce and divide between 4 individual bowls. Set aside.

Heat the oil for deep-frying in a large saucepan or deep-fat fryer to 160–180°C/325–350°F.

To make the batter, mix the iced water, egg and flour together in a medium bowl and leave to chill in the refrigerator. When ready to deep-fry, check the oil temperature – when a drop of batter sinks halfway down, then sizzles up to the surface rapidly, it is ready.

Stir the batter and dip the prepared vegetables in it, a few pieces at a time (by hand or with tongs – see tip in *Pakora* recipe on page 242), and deep-fry until light golden, then drain on kitchen paper (paper towels). Serve with bowls of dipping sauce.

Vegetable or sunflower oil for deep-frying

**For the dipping sauce:**
250 ml/8 fl oz/1 cup *shiitake dashi* soup stock (see opposite)
3 tbsp mirin (Japanese cooking wine)
4 tbsp dark soy sauce

**For the batter:**
250 ml/8 fl oz/1 cup iced water
1 organic egg
130 g/4½ oz/1 cup plain (all-purpose) flour

**Assorted vegetables (these are my favourites, but you can use whatever you wish):**
Onion, sliced into thick rings
Green and red (bell) pepper, cut into 1-cm/½-inch wide strips
Courgette (zucchini), halved and cut into diagonal half-moon shapes
Sweet potato, peeled and cut into 5-mm/¼-inch thick slices
Whole fresh green chillies (chilies)

**Serves 4**

This contemporary Japanese fast food is commonly referred to as a "Japanese Pizza". It is flat and round, but there the similarity stops. "*Okonomi*" actually means "as you like it", so it is as variable as any pizza is likely to be. One distinction is that the *Okonomiyaki* of Hiroshima, unlike this Osaka version, will be cooked with soba noodles in the mix. This one is light and quick, despite the multiple stages.

# Okonomiyaki
# Cabbage Pancake Osaka, Japan

For the *okonomiyaki*, place the dried shiitake mushrooms in a bowl and pour over enough boiling water to cover them. Use a spoon to push them underwater. Leave to rehydrate, about 20–30 minutes, then squeeze out the excess moisture and slice. (If using fresh shiitake, remove the stems and slice.)

To make the sauce, whisk everything together in a small saucepan and bring to the boil. Boil for 30 seconds. Spoon into a small serving bowl and leave to cool until ready to serve.

To make the *wasabi* mayo, mix the mayonnaise, wasabi and water together in a small serving bowl and set aside. It should be about the same consistency as the sauce – add more or less water accordingly.

Prepare the garnish. Toast the sesame seeds in a dry frying pan until golden and popping. Wave the nori, if using, over a naked flame or heat source until it stiffens and crumbles, taking care not to burn. Crumble to a flaky powder and set aside.

To make the *okonomiyaki*, combine the sliced mushrooms, cabbage, spring onions, eggs, flour and mirin or sherry in a bowl and add a good couple of pinches of salt. Stir until evenly mixed.

Heat a frying pan over a medium heat and add 2 tbsp of the oil. Place the cabbage mixture in the pan and form into a round pancake no more than 1 cm/½ inch thick. Cook, pressing the top with the back of a spatula from time to time, until golden and crispy underneath, about 5 minutes. To flip over, first slide on to a plate. Place another plate on top and flip both over. Heat the remaining 1 tablespoon of oil in the pan, then return the *okonomiyaki* to the pan and cook the other side, again pressing the top, until golden and crispy, another 5 minutes.

When thoroughly cooked throughout, slide it on to a board. Spoon the two sauces over the *okonomiyaki* in an attractive pattern. Sprinkle with the toasted sesame seeds and nori flakes, if using. Cut into 4 wedges and serve.

**For the *okonomiyaki*:**
20 g/¾ oz dried shiitake mushrooms (alternatively, use 50 g/2 oz fresh)
150 g/5 oz/2 cups finely shredded Savoy cabbage
4 spring onions (scallions), chopped
2 eggs
75 g/3 oz/⅔ cup plain flour
1 tbsp mirin (Japanese cooking wine) or sherry
Salt
3 tbsp sunflower oil

**For the sauce:**
2 tbsp tomato ketchup
1½ tsp tamari (dark soy sauce)
½ tsp Dijon mustard
1 tbsp mirin (Japanese cooking wine - see page 197) or sherry

**For the *wasabi* mayo:**
2 tbsp mayonnaise
½ tsp wasabi (hot green horseradish), or to taste
2 tsp water

**To garnish:**
2 tbsp sesame seeds
1 sheet nori seaweed (see page 196) (optional)

**Serves 4 as a first course or snack or 2 as a main course**

Since ancient times, the Japanese have been saying, "A bowl of miso a day keeps the doctor away." Indeed the Japanese have the longest-lived population in the world and their diet is the reason! Miso soup is enjoyed on a daily basis, first thing in the morning or as part of the main meal. The soup may be as simple as miso in stock alone, or it can be a chunky melange of potatoes, carrots, seaweed and mushrooms. You may add whatever you like to the soup base – if you happen to be making *Tempura* (see page 199), a handful of the stray bits of crispy batter are delectable in the soup.

Be aware that the miso will take on the appearance of a mass of nebulous clouds if it is added to boiling broth – so add it before boiling point, or after the broth has been taken off the heat. This recipe uses the light-coloured miso, which is subtler, less salty and sweeter than the dark. Dark is quite acceptable for soup, but you may wish to use slightly less. Miso differs greatly in strength and flavour, so use the quantity below as a guideline. (See more notes on miso, page 197.)

# Tofu no Miso-shiru
# Miso Soup with Tofu Japan

Bring the stock to a gentle simmer in a saucepan.

Meanwhile, place the mushrooms, if using, and tofu in a large bowl and pour over enough boiling water to cover, to warm them through.

In a small bowl, dilute the miso to pouring consistency with a little of the warm stock as it heats up.

Once the stock is simmering, turn off the heat and wait a minute or two.

Drain the mushrooms and tofu and divide between 4 small bowls. Sprinkle each with some sliced spring onions.

Stir the diluted miso into the slightly cooled stock until evenly combined. Taste for seasoning and add more miso if liked (or add hot water if less is desired). Ladle into bowls and serve immediately.

500 ml/16 fl oz/2 cups *shiitake dashi* soup stock (see page 198)

2–3 mushrooms from the stock-making, thinly sliced (optional)

150 g/5 oz firm silken tofu, or ordinary fresh tofu, drained and dried, cut into 1-cm/½-inch cubes

2 slightly heaped tbsp light-coloured miso (about 50 g/2 oz)

1 spring onion (scallion), diagonally sliced

**Serves 4**

Traditionally the aubergines are deep-fried before grilling (broiling), but I find this baked version much lighter and fuss-free. You will probably have some of this delicious, dark *Dengaku* glaze leftover, but it will keep for several days in the refrigerator. It also makes a gorgeous barbecue marinade for any vegetable. Small, light purple Japanese aubergines are the ideal vehicle for *Dengaku* in this recipe. Serve with plain boiled rice and Salt-pickled Cucumbers (see page 198).

# Nasu No Dengaku/Tofu Dengaku
# Aubergines (Eggplants) and Tofu in Miso Glaze Japan

Preheat the oven to 200°C/400°F/Gas Mark 6. Remove the stalk from the aubergines and cut in half from top to bottom. Use a small sharp knife to score the flesh of the aubergines in a diagonal grid pattern. Brush a baking tray generously with oil and arrange the aubergines on it, skin-side down. Brush the flesh generously with oil and roast in the oven until golden and soft throughout, about 30 minutes.

Towards the end of the aubergine cooking time, place the tofu on another lightly oiled baking tray and bake for 5 minutes, just to firm up slightly, then remove from the oven and switch off.

Meanwhile, make the glaze. Combine all the ingredients for the glaze in a small saucepan. Place over a low heat and cook, stirring constantly, until thick and smooth, but do not let it boil or the egg may curdle. Scrape into a bowl and set aside.

Preheat the grill (broiler) to its highest setting. Spread a teaspoon of glaze over the top of the tofu and all over the surface of the aubergine halves. Grill (broil) until slightly puffed, about 4–5 minutes. Sprinkle a little crumbled nori and a few poppy seeds over the glaze, if desired. Serve warm or at room temperature.

2 medium or 3 small aubergines (eggplants), about 500 g/1 lb 2 oz
Sunflower oil for brushing
250 g/9 oz firm tofu, drained, dried and cut into 12 pieces, 1-cm/½-inch thick

**For the dengaku miso glaze:**
110 g/3¾ oz/4 tbsp light miso paste
110 g/3¾ oz/4 tbsp dark miso paste
2 egg yolks
2 tbsp sugar
2 tbsp sake
2 tbsp mirin (Japanese cooking wine – see page 197)

**To garnish (optional):**
Crumbled nori
Poppy seeds

**Serves 4–6**

The art of expert sushi making requires a long apprenticeship. These rice-stuffed pockets are one of the simpler forms, and no raw fish in sight. The tofu pockets themselves arrive ready-to-use in a small can or vacuum-pack, absolutely singing with flavour. In Japan, children get these in their lunch boxes, lucky things. Often they are filled just with rice, but colourful fillings make them more exciting, and as the Japanese say, "You eat first with your eyes". It is important to use sushi rice only, and the cooking technique outlined below will make it suitably sticky. These are great as a snack or first course, or even as a light meal in itself.

# Inari-sushi
# Tofu Pocket Sushi Japan

Place the rice in a sieve (strainer) and rinse under cold running water until the water runs clear. Leave to stand for at least 30 minutes. Place the rice in a heavy-based saucepan. Measure the water by placing your fingers flat on the surface of the rice without pressing down. There should be enough water in the pan to come halfway up along your index finger. Bring to the boil, reduce the heat to a simmer and cook, covered, until all the water is absorbed, about 15 minutes. Remove from the heat, place a clean tea (dish) towel under the lid and leave to stand for a further 10 minutes.

If a brown skin has formed in the pan, scrape the rice away from it. Empty the rice into a large (preferably non-metallic) bowl. Stir in the vinegar, a pinch of salt and the mirin. For perfectly sticky rice, stir the rice until cool. (This process will be very quick if you stand in front of an electric fan or have someone fan you while you stir.)

Fill a bowl with water for wetting your hands. To make the sushi, open out a tofu pocket and use wet hands to handle the rice. Fill half the pocket with rice. Sprinkle sesame seeds over the rice, then add strips of each vegetable and ginger. Finish with enough rice to fill, then seal the gap. Using a sushi mat or strong foil, roll the parcel gently back and forth to perfect the shape. Place on a plate, seam-side down. Typically, these are served whole, but you can cut them in half to reveal the beautiful filling, if liked. Serve with Japanese soy sauce and wasabi.

200 g/7 oz/1 cup sushi rice

2–3 tbsp sushi vinegar (flavoured rice vinegar)

Pinch of salt

1 tbsp mirin (Japanese cooking wine)

1 tbsp black sesame seeds or toasted sesame seeds

1 x 284 g/10 oz can inari-sushi tofu pockets, drained

5-cm/2-inch piece cucumber, de-seeded and cut into thin strips

1 piece orange (bell) pepper, cut into thin strips

Shredded pickled ginger

**To serve:**
Japanese soy sauce
Wasabi (hot green horseradish)

**Makes 12–14, serves 4–6**

One of the classic minimalist forms of sushi, this is the perfect springboard for the sushi-making novice. Despite its simplicity, it is still satisfying to create such a beautiful thing – the graduating green hue of the cucumber wedge against the white rice background, framed in a thin black sheath of nori seaweed. Once you've mastered this, you can start adding more filllings such as strips of red pepper, carrot, avocado or yellow pickled radish.

# Kappamaki
# Cucumber Roll Sushi Japan

First lightly toast the nori by waving it over the low flame of a gas burner for a few seconds. Cut each piece in half, making 2 x 10 x 19-cm/4 x 7½-inch pieces. Have a bowl of water ready for wetting your fingers.

To make the sushi rolls, place a piece of nori, rough side up, on a sushi mat or a piece of strong foil, about 20 x 29 cm/8 x 11 ½ inches. Using wet hands, press a couple of handfuls of the cooked rice on to the nori, making a rectangle of rice about 1 cm/½ inch thick, leaving a 2 cm/¾ inch border at the top. Make a horizontal indentation with your wet finger across the middle. Smear with a small amount of wasabi, then lay strips of cucumber on top, end to end. Sprinkle with a few sesame seeds, then rinse your fingers in the water bowl.

To roll up the sushi, start rolling away from you, rolling first the mat and holding the sushi in place with your fingertips. Use your thumbs on the mat to guide the rolling, while lifting it before it gets rolled into the sushi. When you have rolled the nori around the rice and you have reached the border, wet the border, finish rolling and seal. (It's a bit like rolling a cigarette.)

Leave to stand for a few minutes to allow the nori to moisten. It will be ready to eat after about 5 minutes, when the nori feels springy like skin. Trim off the ends and slice into 2.5-cm/1-inch pieces or smaller. Serve with soy sauce for dipping, accompanied by pink pickled ginger and wasabi. The sushi can be made several hours ahead, left whole, wrapped in clingfilm (plastic wrap) and refrigerated, but do eat on the day of making.

3 large sheets nori seaweed
  (see page 196)
Cooked sushi rice, as prepared for
  *Inari-sushi* (see page 205)
Wasabi (hot green horseradish),
  plus extra to serve
10-cm/4-inch piece cucumber,
  de-seeded but unpeeled, cut into
  thin triangle-shaped wedges along
  the length
Toasted sesame seeds, or black sesame
  seeds (optional)

**To serve:**
Japanese soy sauce
Pink pickled ginger

**Makes 20–30 pieces, serves 4–6**

A sensational treatment of tofu – a gorgeous savoury sauce blanketing a crisp coating, which then reveals a fresh and creamy interior – my nickname for this dish is "glorified tofu". I'm afraid the deep-frying is part of the glorification process, though the tofu does not absorb any oil, but acquires a beautiful texture. If at all possible, get your tofu for this dish from a Japanese, Chinese, Thai or other Asian market where they appreciate the virtues of the mighty curd. This recipe makes a quantity which is perfect for two as a main course, or it will serve four as part of a larger spread; multiply as desired. Serve with rice, Salt-pickled Cucumbers (see page 198) and steamed or stir-fried vegetables.

# Agedashi-dofu Deep-fried Tofu with Amber Sauce Japan

Wrap the tofu in a clean kitchen cloth. Place on a plate and put 2 dinner plates on top. Leave to press for 30 minutes.

Meanwhile, prepare the sauce and garnish. Combine the soup stock, soy sauce and mirin in a small saucepan and set aside. In a cup or bowl, mix the cornflour and water together. Mix the grated mooli (daikon) with the cayenne and slice the spring onion very thinly on the diagonal. Place them in a small dish.

Heat a 5-cm/2-inch depth of oil in a wok, saucepan or deep-fat fryer to 160°C/325°F, or until a small chunk of bread crisps in 10 seconds. Unwrap the tofu and cut into 6 chunks. Scatter cornflour over a large plate and roll the tofu in it, coating evenly all over. Shake off excess, then deep-fry the tofu for about 5 minutes until light golden and crisp. Drain on kitchen paper (paper towels).

Meanwhile, finish the sauce. Heat the stock mixture to boiling point in a saucepan, then reduce to a simmer. Stir the cornflour mixture and add to the pan while stirring. Stir while it thickens, then remove from the heat.

Place the fried tofu on a plate or shallow bowl and pour the sauce over. Serve immediately with the garnishes.

250 g/9 oz fresh firm tofu, drained
Oil for deep-frying
Cornflour (cornstarch) for dusting

**For the sauce:**
125 ml/4 fl oz/½ cup shiitake dashi soup stock (see page 198)
1 tbsp dark soy sauce
1 tbsp mirin (Japanese cooking wine – see page 197)
2 tsp cornflour (cornstarch)
2 tsp cold water

**To garnish:**
2.5-cm/1-inch piece mooli (daikon radish – see page 144), finely grated
Large pinch of cayenne pepper
1 spring onion (scallion), sliced

**Serves 2–4**

This is a pared-down, serenity-inducing, main-course dish of noodles in broth. A poached egg on top looks up towards the moon, especially to be enjoyed at moon-appreciation gatherings in late summer. Udon noodles are thick, round and white, and most often sold ready-cooked in packets; soba noodles are also commonly used for this dish – as they are usually sold dry, allow 5–6 minutes cooking time and use 50–75g per person.

# Tsukimi Udon
# Moon-viewing Noodles Japan

Bring a medium saucepan of water to the boil. Warm 4 soup bowls in the oven, or by pouring boiling water into them.

Place the soup stock, ginger, soy sauce and mirin or sherry in a large non-stick frying pan with a lid. Alternatively, use a wide saucepan. Bring to the boil, then reduce to a simmer.

Blanch the spinach in the saucepan of water by plunging it in and removing after 30 seconds with a slotted spoon. Set aside. Add the cooked noodles to this pan and turn off the heat.

Break an egg into a teacup and slide it into the simmering soup stock. Add all the eggs to the stock in this way. Cover and poach until cooked to your liking.

Meanwhile, drain the noodles and divide between the warmed bowls. Add a cluster of blanched spinach to one side of each bowl. Remove the cooked eggs from the broth with a slotted spoon, adding one to each bowl. Pour over the stock and serve immediately.

1 litre/1¾ pints/4 cups *shiitake dashi* soup stock (see page 198)

1-cm/½-inch piece fresh root ginger, peeled and finely grated

2 tbsp dark soy sauce

1 tbsp mirin (Japanese cooking wine – see page 197) or sherry

150 g/5 oz/3¼ cups fresh spinach, well-washed, shredded

250 g/9 oz cooked udon or soba noodles

4 organic eggs

**Serves 4**

Traditionally eaten on Chinese New Year's Day, by vegetarians and non-vegetarians alike, this dish delights the Buddha by its absence of meat, and by the vital symbolism of each of the ingredients – birth, wealth, health and longevity. The contents of each recipe variation differs greatly – some have as many as 28 special ingredients, each with its own significance. I'm sure you will be forgiven for leaving out some of the more obscure items here, but they do make for an interesting dish and it's a great way to celebrate the Chinese New Year. You should find items like dried bean curd skin and ready-fried tofu in any Chinese supermarket – well worth a visit for the uninitiated, not least for the entertainment value of discovering a fascinating array of weird and wonderful foods.

# Lo-Han Jai
# Buddha's Delight China

Place the dried Chinese mushrooms in a bowl, pour over the boiling water and leave to soak for 20–30 minutes. In another bowl, soak the noodles in boiling water to cover for 1 minute, then drain – they should be softened but not completely cooked as they will cook in the wok. Rinse the noodles under cold running water until cool, then dress with a few drops of oil to stop them sticking. Soak the dried bean curd skin in a bowl of hot water for 5–7 minutes, or until pale and soft, then drain.

In a large bowl, combine the bamboo shoot strips, fried bean curd slices, water chestnuts, spring onions, Chinese cabbage and carrot. Drain the mushrooms, reserving the liquor; slice them thinly and add to the bowl. Add the noodles and dried bean curd to the bowl. Mix everything together thoroughly with your hands, pulling the noodles apart and mixing them through.

Turn the oven on to warm, in case you have to cook in batches. Mix the mushroom liquor, soy sauce, sesame oil, sugar, salt, rice wine and cornflour paste together in a bowl.

Heat a wok over a high heat. Add the sunflower oil, swirl around the wok and tip in the bowl of ingredients. (Cook in batches if your wok is too small.) Stir-fry briskly until the cabbage is slightly wilted, about 5 minutes. It may help to use tongs to toss everything around. Pour in the mushroom liquor mixture and stir-fry until the sauce is thickened. Garnish with sliced spring onions and chopped coriander and serve immediately with boiled rice.

8 dried Chinese black or shiitake mushrooms

300 ml/10 fl oz/1¼ cups boiling water

100 g/3 ½ oz/1 packet cellophane noodles (mung bean threads), string snipped off

Few drops of oil

4 x 20-cm/8-inch pieces dried bean curd, broken into chunks

75 g/3 oz/⅓ cup bamboo shoot strips

200 g/7 oz fried bean curd (tofu), sliced

1 x 220 g/7½ oz can water chestnuts, drained

6 spring onions (scallions), thinly sliced

½ Chinese cabbage (napa cabbage), about 350 g/12 oz, coarsely chopped into 2-cm/¾-inch squares

1 medium carrot, peeled and thinly sliced into coins

80 ml/2¾ fl oz/⅓ cup light soy sauce

2 tbsp sesame oil

2 tsp sugar

1 tsp salt

2 tbsp Chinese rice wine or dry sherry

2 tbsp cornflour (cornstarch) mixed with 2 tbsp cold water

4 tbsp/¼ cup sunflower oil

Boiled rice, to serve

**To garnish:**

2 spring onions (scallions), thinly sliced

3 tbsp coarsely chopped fresh coriander (cilantro)

**Serves 6–8**

Szechuan is a huge, mountainous province, the most heavily populated in China and also one of the wealthiest. There is an ancient tradition of Buddhism in the sacred mountain monasteries there, and much original Szechuan cuisine is vegetarian. Its most famous characteristic, however, is the use of chillies, which didn't arrive until after Columbus's discovery of the New World, but were accepted with much more enthusiasm here than the rest of China. This is one of the few classic spicy vegetarian Chinese dishes.

# Ma-Po Tofu
# Tofu in Black Bean and Chilli Sauce

Szechuan, China

Place the dried mushrooms in a small bowl and pour the 200 ml/7 fl oz/ ⅘ cup boiling water over them.

For the sauce, place the salted black beans, if using, in another small bowl and pour over enough boiling water just to cover.

After 30 minutes, drain the mushrooms, reserving the water, then slice the mushrooms. Drain the black beans and mash with a fork. Add the remaining sauce ingredients to the mashed beans, combine thoroughly and set aside. (Add the black bean sauce to this mixture if not using the dried black beans.)

Meanwhile, drain the tofu and wrap in kitchen paper (paper towels) to soak up extra moisture until ready to use, then cut into 2-cm/¾-inch strips.

Heat a wok over a high heat and add the oil. Add the mushrooms, green pepper, chilli and garlic and fry, stirring constantly, until the garlic is golden, about 2 minutes. Add the sauce mixture and cook, stirring constantly, until thickened and bubbly, about 1–2 minutes. Stir the cornflour into the cooled mushroom water and pour into the wok. Cook, stirring, until thick. Add the tofu and stir until well coated with the sauce and warmed through. Serve with boiled rice.

30 g/1 oz dried shiitake or Chinese mushrooms (a generous handful)
200 ml/7 fl oz/⅘ cup boiling water
500 g/1 lb 2 oz fresh firm tofu
3 tbsp sunflower oil
1 green (bell) pepper, chopped into chunks
1 large fresh red chilli (chili), de-seeded and sliced
2 plump garlic cloves, sliced
1 tbsp cornflour (cornstarch)
Boiled long-grain rice, to serve

**For the sauce:**
1 tbsp salted black beans or 2 tsp black bean sauce
3 tbsp light soy sauce
1 tbsp hoisin sauce (see page 197)
1 tbsp sweet chilli (chili) sauce
1 tbsp tomato purée (paste)
1 tbsp Chinese rice wine or dry sherry
1 tsp sugar

**Serves 4**

*Chow Mein* simply means "fried noodles", a dish popularized by Chinese immigrants in the USA, though the dish is known throughout the world. The traditional proportion of noodles to vegetables should be 4:1. The vegetables used are entirely flexible and you may wish to add or substitute beansprouts, bamboo shoots etc., the desired effect being soft, hot, lightly seasoned noodles studded with crunchy vegetables. On top of this goes a delectably rich mushroom sauce and fried tofu strips with garlic. It helps to have a capacious wok for this – if yours is small you may need to cook the noodles in batches.

# Chow Mein Vegetable Fried Noodles with Mushroom Sauce and Garlic Tofu China

For the mushroom sauce, place the dried mushrooms in a bowl and pour boiling water over them just to cover. Leave to soak for 20–30 minutes. Squeeze the mushrooms dry and reserve the water, then slice them. Mix 6 tbsp of the soaking water with the soy sauce, hoisin sauce and rice wine or sherry. Set aside.

Preheat the oven to 110°C/225°F/Gas Mark 1/4 for keeping warm. Bring a large saucepan of water to the boil. Add the noodles and cook for 4 minutes, or follow the packet instructions. Drain and cool under cold running water. Set aside.

Have ready a plate lined with kitchen paper (paper towels). Heat a large wok over a high heat and add 2 tbsp of sunflower oil. Add the tofu with the pinch of salt and fry until light golden. Add the crushed garlic and immediately remove the wok from the heat. Scrape the entire contents of the wok on to the lined plate. Place in the oven to keep warm.

Reheat the wok and add another 3 tbsp of sunflower oil. Add the onion, celery, cabbage, broccoli and water chestnuts and stir-fry for about 3 minutes, or until lightly cooked. Add the cooked noodles, soy sauce and sugar. Stir-fry until warmed through – it may help to use tongs. If your wok is too small to accommodate the noodles, cook in batches. Scrape everything into a large roasting tin (pan) or heatproof bowl, cover with foil and keep warm in the oven.

To make the mushroom sauce, first stir a little of the reserved soy sauce mixture into the cornflour, then stir the paste into the sauce. Reheat the wok over a high heat and add the 1 tbsp of sunflower oil. Add the fresh and reconstituted mushrooms and stir-fry until slightly collapsed. Pour in the sauce mixture and stir while it thickens. Pour the sauce over the noodles, top with the tofu and serve immediately.

300 g/11 oz medium egg noodles

5 tbsp sunflower oil

250 g/9 oz tofu, drained and dried, cut into 5-cm/2-inch long and 5-mm/¼-inch wide strips

Pinch of sea salt

3 garlic cloves, crushed

1 medium onion, finely sliced

2 celery sticks, diagonally sliced

100 g/3½ oz/2 cups cabbage, about 5 leaves, shredded

100 g/3½ oz broccoli florets, sliced

70 g/2¾ oz/½ standard can water chestnuts, drained

1 tbsp soy sauce

1 tsp sugar

Sesame oil, to taste

**For the mushroom sauce:**

20 g/¾ oz/about 1 cup dried shiitake mushrooms

2 tbsp dark soy sauce

1 ½ tbsp hoisin sauce

2 tbsp Chinese rice wine or dry sherry

2 tsp cornflour (cornstarch)

1 tbsp sunflower oil

200 g/7 oz fresh mushrooms, sliced

**Serves 4–6**

This soothing egg and tofu dish has a multi-dimensional flavour and a quick cooking time. It serves as a sauce for rice, or can be eaten as a melt-in-the-mouth porridge on its own — perfect for a high-protein breakfast or a restorative snack. Please note that the eggs are "running" not "runny", in case you are not partial to undercooked eggs. That said, they musn't be overcooked into rubbery curds either. Adapted from Kenneth Lo's *Chinese Vegetarian Cooking*.

# Liu Huang Tsai
# Flowing Running Eggs Peking, China

In a medium bowl or measuring jug, mix the cornflour to a paste with a little of the stock, then blend in the rest of the stock. Add the eggs and seasoning and beat until smooth. Heat the butter and 1 tbsp of oil together in a saucepan over a low heat. Add the egg mixture and stir frequently until thickened and cooked, but not dry.

Meanwhile, heat a wok or saucepan over a medium heat and add the oil, then the mushrooms and garlic. Cook until the garlic is fragrant, then add the peas, mashed tofu, sesame oil and rice wine or sherry, with a pinch of salt. Stir-fry for 2 minutes, then remove from the heat and set aside.

Combine the thickened eggs with the tofu mixture and taste for seasoning. Serve immediately in warmed bowls, with or without rice.

**For the egg mixture:**

1 tbsp cornflour (cornstarch)

125 ml/4 fl oz/½ cup shiitake dashi soup stock (see page 198), cooled

5 organic eggs

Sea salt and freshly ground black pepper

30 g/1 oz/2 tbsp butter

1 tbsp sunflower oil

**For the tofu mixture:**

2 tbsp sunflower oil

6 shiitake or other flavourful mushrooms, fresh or dried and reconstituted, coarsely chopped

2 garlic cloves, chopped

4 tbsp fresh or frozen peas

200 g/7 oz firm tofu, mashed

2 tsp sesame oil

1½ tbsp Chinese rice wine or dry sherry

Pinch of sea salt

Boiled rice, to serve (optional)

**Serves 2–4**

Kimchi divides people. Nearly 41 million South Koreans and their offspring throughout the world couldn't imagine a meal without it. I certainly can't get enough of the stuff – in stir-fries, on top of noodles and in soups like this one. Part of its appeal is its convenience – open a can or a packet and you get an instant, strong flavour sensation.

Perhaps its strength is also its weakness. It has a tendency to overwhelm and, if you don't love it, you probably can't be persuaded. Jeffrey Steingarten, in his hilarious book *The Man Who Ate Everything*, lists kimchi as one of the foods "I wouldn't touch even if I were starving on a desert island…(Koreans) say 'kimchi' instead of 'cheese' when someone is taking their picture; I say, 'Hold the kimchi'". Love it or hate it, this soup is, at least, authentic. (See notes on kimchi, page 197.)

# Kimchi Kuk
# Pickled Cabbage Soup Korea

Drain the tofu and pat dry with kitchen paper (paper towels). Cut into 1-cm/½-inch cubes.

Drain the kimchi liquid into a saucepan. Chop the kimchi and add to the pan with the tofu, vinegar, soy sauce, 1 tsp sesame oil and the water. Place the saucepan over a medium heat, cover and bring to the boil, then reduce to a simmer and leave to simmer for 15 minutes. Taste the liquid and adjust seasoning to taste with soy sauce and cayenne pepper, if liked. Divide between 4 warmed bowls. Garnish each with a few drops of sesame oil and a sprinkling of spring onions.

150 g/5 oz firm tofu
350 g/12 oz kimchi (see page 197), with liquid
1 tbsp rice vinegar
1 tbsp light soy sauce
1 tsp sesame oil, plus extra to garnish
500 ml/16 fl oz/2 cups water
Light soy sauce, to taste
Cayenne pepper, to taste
2 spring onions (scallions), sliced, to garnish

**Serves 4**

A crunchy sweet and sour salad with an assertive sesame flavour, this recipe typifies Korean food. As with so many of China's neighbours, there is an ancient tradition of Buddhism – meat is not always on the menu and sesame is heavily relied upon, both for flavour and nutrition. Koreans base their food on the Five Flavours principle – a balance of sweet-sour-salty-hot-bitter. In addition, many Korean dishes follow an arrangement of five colours: red, green, yellow, white and black. This salad is an example, with the sesame representing the black element.

# Sook Choo Na Mool
# Beansprout and Sesame Salad Korea

Place the beansprouts in a bowl and pour over enough boiling water to cover. Leave for 2 minutes, then drain thoroughly.

To make the dressing, place the sesame seeds in a small, dry frying pan over a medium-high heat. Cook, shaking the pan frequently, until golden and popping, 3–5 minutes. Remove to a small bowl to cool.

Reserve a large pinch of toasted sesame for the garnish, then place the remaining sesame seeds, vinegar, soy sauce, sugar, salt and pepper and garlic in a bowl and beat together. Beat in the oil in a slow and steady stream to emulsify.

Toss the red (bell) pepper and spring onions through the beansprouts. Toss the dressing through the mixture and leave to chill in the refrigerator for 1 hour. Sprinkle with the reserved sesame seeds and serve.

*lettuce*

300 g/11 oz/6 cups beansprouts
1 red (bell) pepper, cored and thinly sliced
2 spring onions (scallions), diagonally sliced

**For the dressing:**
3 tbsp sesame seeds
2 tbsp rice vinegar
2 tbsp light soy sauce
1 tbsp caster (superfine) sugar
½ tsp salt
½ tsp finely ground black pepper
1 garlic clove, crushed
4 tbsp sunflower oil

**Serves 4**

Madhur Jaffrey was served this delectable salad in a Hong Kong restaurant, and re-created it in her book *Eastern Vegetarian Cooking*. The aubergine, as it is like a sponge, acts as a delivery system for assertive flavours, as well as having a unique texture and delicate flavour all its own. Also, having a high water content means it responds well to microwave cooking, essentially steaming in its own juice. Both microwave and steaming instructions are given below. This is a lovely accompaniment to *Lo-Han Jai* (see page 209), *Tse Tofu* (see page 219) or any simple stir-fry.

# Lian Ban Che Zhe
# Cold Salad of Steamed Aubergine (Eggplant) Hong Kong

First cook the aubergines. To microwave, place the aubergine pieces in a microwave-safe bowl and toss the salt through them. Cover and cook on high power for 5 minutes, then stir. Cover and cook again for 3 minutes, then leave to stand for 3–5 minutes. Check that every piece of aubergine is thoroughly soft; if not, cook a little longer, then drain. Alternatively, steam the aubergines for 20–25 minutes until completely soft.

Beat all the dressing ingredients together in a large bowl, then add the hot aubergines. Toss and crush slightly, keeping it chunky, until well mixed. Leave to cool, then chill in the refrigerator. Serve cold, sprinkled with sliced spring onions and chopped coriander.

2 medium aubergines (eggplants), about 500 g/1 lb 2 oz, peeled and cut into 2.5-cm/1-inch pieces

½ tsp salt

**For the dressing:**

1½ tbsp light soy sauce

1 tbsp rice vinegar or white malt vinegar

2 tsp sesame oil

1 plump garlic clove, crushed

½ tsp crushed dried chilli (dried red pepper) flakes, cayenne pepper or hot chilli (chili) oil, or to taste

**To garnish:**

2 spring onions (scallions), finely sliced

Small handful of fresh coriander (cilantro), finely chopped

In our supermarket-ready world, it may seem an anathema to make noodles when you can get them out of a packet cheaply, quickly, and easily. I invite you to take a little adventure in noodle making – but for these "pulled" noodles you won't need a machine, a rolling pin or any skill at all, and there's no mess or fuss. In fact, these could be made on your knee by the fire at base camp in the Himalaya, that's how simple they are! A bit like unstuffed ravioli, they have a wonderful, toothsome texture, suspended in a spicy broth, to which you can add any vegetables or spices you wish. An inspiring technique, as found in *The Lhasa Moon Tibetan Cookbook*.

# Tse Tentuk
# Pulled Noodles in Vegetable Broth Tibet

To make the noodle dough, mix the flour and salt together in a bowl, then stir in the water. Start mixing and squeezing with your hand to form a dough. Knead on a clean dry work surface for 3–4 minutes until smooth and elastic. Roll into a long sausage-shape about the thickness of your finger. Coil on a plate and brush or rub with a little oil, then cover with clingfilm (plastic wrap) and set aside while you prepare the broth.

To make the broth, heat a saucepan over a medium-high heat and add the oil. Add the onion, garlic and chillies and stir-fry quickly until fragrant and soft, about 2 minutes. Pour in the stock or water, cover and bring to the boil, then reduce to a simmer. Add the soy sauce, lemon juice or vinegar and rice wine or sherry and taste for seasoning, adjusting the sweet/salt/sour balance to your liking.

Take the dough in your hands and flatten the end by squashing it between your thumb and fingers to about 2 mm/⅛ inch thick, then pull off pieces about the size of your thumb joint and toss them into the broth. The noodles will rise to the surface when they are cooked, which only takes a couple of minutes.

Finally, stir in the spinach, tomato and spring onions and serve.

**For the noodles:**
140 g/4½ oz/1 cup plain
   (all-purpose) flour
½ tsp salt
80 ml/2¾ fl oz/⅓ cup tepid water
A little sunflower oil

**For the broth:**
1 tbsp sunflower oil
1 small onion, finely chopped
3 garlic cloves, finely chopped
1–2 fresh green chillies (chilies), de-seeded if
large, finely chopped
1 litre/1¾ pints/4 cups vegetable stock
   or water
4 tbsp dark soy sauce, or to taste
1 tbsp lemon juice or cider vinegar
2 tbsp Chinese rice wine or dry sherry
100 g/3½ oz/2⅛ cups fresh spinach or
   other quick-cooking greens, shredded
1 large tomato, finely chopped
2 spring onions (scallions), chopped

**Serves 4**

This recipe illustrates the geographical position of Tibet, fusing India with China. Few authentic recipes elsewhere combine tofu and soy sauce with Indian spices, but the combination works a treat. I've tried this with smoked tofu and it works especially well with the Indian flavourings, as well as having a good firm texture. Serve on a bed of boiled egg noodles or plain rice.

# Tse Tofu
# Tofu with Greens and Spices Tibet

Heat a wok with a lid over a high heat and add the oil. Add the spring onions, garlic and ginger and stir-fry until fragrant, about 1 minute. Add the chilli, spices and tofu and stir-fry for 2 minutes. Add the soy sauce, sugar, tomato, peas and spinach and stir-fry for 1–2 minutes until the greens are cooked and the tomato starts to collapse. Serve immediately with boiled rice or noodles.

2 tbsp sunflower oil

3 spring onions (scallions), chopped

3 garlic cloves, sliced

1-cm/½-inch piece fresh root ginger, finely chopped

1 fresh green chilli (chili), slit in half

½ tsp paprika

½ tsp ground cumin

½ tsp garam masala ( see recipe on page 181)

300 g/11 oz tofu, fresh or smoked, drained and cut into 1-cm/½-inch cubes

2 tbsp soy sauce

½ tsp sugar

1 large tomato, quartered

4 tbsp fresh or frozen peas

300 g/11 oz/6¾ cups spinach or other leafy greens (trimmed weight), stems removed, torn

Boiled rice or noodles, to serve

**Serves 4**

# chapter nine
# The Indian Subcontinent and Central Asia

This chapter begins in Sri Lanka and ascends all the way to Afghanistan, drawing a wide border around India, the vegetarian capital of the world. The vegetarian culture forged by Hinduism in this region is so highly developed that this chapter was by far the most difficult to compile. The region is as varied as the whole of Europe, with enduring influences from millennia of invasions and ruling empires, making it quite a challenge to select just 20 recipes.

Spice is the thread that links the cuisines of Afghanistan, Pakistan, India and Sri Lanka, and the sophistication in its use is unrivalled. The earth's most important spice commodity, black pepper, was being cultivated in India and traded in the Middle East as far back as 2,000 BC. Hindus, Indian Buddhists

and Jains, all traditionally vegetarians, were very active in facilitating the flow of spices from the Far East to the Arab world through the heyday of the spice trade. With such a staggeringly long and rich history, one can appreciate how advanced their understanding of flavour must be.

"If the diet is pure, the mind will be pure, and if the mind is pure, the intellect will be pure."

Manu, Hindu lawgiver

# meet the expert:
# Das Sreedharan – Keralan Cuisine

Das Sreedharan grew up in a small village in Kerala, South India. He is the founder and proprietor of Rasa restaurants in London, and the author of several books on Keralan food including *The New Tastes of India*. The first time I met Das was in early 2001. I had just returned to London from several weeks in Kerala, India's palm-strewn south-western state along the Malabar coast, and I was utterly intoxicated by the experience. I wanted the feeling to last – I wanted to breathe Keralan air, eat Keralan food and spend time around Keralans. So, I presented myself at the doorstep of one of Das's acclaimed restaurants as a vegetarian chef and food writer who was passionate about Kerala, and he graciously welcomed me.

We've kept in touch, and since then Das's business has been growing fast. As he makes preparations to open yet another restaurant in his award-winning chain, it is obvious that Londoners are catching on to the unique, fresh style of authentic Keralan food that Das serves at Rasa. "Kerala offers the most spectacular array of vegetarian dishes, due to the tropical weather and natural beauty," says Das. The food is fragrant with coconut, sweet mangoes, green bananas, cardamom and black pepper from the hills, and the signature ingredient of the South, curry leaves. "In terms of variety, colour, texture, healthiness and imagination, Kerala is best vegetarian destination in India. When it comes to vegetarian food, Indian people always think of South India. Of Kerala's 31 million population, I would say about 25 per cent are still totally vegetarian."

Another distinctive aspect of South Indian food is "tiffin", or snacks enjoyed throughout the day from teashops, on trains, and from street vendors. "True 'eating out' in India is not geared towards restaurant meals, but a variety of snacks eaten all day long. Even though cooking is a regular and never-ending duty at home, people can't resist the temptation of snack places, where they can get *vadai*, *idli* and *dosai*." (*Vadai* are silky deep fried dumplings, a bit like savoury doughnuts, spiked with chilli and ginger.

You'll find recipes for *Idli* and *Masala Dosa* on pages 227 and 230.)

A lot has changed in India since Das's youth. "It's unfortunate to see the decline of proper farming and good healthy eating in India, and even Kerala is becoming a completely consumer-driven state. The population is very educated, there's a lot of foreign money from people working abroad, and there is a lot of competition to be the most modern. Even though modern eating has changed a great deal in Kerala, people still enjoy a wonderful vegetarian meal most days. Though if you want to enjoy true Kerala vegetarian food, you will have to go a nice family home where people are very passionate about their cooking."

When I was in Kerala, I certainly ate well – the unbelievably generous and complex vegetarian *thali*, for example, a selection of up to 30 different dishes served on a banana leaf, was a regular favourite. "People in Kerala are used to elaborate meals three times a day," says Das, "and that demands a huge variety of flavours and textures. We have the most imaginative mothers when it comes to cooking! They always manage to create wonderful flavours with fresh ingredients like ginger, coconut and curry leaves from their gardens."

So in a rapidly changing society, what does the future hold for the vegetarian world capital? "The Hindu community has always believed in food from nature and respect for all living creatures," Das emphasizes. "While some remain loyal to their faith and style of cooking, vegetarian food is considered old cooking – you wouldn't find modern vegetarian restaurants in Kerala, experimenting with new dishes. When people want to eat vegetarian food they want traditional food. There aren't many vegetarian chefs there who have a vision to take it to the next level for the future." Meanwhile, Das is busy refining true Kerala style in his UK restaurant empire. Luckily for me, it may be that some of the best of world vegetarian cuisine is right here in London, where I live.

"The full use of taste is an act of genius."
John La Farge, American artist

# focus on ingredients

Dal – lentils – Dal is the word used in India to describe any lentil or legume, and a whole host of types are used in Indian cooking. Generally, small, split lentils do not have to be soaked before cooking (red, yellow, urad or black, green, brown). Larger lentils should be soaked for at least 4 hours (chana, toovar). Chana dal is another name for dried chickpeas, which have been hulled and split. Dal should never be eaten raw, but sometimes they are cooked, from dry, very briefly in oil to add a crunchy, nutty accent to a

thick it is. To make tamarind water, place 50 g/2 oz x 3-cm/1¼-inch cube of compressed tamarind in a pan and mash slightly. Add 250 ml/8 fl oz/1 cup water, bring to the boil and simmer for 10 minutes, stirring occasionally. Cool slightly, then push through a sieve (strainer). You should have about 175 ml/6 fl oz/¾ cup tamarind water. To make a thicker pulp, use less water.

Curry Leaves – *meetha neem, kadhi patta* – these have a unique flavour, reminiscent of toasted

Curry Leaves

Dal

chutney or snack mix. All lentils are high in protein and of high value in a vegetarian diet.

Tamarind – *imli* – This is used primarily as a souring agent, but has sweet and salty elements as well. It grows on trees in long, curved pods, about 10–15 cm/4–6 in long. The pods are cinnamon-coloured and easy to break away, revealing the flesh, which encases large, shiny brown seeds and fibres. Tamarind is most often sold in a compressed, chocolate-coloured block. The tasty flesh must be extracted from the seeds and fibres before use – then it is called tamarind pulp, or tamarind water, depending on how

nuts and onions, but there is really no substitute. Some compare them to bay leaves as they are added whole to dishes to emanate flavour. They are quite soft and edible, unlike bay, though some people push them to the edge of the plate. They are used on a daily basis throughout India and especially in the South, where they are fried with mustard seeds as the first stage of cooking, or at the end as a separate garnish, again fried with mustard seeds. Curry leaves are available fresh from Asian food stores, usually in quite large quantities. The good news is that they freeze brilliantly so you can always have some to hand. Dried curry leaves are quite inferior but acceptable if essential.

**Mango** – The mango's bewitching perfume and creamy flesh has long secured its position as the world's finest fruit. They've been cultivated in India since before 2000 BC, and India and Pakistan are major exporters as well as providers for their own massive demand. There hundreds of varieties of mango, different sizes, shapes and colours, the best of which have a thin skin and sweet flesh without fibres. The Alphonso variety from India is a personal favourite and is well worth seeking out. Unripe mangoes are small and green, with a tart yet fragrant quality that makes a wonderful fresh chutney. They are also used in curries (see Mango Curry on page 233), and the skin has a flavour all its own and can be left on in cooking. Mangoes

Jains, whose extremely strict diet forbids eating onions and garlic, use this spice as a substitute. A pinch is all that's needed in cooking and it is considered to be an anti-flatulent, which is why it is so often added to bean dishes. Buy asafoetida in small quantities and keep in a small jar with a tight-fitting lid.

**Ginger** – Fresh ginger appears in nearly every recipe in this chapter, and many others. It adds fragrance, pepperiness and a crunchy texture. When it's very fresh or "green", it's still mild and juicy and hasn't developed fibres – then it can be used more like a vegetable than an aromatic when peeled and cut into julienne strips. As it ages, it becomes more peppery

**Mangoes**

**Tamarind Pods and Block**

are messy to prepare if they are fully ripe – the easiest trick is to stand the fruit on its stem end, slice whole "cheeks" off the fat sides, then score the cut side of each cheek right down to the skin but not through it, then turn it inside-out and cut off the cubes of flesh.

**Asafoetida** – *hing* – Possibly the most pungent spice of them all, this has a strong onion smell, which leaps out of the jar and travels for yards in seconds. It is used mainly in India but it is grown in Afghanistan and Iran. The spice is derived from a rhizome or taproot, from which a highly aromatic milk is tapped, dried and powdered. Certain Hindu high priests and

and fibrous, but it is still fine to use even when it's looking a bit shrivelled – as long as it's not mouldy, it's still useful. The easiest way to peel ginger is to use the tip of a teaspoon to scrape off the skin. It calms the stomach and ginger tea is an instant cure for a stomach ache – simply steep grated ginger in boiling water, add a little lemon and honey and drink.

**Ghee** – This is plain clarified butter – the fat left after the milk solids are removed. It is preferred in Indian cooking for its rich flavour, while being able to sustain high cooking temperatures. It is sold ready-made in long-life cans and jars.

A Tamil speciality, this tangy, fiery soup definitely pushes the appetite accelerator pedal – a great way to start a meal. It's the tamarind and blend of spices that really work their magic here. *Rasam* is often described as a "thin lentil soup" but I think "hot and sour" is a better description of the dominant characteristics of this one, which is based on a Sri Lankan version I have eaten. Sometimes *Rasam* is made into a complete light meal, becoming a thin gravy for rice, with a dollop of yogurt.

# Rasam
# Hot and Sour Tomato Broth Sri Lanka/South India

Rinse the lentils, place in a small saucepan with 175 ml/6 fl oz/¾ cup water, and bring to the boil. Simmer for 15 minutes, or until tender throughout, checking regularly that it is not burning or drying out (add a little more water if necessary). Do not drain.

Place the tamarind in another saucepan and mash slightly. Add 250 ml/ 8 fl oz/1 cup water, bring to the boil and simmer for 10 minutes, stirring occasionally. Cool slightly, then push through a sieve (strainer). You should have about 175 ml/6 fl oz/¾ cup tamarind pulp.

Heat a wok or large saucepan over a medium heat. Add the oil, the mustard seeds, cumin seeds, fennel seeds, black pepper, asafoetida, if using, and the curry leaves, if using. Fry briefly until the mustard seeds pop, then add the tomatoes, chillies, ginger and garlic. Cook, stirring, until the tomatoes collapse, about 2 minutes. Add the cooked lentils with their water, tamarind, turmeric, water and salt and bring to the boil. Simmer for 5 minutes and taste for seasoning.

3 tbsp red split or yellow lentils
175 ml/6 fl oz/¾ cup water
50 g/2 oz tamarind, about
    3-cm/1¼-inch cube
250 ml/8 fl oz/1 cup water
1 tbsp sunflower oil
1 tsp mustard seeds
1 tsp cumin seeds
1 tsp fennel seeds
Freshly ground black pepper
½ tsp asafoetida (optional)
20 curry leaves (optional)
4 plump vine-ripened tomatoes, about
    500 g/1 lb 2 oz, finely chopped
2–3 fresh thin green chillies (chilies), or
    to taste, slit lengthways
2.5-cm/1-inch piece fresh root ginger,
    finely chopped
2 garlic cloves, finely chopped
½ tsp turmeric
675 ml/1⅛ pints/2¾ cups water
1½ tsp sea salt, or to taste

**Serves 4–6**

"Hopper" is an Anglicization of the word "*appam*", which is the Tamil word for the pancake, best described by Madhur Jaffrey in *Eastern Vegetarian Cooking*: "If a French crêpe were to marry an English crumpet, the couple would probably become the proud parents of a Sri Lankan hopper." The yeasted batter is moistened with coconut milk, giving it a luscious creamy flavour. Authentic hoppers, typically a breakfast food, are cooked in a wok-like pan, and they come out lacy and bowl-shaped – difficult to achieve unless your wok is expertly seasoned. Use your best non-stick frying pan for guaranteed results.

# Hoppers with Sambol
# Coconut Pancakes with Hot Coconut Relish Sri Lanka

To make the hoppers, sift both flours into a large bowl and stir through the yeast and salt. Pour in the coconut milk, then add enough warm water to make a thick batter, about the consistency of a cake mixture (batter). When well mixed, cover with clingfilm (plastic wrap) and leave in a warm place for at least 1 hour.

When ready to cook, select a small non-stick frying pan if possible and a lid which will fit over it. Smear with a little oil and heat over a low-medium heat. Scoop about 80 ml/2¾ fl oz/⅓ cup of batter into the pan and quickly swirl to the edges. Alternatively use the back of a soup spoon to spread the batter, making a pancake about 3–4 mm/⅛ inch thick. Cover the pan and cook until the base is golden and slightly crisp, and the top is no longer pale and wet, but dry and cooked through. Repeat with all the batter to make about 8 hoppers.

To make the sambol, pour boiling water over the coconut and leave to cool. Add to blender with the onion or shallot, garlic, lime juice, salt, chilli or cayenne and paprika and blend until smooth and peach-coloured. Serve with the hoppers.

**For the hoppers:**

175 g/6 oz/1¼ cups plain (all-purpose) flour

50 g/2 oz/⅜ cup rice flour

1 x 7 g/¼ oz packet easy-blend dried yeast (active dry yeast)

1 tsp sea salt

250 ml/8 fl oz/1 cup coconut milk

Sunflower oil for frying

**For the sambol:**

250 ml/8 fl oz/1 cup boiling water

100 g/3 ½ oz/1 cup unsweetened desiccated coconut (dry unsweetened coconut)

½ medium onion or shallot, very finely chopped

1 clove garlic, degermed

2 tbsp lime juice

1 tsp sea salt

1 small red chilli (chili) or ½ tsp cayenne pepper, or to taste

½ tsp paprika

**Serves 4–6**

Cows are considered sacred to Hindus, and while dairy products abound in India, there is only really one Indian cheese and this is it – fresh cheese for cooking. In a tropical climate before the days of refrigeration, dairy products could not be kept for long, so maturing the cheese was never an option. This is the first stage of how all cheese-making is done: separating milk into curds and whey, and it is remarkably easy. The curds are fluffy and light at first and very quickly become a solid mass when pressed and chilled, resulting in a high-protein ingredient with a creamy yet chewy texture. The whey can be saved to make *Matar Paneer* (see page 240) or used for making *roti* (Indian breads). Manufactured paneer is sold in some supermarkets and Asian food stores, but home-made is much lighter and creamier.

# Paneer
# Home-made Curd Cheese India

Bring the milk to the boil in a large saucepan. Watch it carefully, and just as it starts to scale the sides of the pan, turn off the heat. Stir in the lemon juice. Cover the pan and leave to stand for 10 minutes.

Drain the curds in a colander lined with a new re-usable kitchen cloth, a piece of muslin (cheesecloth) or a clean tea (dish) towel. (Save some of the whey if you want to make *Matar Paneer* on page 240; otherwise, discard.) Squeeze out the excess moisture and leave to cool and drain further, then leave to chill in the refrigerator.

The paneer can be used once cool, though it will have a very crumbly texture. It will harden within an hour in the refrigerator so that is a slicing consistency. For best results in cooking, leave to solidify for further 3–4 hours.

3.5 litres/6 pints/14¾ cups full cream (whole) milk
100 ml/3 fl oz/generous ⅓ cup fresh strained lemon juice (about 3 lemons)

**Makes about 300 g/11 oz**

## variations

**Spiced Paneer:** Add whole spices such as cumin, fennel or chilli (dried red pepper) flakes to the fresh curds, then solidify as instructed.

**Paneer Pakora:** For a seriously wicked treat, take two equal-sized slices of paneer and make a sandwich with some chutney spread in between, such as *Chutni Gazneesh* (see page 245) or mango chutney from a jar. Dip in *Pakora* batter (see page 242) and deep-fry until golden.

"*Idli! Idli!*" is the familiar cry from the *idli walla*, heard from dawn onwards on passenger trains and in the streets in South India. Served with eye-opening spicy chutneys, these light yet substantial dumplings are a favourite breakfast finger food. Personally, I love them any time of day.

Traditional *idli* are made from rice and lentils ground together into a batter, which is fermented for hours in the tropical heat, to achieve a slight tang. The quick method here, using wheat semolina and low-fat yogurt for sharpness, is a trick I picked up from Madhur Jaffrey in her book *Eastern Vegetarian Cooking*. Most South Indian kitchens are equipped with a special apparatus for making *idli*, which steams them in several tiered moulds. Just in case you don't have an *idli*-maker, I devised this method in the oven, using your standard mince pie or muffin tins (pans), ideally non-stick. This makes a gluttonous quantity, but they freeze brilliantly and can be microwaved from frozen for an instant breakfast or snack. At least one of the fresh chutneys (overleaf) is an essential accompaniment, but as you'll see, they can be whizzed up in moments.

# Idli Steamed Dumplings Kerala, South India

Preheat the oven to 200°C/400°F/Gas Mark 6.

Heat the oil in a non-stick frying pan over a medium heat and add the mustard seeds. When they start to pop, reduce the heat and add the semolina. Stir and cook gently for 2 minutes – the semolina should not brown. Remove from the pan and transfer to a heatproof measuring jug. Leave to cool.

Stir the coconut, salt, chilli and baking powder through the semolina. Add the yogurt and mix to a thick batter.

Brush several mince pie tins (pans) with a little oil. Pour the batter into the moulds. (Tin sizes will vary. You may fill more than 12 holes with this quantity.) The batter will rise, so do not overfill. Place a curry leaf, if using, on top of each. Make a bain-marie for the idli. Place the tins in a large oven tray and pour in boiling water to create a pool, which sits under the tins without dribbling over. Brush a piece of foil with oil and cover the mince pie tins, oiled-side-down. Place carefully in the oven and leave to steam for 20 minutes, or until set throughout. Serve with fresh chutneys (see overleaf).

2 tbsp sunflower oil, plus extra for oiling

1 tsp black mustard seeds

180 g/6½ oz/¾ cup semolina or cream of wheat cereal

3 tbsp desiccated (dry) unsweetened coconut

½ tsp salt

1 fresh green chilli (chili), de-seeded if large, chopped

1 tsp baking powder

500 ml/16 fl oz/2 cups very low-fat yogurt (for extra tang)

Fresh curry leaves, to garnish (optional)

Chutneys, to serve (see recipes overleaf)

**Serves 4**

This classic chutney is also essential with Masala Dosa (see page 230). In South India it's made with fresh coconuts, which are everywhere, but dried coconut will suffice.

# Coconut Chutney South India

Place the coconut in a bowl and pour over just enough boiling water to cover. Leave to swell until cool. In an electric blender, process the coconut, green chillies, ginger, salt and yogurt to a fine paste. Transfer the mixture to a bowl and set aside.

Heat a small frying pan over a medium heat and add the oil. Add the mustard seeds and curry leaves. When the mustard seeds begin to pop, remove from the heat and stir the contents of the pan through the coconut mixture.

100 g/3½ oz/1 cup unsweetened desiccated (dry) coconut

2 fresh green chillies (chilies), de-seeded if large

2.5-cm/1-inch cube fresh root ginger, peeled and coarsely chopped

½ tsp salt

3 heaped tbsp natural (plain) yogurt

2 tbsp oil

1 tsp black mustard seeds

10 fresh or dried curry leaves (optional)

**Serves 4–6**

You might just fall over with delight when you taste this. It's one of the best combinations I know. No need to save it for *Idli* (see previous page) – serve with vegetables or poppadums for dipping, or as a sauce for anything with rice.

# Tomato and Cashew Chutney South India

Heat a frying pan over a medium-high heat and add the oil. Add the tomatoes and garlic and fry briskly until slightly softened. Set aside to cool.

Heat a separate dry pan over a medium heat. Add the cashews, sesame seeds, cumin seeds and chillies and toast until the sesame seeds pop. Leave to cool slightly, then combine everything in an electric blender, adding the sugar and salt and purée until smooth. Serve immediately.

1 tbsp sunflower oil

300 g/11 oz tomatoes, quartered

4 whole garlic cloves

Handful of cashews, about 25 g/1 oz/⅛ cup

1 tbsp sesame seeds

1 tsp cumin seeds

2 small dried chillies (chilies), or to taste

1 tbsp dark brown sugar

½ tsp salt

**Serves 4–6**

*right Idli* (see page 227), served with Tomato and Cashew Chutney (left) and Coconut Chutney (right).

The mighty *Masala Dosa* is the ambassador dish of South India, popularized throughout India and making an impression the world over. The *dosa* itself is traditionally made from hulled, split black lentils (urad dal) and rice, soaked separately overnight, blended together into a batter and then fermented for several hours in the tropical heat to achieve a wonderful sour flavour. Here I offer you a quick and highly effective shortcut.

# Masala Dosa
# Spiced Potato-filled Rice Pancake

South India

To make the potato masala, place the potatoes in a large saucepan with a lid and cover with water. Bring to the boil and simmer until the potatoes are cooked but firm. Drain and set aside until cool enough to handle. Alternatively, steam until cooked, then leave to cool. Peel the potatoes, then place back in the pan and mash roughly.

Heat the oven to warm. Heat a large frying pan over a medium-high heat. Add the oil and mustard seeds, and as they begin to pop, add the curry leaves and chillies and cook for 30 seconds. Add the onions and cook, stirring, until the onions are well browned. Add the tomato, ginger, turmeric and salt, then reduce the heat and simmer for 5 minutes.

Add the mashed potatoes to the mixture and stir. Cook for 3–4 minutes, then remove from the heat. Taste for seasoning, set aside and keep warm.

To make the *dosai*, mix both flours, yogurt, lemon juice, water, salt and bicarbonate of soda together thoroughly in a large bowl to the consistency of single (light) cream.

Choose your best large, non-stick frying pan. Pour a little oil into a saucer and place the onion in it, cut-side-down; also have ready a cup of oil with a teaspoon. Heat the frying pan over a medium heat. Use the oiled onion to lightly oil the frying pan by rubbing it all over the surface. Pour about 100 ml/3 fl oz/⅓ cup of the batter into the centre of the pan and quickly swirl to thinly coat the base. Take a tsp of oil and dribble it around the edges of the *dosa*, giving it a crispy edge. When the base of the *dosa* looks golden and crisp and the edges are curling up, take your potato masala and place a couple of spoonfuls on one side of it. Fold the *dosa* over into a half-moon shape, or you can try rolling the filling up inside. Keep warm while you make the rest, lightly oiling the pan with the onion each time. Serve as soon as possible, with the accompaniments mentioned on the right.

**For the potato masala:**

700 g/1½ lb potatoes, scrubbed and unpeeled

3 tbsp sunflower oil

1 tsp black mustard seeds

20 curry leaves

2 fresh green chillies (chilies), de-seeded if large, finely sliced

2 medium onions, finely sliced

1 medium tomato, chopped

1-cm/½-inch piece fresh root ginger, peeled and finely chopped

½ tsp turmeric

Sea salt

**For the *dosai*:**

140 g/4¾ oz/scant 1 cup plain (all-purpose) flour

60 g/2¼ oz/½ cup rice flour

6 tbsp low-fat yogurt

2 tsp fresh lemon or lime juice

375 ml/13 fl oz/1½ cups water

½ tsp salt

1 tsp bicarbonate of soda

Sunflower oil for frying

½ medium onion, peeled, top intact (don't chop it off!)

**To serve:**

Coconut Chutney (see page 228)

Dal (Sambar) (see page 228)

**Makes 8–10, serves 4–6**

As Camellia Panjabi informs me in her wonderful book *50 Great Curries of India*, egg curry is made all over India, simply by cooking a basic home-style curry and adding hard-boiled (hard-cooked) eggs at the end. This quick-cooking variation, with its mustard seeds and curry leaves, is typical of South Indian curries. Rather than hard-boil the eggs, I prefer to cook them "butter-yolked" – cooked through but with a yolk that is barely oozing in the middle.

# Egg Curry South India

Place the eggs in a saucepan and cover with cold water. Bring to the boil and simmer for 5 minutes. Drain, cool and remove shell.

Heat a wok or large saucepan until very hot and add oil. Add the mustard seeds and curry leaves. When the mustard seeds begin to pop, add the onion and fry briskly until golden. Add the garlic, ginger, chillies, turmeric, cumin seeds, coconut and salt and pepper to taste. Fry for a couple of minutes until fragrant, then add the tomatoes and the whole eggs. Heat through and remove from the heat. Stir the yogurt through the mixture. Cover and leave to stand for 2–3 minutes. Sprinkle with whole coriander leaves. Serve with rice or chapatis.

4 organic eggs

2 tbsp sunflower oil

2 tsp black mustard seeds

Handful of curry leaves

2 large onions, finely sliced

3 garlic cloves, sliced

5 cm/2 in thumb fresh root ginger, chopped

4 thin green fresh chillies (chilies), halved lengthways

2 tsp turmeric

2 tsp cumin seeds

3 tbsp desiccated coconut (dry unsweetened coconut)

Sea salt and freshly ground black pepper

4 plump vine-ripened tomatoes, chopped

200 ml/7 fl oz/⅘ cup natural (plain) yogurt

Fresh coriander (cilantro) leaves, to garnish

Boiled basmati rice or chapatis, to serve

**Serves 4**

As with most South Indian curries, this one is cooked in minutes. One theory is that the tropical climate makes it too hot to hang around in the kitchen for long. Quick-cooking curries always taste zesty and fresh and never heavy. This delectably sweet and creamy curry entertains a couple of unusual methods in the preparation.

First, the mango is not peeled; this is because the skin has a peppery flavour all its own. (See notes on mangoes on page 223). Firm-fleshed varieties are best for this recipe. Taste the skin, and leave it on if you don't find it disagreeable.

Second, the chillies are not chopped or sliced, but simply cut in half lengthways. This way, they impart a slight overtone of heat to the dish. Those who like a powerful chilli hit can, of course, eat the chilli. This is a great way of pleasing several palates with differing chilli tolerances.

# Mango Yogurt Curry South India

Heat a wok or large saucepan and add oil. Add the mustard seeds and fry until they pop, then add the curry leaves, turmeric, ginger, garlic, onion, chillies and some salt. Fry until the onion starts to brown, then add the tomatoes and mango. Fry until the tomato just starts to soften, only 1–2 minutes. Remove the wok from the heat and stir in the yogurt. Cover for a minute or two to warm through, then serve with rice.

2 tbsp sunflower oil

1 tsp black mustard seeds

Handful of fresh or dried curry leaves

2 tsp turmeric

Large thumb of fresh root ginger about 5 cm/2 inches, chopped

3 plump garlic cloves, chopped

1 large red onion, finely sliced

2–3 fresh green chillies (chilies), halved lengthways

Salt

300 g/11 oz tomatoes, cut into chunks

1 large, firm, mango, washed, unpeeled and cut into chunks

750 ml/1¼ pints/3 cups natural (plain) low-fat yogurt

Boiled rice, to serve

**Serves 4**

*Rai* means mustard seeds and in Gujarat, they are an essential ingredient for this cooling accompaniment. Apart from being cool in temperature, the casein in yogurt counteracts the fire of chillies, and as well as easing digestion, raita provides a perfect foil for a selection of spicy dishes. In the South, yogurt salads are called *pachadi*, and often contain coconut.

# Raita Yogurt Salad Gujarat

Mix the yogurt, vegetables, chilli, coriander and mint together in a bowl and add the lemon juice and salt and pepper to taste. Scoop into a serving bowl.

This part is optional but delicious and authentic: Heat a frying pan over a medium-high heat. Add the oil, then the mustard seeds, cumin seeds and curry leaves. When the mustard seeds begin to pop, pour the contents of the pan over the yogurt mixture.

500 ml/16 fl oz/2 cups natural (plain) yogurt
1 medium tomato, thickly sliced and cut into strips
1 small onion, halved and thinly sliced
5-cm/2-inch piece cucumber, peeled, de-seeded and cut into matchstick strips
1 fresh thin green chilli (chili), sliced
1 tbsp finely chopped fresh coriander (cilantro)
1 tbsp finely chopped mint
1–2 tbsp fresh lemon juice, to taste
Sea salt and freshly ground black pepper

**To garnish (optional):**
1 tbsp sunflower oil
1 tsp black mustard seeds
½ tsp cumin seeds
8–10 curry leaves (optional)

**Serves 4–6**

Every style of *dal* throughout India is different, but one thing is consistent: *dal* will be eaten almost every day as an essential part of the main meal, which is usually made up of several vegetable dishes, chutneys and rice. I call it a "soup" because that is descriptive of its consistency, but it does not define its identity. The function of *dal* is more to lubricate the rice and provide a contrast to the vegetable dishes, as well as providing extra protein (see page 222).

This Gujarati-style *dal* differs from other parts of India, characterized by a distinctive sweet-sour flavour – the sweet from palm sugar or jaggery, the sour from kokum flowers or lemon juice. Gujarati *dal* is made with toovar dal, which is actually a hulled, split pigeon pea. It should have the consistency of a light tomato soup, and can take the place of a *sambar*, which is normally served with *Masala Dosa* (see page 230). All the ingredients here make up a very authentic *dal*. If you can't get hold of all of them, don't let that stop you making it – just use what's available to you.

# Dal
# Spiced Lentil Soup Gujarat

If using toovar dal, soak it first in a bowl of hot water for 3 hours. Drain. If using red lentils, there is no need to soak.

Place the dal in a large saucepan with the water and bring to the boil. Skim any foam that appears on the surface. Cook rapidly uncovered for 10–15 minutes, then reduce the heat and simmer until very tender, about 40–50 minutes, depending on the type of dal used and its age. Purée with the water, using a hand-held blender, or pass the mixture through a sieve (strainer).

Heat another large saucepan (or the rinsed and dried pan) over a medium heat and add the oil. Add the spices and fry for 1 minute, or until the mustard seed pops, then add the tomatoes, ginger and garlic. Cook until the tomato collapses, then add the fenugreek and salt and cook for about 30 seconds (it is very important that fenugreek does not overcook, as it becomes very bitter). Pour in the lentil broth. Add the sugar, lemon juice and turmeric. Bring to the boil, then simmer for about 30 minutes, or until reduced to a tomato-soup consistency. Add a little water if it becomes thick. Taste for seasoning and serve.

100 g/3½ oz/½ cup toovar dal, or split red lentils

1.5 litres/2½ pints/generous 6⅓ cups water

2 tbsp sunflower oil

Large pinch of asafoetida

8–10 curry leaves

½ tsp black mustard seeds

½ tsp cumin seeds

4-cm/1½-inch piece cinnamon stick, or a few shards of cassia bark

8 cloves

1 large vine-ripened tomato, finely chopped

2.5-cm/1-inch piece fresh root ginger, finely chopped

2 plump garlic cloves, finely chopped

½ tsp fenugreek

1½ tsp salt

2 tbsp chopped palm sugar (jaggery) or light brown sugar

2 tbsp lemon juice

½ tsp turmeric

**Serves 4–6**

I first became addicted to these at a restaurant in Southall, the "Little India" of London – a noisy and colourful place where you can get transported to India for the afternoon and enjoy some seriously good food. When I went to the real South India, I was delighted to find them sold as street food and tasting much the same. But it continued to mystify me how to make them – trying to re-create them at home, they always fell apart in the frying. I finally worked it out, thanks to Yamuna Devi in *Lord Krishna's Cuisine: The Art of Indian Vegetarian Cooking*, my bible. The key? Almost no oil and a long, slow cook in the pan.

# Aloo Tikki Chana Chat
# Potato Cakes with Chickpeas and Tamarind Sauce South India

Place the potatoes in a large saucepan, cover with water and add salt. Bring to the boil and cook until tender throughout. Drain and cool.

Meanwhile, make the tamarind sauce. Place the tamarind in a small saucepan and pour over the boiling water. Bring to the boil, then simmer for 10–15 minutes, or until the flesh falls off the seeds. Strain into a bowl, then return the tamarind water to the pan. Add the ginger, cumin and sugar and stir. Bring to the boil, then reduce to a simmer and cook until thick, about 10–15 minutes. Remove the pan from the heat and set aside.

Place the cooled potatoes with the garlic, chilli, 1 tsp of salt, pepper, nutmeg, chopped coriander, lemon juice and gram flour in a large bowl and mix thoroughly. Rub your hands with a little oil and form the mixture into balls about the size of a lime, then flatten into thick cakes. The mixture should make 8 cakes.

Heat a wide, non-stick frying pan over a low heat and add a tiny smear of sunflower oil. (Don't be tempted to shallow-fry, as the cakes won't hold together.) Cook the cakes slowly, about 15 minutes each side, until crisp and golden.

If using spinach, arrange a few leaves on 4 serving plates. Serve 2 cakes per person with a sprinkling of chickpeas, a couple of tablespoons of thinned yogurt and the warm tamarind sauce. Garnish with chopped coriander leaves.

500 g/1 lb 2 oz floury (mealy) potatoes, peeled and cut into large chunks
Salt
1 garlic clove, crushed
2 small fresh red chillies (chilies), finely chopped
Freshly ground black pepper
Generous grinding of nutmeg (half a whole nutmeg)
2 tbsp chopped fresh coriander (cilantro)
1 tbsp fresh lemon juice
3 tbsp gram flour (see page 170)
Sunflower oil
Fresh coriander (cilantro) leaves, to garnish

**For the tamarind sauce**
100 g/3½ oz tamarind, about 5 x 5-cm/2 x 2-inch piece
250 ml/8 fl oz/1 cup boiling water
1 tsp finely grated fresh root ginger
1 tsp ground cumin
2 tbsp dark brown sugar

**To serve:**
Handful of baby spinach leaves (optional)
½ x 400 g/14 oz can chickpeas, drained and rinsed
8 tbsp natural (plain) yogurt, thinned with a little water to dribbling consistency

**Serves 4**

These delicious little morsels are a really special treat. The batter is quite different from *Pakora* (see page 242) but, like all Indian batters, it is made from chickpea flour. The batter and filling can both be prepared well in advance and the frying done at the last minute. Consistency is paramount – if the batter is too runny it will slide off the potato mixture, but if it is too thick, it will crack open, letting the expanding potato mixture escape. More chickpea flour or water can be added to rectify either of these situations.

# Bateta Wada
# Battered Spiced Potato Balls Gujarat

Place the potatoes in a steamer and steam until tender throughout. While still warm but cool enough to handle, peel and mash the potatoes in a large bowl. Add the salt, sugar, fresh ginger, green chillies and lemon juice. Leave the mixture to cool, then add the fresh coriander. Taste for seasoning. Divide into 24 balls and leave to chill in the refrigerator until needed.

To make the batter, sift the flour into a bowl. Slowly add the cold water to the flour, ensuring that there are no lumps. Mix in the salt, asafoetida, if using, and cayenne. The texture should be like thick double (heavy) cream.

Heat the oil for deep-frying in a large saucepan or deep-fat fryer to 160°C/350°F. As the oil begins to warm up, take 1 tbsp from the pan and mix it into the batter.

Once the oil has heated, drop a few potato balls into the batter and remove with a soup spoon or by hand, then drop into the hot oil. Deep-fry to a light golden brown colour and drain on kitchen paper (paper towels). Cool for a few minutes before eating. They taste best served immediately, but they could be reheated in a medium oven. Serve with *Chutni Gazneesh* or chilli sauce.

500 g/1 lb 2 oz floury (mealy) potatoes, scrubbed but left unpeeled

1½ tsp salt

1 tbsp caster (superfine) sugar

1-cm/½-inch piece fresh root ginger, peeled and finely grated

1–2 thin green fresh chillies (chilies), or to taste, finely chopped

2 tbsp lemon juice

3 tbsp finely chopped fresh coriander (cilantro)

Sunflower oil for deep-frying

**For the batter:**

100 g/3½ oz/scant 1 cup chickpea flour

125 ml/4 fl oz/½ cup cold water

¼ tsp salt

Large pinch of asafoetida (optional)

Large pinch of cayenne pepper

1 tbsp warm sunflower oil (see below)

**To serve:**

*Chutni Gazneesh* (see page 245)

Chilli (chili) sauce

**Serves 4–6**

*Charchari* refers to the cooking method for many types of vegetables, where they steam in an aromatic broth, which reduces to a thick glaze, and finally becomes a slightly charred crust with an intense flavour. That is not to say burnt – it nearly comes to this, but not quite – you take it to the outer limits, then bring it back. This is a "dry" dish – that is, it provides a perfect contrast to saucy curry dishes, which might be served alongside it such as *Dal* (see page 235) or *Khatta Baigan* (see page 241). A good, large non-stick frying pan will deliver perfect results. The golden rule of cooking a *Charchari*: do not stir.

# Baigan Aloo Charchari
# Char-crusted Aubergines (Eggplants) and Potatoes  Bengal

In a large non-stick frying pan off the heat, arrange the aubergine and potato chunks in an even layer. Evenly distribute the coriander seeds, cumin seeds, turmeric, salt, pepper, chillies, fresh coriander, asafoetida and curry leaves, if using. Sprinkle over the lemon zest and juice. Pour in the water and dot with ghee or butter. Cover, place over a high heat and bring to the boil. Shake the pan a few times, then reduce the heat to a simmer. Cook, covered and without stirring, for about 20 minutes, checking from time to time that the water has not dried out – if it has, add a little more.

After 20 minutes, the aubergines should be buttery soft, the potatoes tender and the liquid should have reduced to a thick glaze. Do not stir. Remove the lid and increase the heat. Reduce the sauce until it just starts to form a crust on the base of the pan. Remove the pan from the heat.

Leave to stand for 2 minutes, then stir the crust through the mixture. Fry a little more to achieve more crusty bits, if liked, or serve immediately. Serve hot or cold.

1 medium aubergine (eggplant), about 250 g/9 oz, cut into 2.5-cm/1-inch pieces

2 medium-large potatoes, about 400 g/14 oz, peeled and cut into 1-cm/½-inch cubes

2 tsp coriander seeds, lightly crushed

1 tsp cumin seeds

½ tsp turmeric

1 tsp sea salt

Freshly ground black pepper

2 thin green fresh chillies (chilies), slit lengthways

Large handful of fresh coriander (cilantro), chopped

Large pinch of asafoetida (optional)

8–10 curry leaves (optional)

Finely grated zest and juice of ½ lemon

250 ml/8 fl oz/1 cup water

50 g/2 oz/4 tbsp ghee (see page 223) or butter, cubed

**Serves 4**

This well-known classic appears on most Indian restaurant menus throughout the world, and on dinner tables in India but especially the Punjab. Every housewife has her own version, possibly with the addition of mint or extra spices. This version uses garam masala, which is a flexible spice mixture that you can make yourself (a Kenyan version, which originated in India, appears on page 181), or buy ready-ground. This dish stands up to being left for a while and even improves with standing – a real boon if you are cooking a multi-dish Indian feast.

# Matar Paneer
# Cheese and Peas in a Spicy Sauce Punjab

Heat a large, non-stick frying pan with a lid over a medium heat and melt the ghee or add the oil. Add the paneer cubes and fry with caution – they splutter considerably so stand well away, turning to brown on all sides. Remove from the pan with a slotted spoon and drain on kitchen paper (paper towels).

Add the onion to the frying pan and fry until soft, then add the garlic and ginger and fry until fragrant, about 1 minute. Pour in a splash of milk or whey and add the spices and salt. Cook, stirring, for 2 minutes, then add the remaining milk and the tomatoes. Cover the pan, bring to the boil, reduce the heat to a simmer and cook for 10 minutes.

Add the peas, the fried paneer and the chopped coriander. Stir well, then cover and cook for a further 10 minutes, stirring occasionally. Serve hot, with extra coriander leaves sprinkled over. Serve with rice.

4 tbsp ghee or sunflower oil

250 g/9 oz paneer, store-bought or home-made (see page 226), cut into 1-cm/½-inch cubes

1 medium onion, finely chopped

3 garlic cloves, finely chopped

2.5-cm/1-inch piece fresh root ginger, peeled and finely chopped

250 ml/8 fl oz/1 cup semi-skimmed (lowfat) milk or whey (see page 226)

1 tsp turmeric

¼ tsp cayenne pepper

2 ½ tsp garam masala (see page 181)

1 tsp ground coriander

1 tsp salt

4 plump vine-ripened tomatoes, about 450 g/1 lb, finely chopped

280 g/10½ oz/2 cups fresh or frozen green peas

1 tbsp chopped fresh coriander (cilantro), plus extra whole leaves to garnish

Boiled rice, to serve

**Serves 4–6**

Here, aubergines melt into an incredibly delicious sauce, sweet with molasses and sharp with tamarind. I'm afraid there is no substitute for the tamarind in this case, as it so fully characterizes the dish. The dish is really more sauce than substance, so it must take its place in a spread with light dishes such as *Navratan Pulau* (see page 243), *Baigan Aloo Charchari* (page 239), *Dal* (page 235) and *Raita* (page 234).

# Khatta Baigan Sweet and Sour Aubergines (Eggplants) Bangladesh

Place the aubergines in a colander and toss the salt through them to coat evenly. Leave to drain for at least 30 minutes, then pat dry with kitchen paper (paper towels).

Heat a wok or large saucepan with a lid over a medium heat and add the oil. Add the aubergine and fry for a few minutes until they are tinged with gold – they do not need to cook fully. Remove the aubergine to a bowl.

Heat another 2 tbsp of oil in the wok and add the onion. Cook until softened, about 2 minutes, then add the garlic and spices. Cook, stirring, for 1 minute. Add the aubergine and stir to coat with the spices. Pour in the water, tamarind and black treacle or sugar. Cover, bring to the boil, then reduce the heat to a simmer and cook very gently for about 1 hour, stirring occasionally, until thick and saucy. Taste for seasoning towards the end, adding more salt if necessary.

3 medium aubergines (eggplants), about 700 g/1 ½ lb, cut into 2.5-cm/1-inch pieces
1 tsp salt
50 ml/2 fl oz/¼ cup sunflower oil, plus extra 2 tbsp
1 medium onion, finely chopped
2 garlic cloves, chopped
½ tsp turmeric
½ tsp cayenne pepper
1 tsp ground cumin
2 tsp ground coriander
½ tsp ground ginger
500 ml/16 fl oz/2 cups water
125 ml/4 fl oz/½ cup tamarind water (see page 222)
80 ml/2 ¾ fl oz/⅓ cup black treacle (molasses) or sugar (about 6 tbsp)

**Serves 6**

*Pakoras* are a passion in this part of the world, where you'll find a *pakora-walla* pushing his cart through every street and railway station. I've often said that you could batter and deep-fry a piece of cardboard and it would taste good, and I'd have to argue that this delicious batter really would make it so – it is so flavourful that no dipping sauce is really necessary. I find it interesting that this is the polar opposite to its Japanese counterpart, *Tempura* (see page 199); it's an interesting illustration of the flamboyant versus the minimalist.

Chopped or shredded vegetables or even fruit can be made into *Pakora*. Of the suggestions below, spinach leaves and onions are my favourites. See *Paneer* on page 226 for a further suggestion.

# Pakora
# Deep-fried Vegetables in Spiced Batter North India/Pakistan

To make the batter, sift the gram flour with the spices and salt over a bowl to remove lumps, then sift again. Beat the garlic, yogurt and water together in a separate bowl, then beat in the flour mixture until smooth. The batter should be a medium consistency: thick enough to coat a sturdy piece of cauliflower, yet thin enough to coat a delicate spinach leaf. Add more water or flour accordingly, until completely smooth. Set aside to rest for 30 minutes.

Heat the oil in a large saucepan or deep-fat fryer to 160°C/350°F, or until a small chunk of bread browns in 10 seconds. Dip the prepared vegetables in the batter (two sets of tongs are useful – one pair for dipping in batter, the other for retrieving from the oil) and deep-fry, a few at a time (do not over-crowd the oil) until golden, puffed and crisp. Drain on kitchen paper (paper towels) and eat right away.

Sunflower or vegetable oil, for deep-frying

**For the batter:**
100 g/3 ½ oz/scant 1 cup gram flour (see page 170)
¼ tsp turmeric
¼ tsp cayenne pepper
½ tsp ground cumin
½ tsp salt
1 plump garlic clove, crushed
300 ml/10 fl oz/1¼ cups natural (plain) yogurt
175 ml/6 fl oz/¾ cup water

**Vegetables for deep-frying:**
Cauliflower florets
Fresh spinach leaves
Sliced onion rings
Aubergine (eggplant) slices
Broccoli florets
Red and green (bell) pepper slices or rings
Sweet potato slices
Whole fresh green chillies (chilies)

**Makes enough for 20–25 pieces of *Pakora*, serves 4–6**

The word *pulau*, also *pilau*, *pullau*, or *pullao*, is the phonetic spelling for the Hindi or Urdu word for a host of variations of rice cooked with vegetables and spices. Navratan refers to "nine jewels" of the court of the Mughal Emperor Akbar, represented by nine vegetables – some say these jewels were ministers, others say courtesans – in any case, the dish reflects the more lavish and rich character of the cooking of this region as opposed to the South. A favourite decorative garnish for *Pulau* is real gold or silver leaf.

# Navratan Pulau
# Vegetable Rice Pakistan/North India

Soak the rice in cold water for 30 minutes, then drain thoroughly.

Heat a large saucepan with a lid over a medium heat and melt the ghee or add the oil. Add the onion and cook until translucent, then add the spices. Cook until fragrant, about 1 minute, then add the vegetables and salt and stir. Cover and let the vegetables release some of their juices for about 5 minutes, stirring once or twice.

Next, add the drained rice and sultanas and stir for 1 minute. Add the saffron and water, stir, cover and bring to the boil. The rice mixture should be just barely submerged in water; if it is not, add a little more. Later in cooking, as the water gets absorbed, the top layer becomes steamed. Simmer, covered, without stirring, for 20 minutes, or until all the water is absorbed and every grain of rice is tender. Check from time to time that it has not dried out completely underneath before rice is cooked.

To make the optional garnish, toast the sesame seeds and coconut in a dry frying pan over a medium heat until golden and the sesame seeds pop. Sprinkle over the cooked *Pulao* and serve.

250 g/9 oz/generous 1¼ cups basmati rice

2 tbsp ghee or sunflower oil

1 medium onion, finely sliced

½ tsp cumin seeds

12 cardamom pods

4 cloves

8–10 curry leaves or 2 bay leaves

4-cm/1½-inch piece cinnamon stick or a few shards of cassia bark

500 g/1 lb 2 oz mixed vegetables, cut if large into bite-sized chunks, such as cauliflower, broccoli, aubergine (eggplant), pumpkin, courgette (zucchini), broad (fava) beans, carrots, French (green) beans

2 tsp salt, or to taste

3 tbsp sultanas (golden raisins)

Large pinch of saffron (about 30 strands)

About 650 ml/1⅛ pints/2⅔ cups water

**To garnish (optional):**

2 tbsp sesame seeds

4 tbsp unsweetened desiccated (dry) coconut

**Serves 6**

This dish has relatives throughout the world – *Frittata* in Italy, *Tortilla* in Spain (page 112), *Markode* in Algeria (page 157) and *Kookoo* in Iran. As with all such egg and vegetable mixtures, the contents are usually dictated by what's seasonal. In this version, you may be surprised that the leeks are not cooked first before going into the eggs, as raw leeks can be a bit tough. If slowly cooked, however, the leeks have just enough time to steam inside the *khagina*, resulting in a clean, refreshing flavour and texture. Unlike most of its cousins named above, the *khagina* has a tiny bit of leavening, which fluffs it up beautifully.

# Khagina Egg Torte Afghanistan

Place the sultanas in a bowl and pour over enough boiling water to cover. Leave to plump for about 20 minutes.

Meanwhile, in a large bowl, beat the eggs with the flour, baking powder, salt and pepper until thoroughly incorporated. Drain the sultanas and add to the egg mixture with the leeks, spring onions, chilli and tomatoes. Combine thoroughly.

Heat a 20-cm/8-inch non-stick frying pan over a low-medium heat and add the oil. Pour the mixture into the pan and distribute the contents evenly. Follow cooking instructions as for *Tortilla de Patatas* (see page 112). Cut into wedges and serve immediately with *Chutni Gashneez*.

2 tbsp sultanas (golden raisins)
6 organic eggs
1 tbsp plain (all-purpose) flour
1 tsp baking powder
1 tsp salt
Freshly ground black pepper
2 leeks, about 225 g/8 oz, finely chopped
8 spring onions (scallions), finely chopped
1 fresh green chilli (chili), chopped
2 ripe tomatoes, chopped
2 tbsp sunflower oil
*Chutni Gashneez* (see below)

**Serves 4–6**

Anyone apprehensive about coriander (love it or hate it) should be begged to at least try this full-throttle sauce – the herb's taste changes radically for the better. As one Afghan taxi driver told me, "It's good with anything at all…like ketchup."

# Chutni Gashneez
# Coriander (Cilantro) Chutney Afghanistan

Place all the ingredients in an electric blender and whiz until smooth, scooping down the sides as necessary to form a thick sauce.

Serve with *Khagina* (see above) and rice, if liked. The chutney will keep for up to 3 days in the refrigerator, though it tends to lose its bright green colour.

1 bunch of fresh coriander (cilantro), stems and leaves, about 100 g/3½ oz, picked through, washed, patted dry and coarsely chopped
2 hot green fresh chillies (chilies), or to taste,
2 garlic cloves, chopped
Handful of walnuts, about 25 g/1 oz

1½ tbsp light brown sugar
125 ml/4 fl oz/½ cup best quality wine vinegar,
1 tsp salt

**To serve (optional):**
*Khagina* (see above)
Boiled rice

**Serves 6**

# chapter ten
# Southeast Asia

In this chapter I have trawled the colourful region from the Bay of Bengal to the Timor Sea, where several distinct cultures have assimilated the best of the rest of Asia. From China, they've adopted the principle of balancing the fundamental five flavours of hot, sour, salty, bitter and sweet, with added emphasis on the sweet. From India, they've borrowed the technique of grinding spices, garlic and chillies (chilies) into curry pastes, placing emphasis on the chillies. To this foundation they apply fresh indigenous aromatics – lemon grass, kaffir lime leaves, sweet basil, pandanus leaf – often suspending these ravishing perfumes in luscious coconut milk. All of this forms a definitive Southeast Asian cuisine, multiple symphonies of flavour, intended for collective feasting, and most often designed to accompany the sacred grain – rice.

"Food is the ultimate social connector. To share food, to make gifts, offerings or exchanges of food, is to connect oneself to family, friends, superiors, inferiors, spirits and gods. Gods and spirits can no more refuse offerings of food than guests can." Bob Love, *Sundays at Moosewood Restaurant: Southeast Asia*

# meet the expert:
# Sri Owen – Indonesian Cuisine

Sri Owen was born and educated in Indonesia. She is a broadcaster, teacher, writer and consultant specializing in Southeast Asian cooking, and is the author of over 10 books, including *Indonesian Regional Food and Cookery* and *The Rice Book*. She lives in London with her husband Roger.

It was a great privilege to be invited to the Owens' house to witness a session of making tempeh, the delicious native-Javanese fermented soya bean (soybean) cake, an ingredient highly prized by Indonesians and Malays, and a gift to vegetarians in the West. Previously, I had only been able to find tempeh in health food stores, but now, Sri and Roger, armed with a vial of rhizopus oligosporus starter and a mass of soaked soya beans, were about to show me how do it myself. "People who know tempeh regard as the best of all soy products," said Sri, "The chewy texture of the beans…it's so much more interesting than tofu."

As Roger began stripping the soya bean skins and splitting them by rubbing and squeezing them through his fingers, Sri began telling me about the food of her homeland. Indonesia is a complex, huge and varied place, made up of 17,000 islands with over 220 million inhabitants. "Indonesian cuisine is one Asian cuisine by itself," says Sri, "but just as three of Earth's tectonic plates meet there, so do three major culinary influences: Arab, Indian and Chinese. Indonesians adopted the Chinese approach of having three textures and five flavours present in a meal, to achieve balance. Traditionally, they were very thrifty, and good health has always been very important. It's always been preferable to cook food they've grown themselves or bartered from neighbours. It's deeply ingrained in the culture to look after your neighbours and family with wholesome food."

The next phase of the tempeh-making was under way. The stripped, split beans went back in the pan. Roger boiled them up in fresh water with vinegar and simmered for an hour, then drained them and spread on a tablecloth to dry. Sri explained, "They should not become bone-dry, nor should they glisten with moisture. Keep moving the beans around, so they cool evenly. When they reach body temperature, it's time to add the starter." She sprinkled a half-teaspoonful of the live starter over the beans and mixed it through by

hand. We then distributed the beans among sealable polythene bags with tiny holes punched in them. They were flattened, then left to incubate for 24 hours in a warm airing cupboard. "Soya beans alone are difficult to digest, Sri explains. "This problem has long been known in the East, and various solutions have been found, most of them depending on some kind of fermentation of the beans; this, as it were, pre-digests them for us."

The next day, the soya beans (soybeans) have a whitish, silky web fusing them into a compressed cake. They have now become tempeh. Removing the bags from the cupboard, it is time to halt the fermentation process and store the tempeh in the refrigerator or freezer. The beautiful tempeh cakes smell of freshly baked bread and are remarkably warm, a mass of thriving micro-organisms, and they continue generating heat long after going in the refrigerator.

"Most Indonesians would, I fear, apologise for serving tempeh to guests, instead of being proud of it, as they should be," says Sri, "but generally Indonesians are getting more confident about their cuisine and about themselves. Outside Indonesia, the cuisine has been misunderstood – real Indonesian food is a far cry from cliché of the Dutch *rijsttafel* (a rather tacky colonial tradition of banqueting); it's lighter, fresher, less complicated. A typical daily meal is healthy and simple – rice cooked without salt, perhaps some fried fish, tofu or tempeh, fresh steamed vegetables and the obligatory *sambal* or chilli sauce for dipping, as well as a saucer of ketjap manis (a sweet soy sauce). As with other Southeast Asian cuisines, Indonesian cooks are conscious of balancing the sweet-sour-salty-hot elements, as well as texture. Today, I still dream of burying the *rijsttafel* and replacing it with an appreciation of this type of good contemporary Indonesian cooking, using the best and freshest ingredients."

Next we sit down to discuss how we'll cook the best and freshest tempeh imaginable. "Most frequently it will simply be sliced and deep-fried," says Sri, "then dressed in a spicy tomato sauce with fried onions – then we call it *Oseng Oseng* (see page 250). Or it can be simmered in coconut milk, or slow-cooked in a *Rendang* (page 256)."

# focus on ingredients

**Bird's eye chillies (chilies)** – bird, *prik kii noo*, Thai chillies – The rule of thumb with chillies is the smaller, the hotter, and this certainly applies to these tiny chillies. This type ranges in size from 5 mm/¼ inch to 2 cm/¾ inch long and though ferociously hot, they have a distinctive herbal note that cuts right through the heat. They are essential to the authentic flavour of Thai green curry paste.

**Galangal** – *galanga*, Java root, Siamese ginger – This rhizome has similar characteristics to ginger, which can be used as a substitute. It has a creamy white appearance with a thin skin and dark pink nodules. It has a lemony fragrance and peppery heat. It should be peeled and chopped before using. Older galangal, like ginger, becomes very fibrous, but has an intensified flavour. It is believed to have many medicinal properties including anti-bacterial and anti-fungal.

Galangal

**Kaffir lime** – The kaffir lime is a citrus fruit, which looks like a lime on a bad hair day, with a crumpled, knobbly skin. Its juice and pulp is too bitter for cooking but is used as an anti-dandruff remedy. The zest of the lime can be used, but it is the leaves of the kaffir lime that have a unique perfume, for which there is really no substitute. It is a shiny green leaf, which exudes an incredible floral fragrance and flavour. It is quite tough and fibrous, and larger leaves have a hard central stem, which should be discarded; the leaf can then be very finely shredded or used like a bay leaf to infuse flavour. Fresh lime leaves freeze beautifully, so you can always have some to hand. Unfortunately dried lime leaves have lost the magic of the fresh, but can be used as a last resort.

**Lemon grass** – citronella, fever grass – Yes, that's the same citronella as the insect-repellent candles. It also used to treat a host of ailments including colds and stomachache. In cooking, it imparts a soft, lemony aroma. The stalks are pale green at the top and creamy white with layers of pink at the base, where it is most flavourful. It has concentric layers, like an onion, which are oily, fibrous and slightly powdery. The outermost layer should be discarded and the base trimmed before using. It should be used as fresh as possible and when cut, its fragrance dissipates quickly, so it should be used at once. It will keep for weeks in the refrigerator but doesn't take well to freezing.

Lemon grass

**Palm sugar** – jaggery, *gula* – The sweetener of choice in cooking throughout Asia, this sugar is derived from the sap of the palmyra palm tree and many other types of palm besides, though the palmyra is the most prized. When the sap is first extracted it is called "sweet toddy", which is boiled down to a solid sugar. If the sap is allowed to ferment, it quickly becomes "toddy", which is one easy, very intoxicating moonshine! Palm sugar can be quite pale and soft or very dark brown and rock-hard. It has a deep caramel flavour and is wonderful for desserts, but it also represents the all-important sweet aspect to the sweet-sour-salty-hot cornerstones of Asian cooking.

**Pandanus leaf** – pandan leaf – This long, shiny, ridged leaf resembles a giant blade of grass. It is used throughout Asia to add delicate flavour to sweet and savoury dishes. Its nutty aroma is activated only by heat. It is also robust enough to be wrapped around food before cooking, a bit like a banana leaf, but it also imparts a distinctive fragrance. A small strip can be added to rice towards the end of cooking to create a whole other dimension of flavour. Pandanus leaves freeze very well and are often sold this way. The fruit of the plant is used as a starchy vegetable in the Philippines.

**Kaffir Lime Leaves**

**Sweet Basil Leaves**

**Sweet basil** – Thai basil, *horapa* – This herb is a cousin of the Mediterranean basil but quite different in appearance and flavour. The leaves are pointed, ridged and slightly dull with hard purple stems. It is not to be confused with holy basil, which has shaggy edges and a peppery flavour. Sweet basil has a distinctive liquorice flavour and adds sweetness to curries and stir-fries. It should be added towards the end of cooking. It is difficult to keep fresh and should be used quickly after purchase, and like its European relative, should never be refrigerated as it thrives in a hot climate.

**Tempeh** – *tempe* – Originating in Java, Indonesia, these cakes of fermented soya beans (soybeans) are greatly loved in Malaysia and Thailand as well. Tempeh doesn't score very high in the glamour stakes, appearing like a cake of compressed peanuts encased in a web-like mould – this comes from the culture it is injected with. It does, however, take prizes for flavour and nutrition – it tastes very nutty and chewy, and is packed with complete protein and many valuable nutrients. When sliced thinly and fried, it has a somewhat bacon-like texture and a nutty flavour. In the West it is most commonly found in health food stores, either fresh or frozen. Tempeh can be made at home; full instructions can be found in Sri Owen's *The Rice Book* (Frances Lincoln, 2003) (see also page 247).

And now for a little lesson in taste. The sense of taste is like an orchestra. It has six main sections, like the horns, strings, etc. These sections respond to the following six aspects of flavour: sweet, sour, salty, hot (as in chilli), bitter and *umami*, the last being the Japanese name for savoury fermented flavours (think aged soy sauce, blue cheese). The bitter factor is one we generally avoid, but sometimes it is nice, in the case of chocolate or tonic water, for example. The individual instruments in our orchestra of taste are the fragrant and pungent flavours – garlic, herbs and spices. Southeast Asian food demonstrates this metaphor beautifully. It tastes good because it addresses all the aspects of taste with impact and good balance. The all-purpose sauce below is a perfect example of how the sweet–sour–salty–hot aspects combine to delicious effect.

# Fresh Sweet Chilli Sauce Southeast Asia

Simply mix everything together in a bowl and set aside to allow the flavours to develop.

80 ml/2 ¼ fl oz/scant ⅓ cup golden syrup or honey
1 tbsp light soy sauce
1 tbsp lime juice
    or rice vinegar

2 fresh red chillies (chilies), or more to taste, finely chopped
1 plump garlic clove, crushed

**Makes about 125 ml/4 fl oz/½ cup**

If you've never tried tempeh, this recipe is a great doorway into the unknown, as it really brings out its best – it's a wonderfully crunchy, tangy pre-meal nibble or canapé.

# Oseng Oseng Tempe
# Fried Spiced Tempeh Java, Indonesia

Thinly slice the tempeh and cut into 5-cm/2-inch pieces.

Heat the oil in a wok or large saucepan until a piece of shallot sizzles immediately. Deep-fry the tempeh slices, gently stirring from time to time. When light golden, add the shallots to the oil and deep-fry until the shallots and tempeh are deep golden and crispy. Remove with a slotted spoon and drain on kitchen paper (paper towels).

Place the tempeh and shallots in a bowl. In a separate bowl, mix together the remaining ingredients. Stir the sauce through the warm tempeh and serve immediately.

250 g/9 oz tempeh (see page 249)
Sunflower or vegetable oil for deep-frying
4 shallots, finely sliced
1 tbsp tomato purée (paste)
2 tsp light soy sauce
½ tsp caster (superfine) sugar
½ tsp dried chilli (dried red pepper) flakes
    or cayenne pepper, to taste
1 tbsp fresh lime juice

**Serves 4**

A richly warming dish, this is the vegetarian version of what is considered one of Indonesia's national dishes, Sambal Goreng, well known throughout Southeast Asia. The word after *Goreng*, meaning fried, always determines the type, whether it's beef, chicken, fish, shrimp or tofu. Hard-boiled (hard-cooked) eggs or vegetables can also be added to the rich, smooth sauce towards the end of cooking. Rice is essential, and a clean-tasting salad or steamed vegetables balances the richness.

# Sambal Goreng Tahu
# Fried Tofu in Spicy Coconut Sauce Indonesia

Place all the paste ingredients in a blender and purée until smooth, adding more water if necessary to get the blades running freely. Scrape into a saucepan (don't rinse blender yet), bring to the boil and cook, stirring constantly, for about 3–4 minutes, or until thickened and taking on a slightly darker shade of pink. Add the hot water (sloshing it in the blender first to get out remaining paste), lemon grass and lime leaves and simmer for 20 minutes.

Meanwhile, drain tofu and dry well with kitchen paper (paper towels). Cut into 2 cm/1 inch cubes. Heat a wok over a high heat, add oil and fry the tofu until golden. Drain on kitchen paper.

Add the tomatoes and chopped creamed coconut to the sauce and cook for a further 2 minutes to dissolve the coconut, then add the tofu. Stir and leave to stand for 5 minutes, then serve with rice and fresh steamed vegetables.

400 ml/14 fl oz/1¾ cups hot water
1 lemon grass stalk, trimmed
2 kaffir lime leaves
Sunflower oil for frying
250 g/9 oz firm tofu
2 large tomatoes, about 275 g/10 oz, chopped
100 g/3½ oz block creamed coconut, chopped

**For the paste**
3 shallots, peeled and quartered
2 garlic cloves, peeled and halved
5-cm/2-inch piece fresh root ginger, coarsely chopped
3 fresh red chillies (chilies), de-seeded and coarsely chopped if large
6 almonds
1 tsp ground coriander
1 tsp paprika
Salt
1 tbsp lemon juice
2 tbsp sunflower or vegetable oil
About 2 tbsp cold water

**To serve:**
Boiled rice
Steamed vegetables

**Serves 4**

This is the most common dish throughout Indonesia. When my husband was travelling there, he found that in the remote areas, it was nearly the only offering for tourists and locals alike, but he never had it the same twice. Sri Owen, in her book *Indonesian Regional Food and Cookery*, gives this perfect, meatless recipe for *Nasi Goreng*. She emphasizes that the rice should be cooked about 2–3 hours before using in the recipe, as still-hot rice will go soggy, and rice from yesterday will be too stale to make the dish first-rate. "There are right and wrong ways of making *Nasi Goreng*," says Sri. "A good one is light, hot, the grains moist but separate and quite fluffy, the garnish fresh and attractive…its textures contrasting with the texture of the rice." This is how it's done, and it is fabulous.

# Nasi Goreng Fried Rice Indonesia

Cook the rice in plenty of boiling water until tender, then drain and leave to cool completely.

Heat a wok or large saucepan with a lid over a medium heat and add the oil and butter. Add the shallots or onion and fry for 1–2 minutes until slightly softened, then add all remaining ingredients except the rice. Stir for 1 minute, then cover and simmer for 5 minutes, or until the carrot is soft.

Uncover and increase the heat to high. Add the rice and stir-fry until the rice is evenly coated with the reddish sauce and thoroughly hot. Serve immediately with garnishes of your choice.

190 g/6¾ oz/scant 1 cup raw long-grain rice

2 tbsp sunflower oil

15 g/½ oz/1 tbsp butter

3 shallots or 1 small onion, finely chopped

3 medium carrots, about 300 g/11 oz, peeled and chopped small

100 g/3½ oz/1 cup button (white) mushrooms, quartered

1 tsp paprika

1–2 tsp *sambal oelek* (Indonesian chilli/chili sauce) or other chilli (chili) sauce, to taste

1 tbsp tomato purée (paste)

2 tbsp light soy sauce

2 tbsp water

**To garnish (optional):**
4 eggs, scrambled
Sliced spring onion (scallion)
Sliced tomatoes
Sliced cucumber
Chopped watercress

**Serves 4–6**

The key to a good *Gado Gado* is a balance of freshly steamed and raw vegetables, providing the backdrop for some crispy fried tofu, some tempeh perhaps, and some wholesome egg — but it's the sauce that's the star of the show. Nobody can resist a good spicy peanut sauce, and to be at its best, it should be made with freshly roasted peanuts, not peanut butter. The selection of salad components is entirely flexible — use what's seasonal and available.

## Gado Gado
# Vegetable and Egg Salad with Hot Peanut-Coconut Sauce Jakarta, Java

To make the sauce, preheat the oven to 200°C/400°F/Gas Mark 6. Place the raw peanuts on a baking tray and roast for 5–7 minutes until golden. Leave to cool completely.

Place the peanuts in a blender with the remaining sauce ingredients and purée until completely smooth. Taste for seasoning.

When ready to eat, scrape into a medium frying pan and heat over a low-medium heat until hot and a shade darker. Serve with your chosen selection of vegetables and garnishes.

**For the sauce:**
250 g/9 oz/1 ⅔ cups raw blanched peanuts
2 garlic cloves, peeled and halved
2 tbsp chopped palm sugar (jaggery) or light brown sugar
1 tbsp cider vinegar
3 tbsp dark soy sauce
4 tsp *sambal oelek* (Indonesian chilli (chili) sauce) or other chilli sauce
½ tsp cayenne pepper, or to taste
1 x 400 ml/14 fl oz can coconut milk

**For the raw vegetable selection:**
½ cucumber, cut into short thin sticks
2 tomatoes, cut into wedges
2 Little Gem (Boston) lettuces, shredded
4 spring onions (scallions), sliced
½ red (bell) pepper, sliced

**For the cooked vegetable selection:**
100 g/3½ oz French (green) beans, steamed
100 g/3½ oz beansprouts, blanched or covered in boiled water and drained
½ small cauliflower, broken into florets, steamed
2 medium potatoes, steamed or boiled whole, sliced
2 medium carrots, peeled and sliced, steamed

**To garnish:**
4 hard-boiled (hard-cooked) eggs
100 g/3½ oz firm tofu, cubed, fried crisp
100 g/3½ oz tempeh (see page 249), sliced, fried crisp
1 medium onion, finely sliced, fried crisp

**Serves 4–6**

In Bali, this is made with fresh grated coconut, and fresh beans, or beans which have been soaked overnight, cooked and cooled. Using dried coconut and canned beans means you can have the salad ready in five minutes, and a mighty delicious salad at that. Sacrilege? In some circumstances, yes – in this case, to my mind, no, as the amount of effort saved eclipses the small amount of flavour lost. This was one of the favourites of my recipe testers and tasters – it has a classic light flavour further lifted by the mint. Adapted from Sri Owen's *Indonesian Regional Food and Cookery*.

# Jakut Murab
# Black-eyed Bean (Black-eye Pea) Salad Bali

Place the coconut in a bowl and pour over the boiling water. Leave to cool.

Mix the lime juice, sugar, chilli and salt through the coconut to form the dressing.

Combine the beans, cucumbers, spring onions and mint in a bowl. Stir through the dressing and serve immediately.

50 g/2 oz/½ cup desiccated (dry) unsweetened coconut

50 ml/2 fl oz/¼ cup boiling water

2 tbsp fresh lime juice

1 tsp light brown sugar

1 fresh hot red chilli (chili), chopped

½ tsp salt, or to taste

1 x 400 g/14 oz can black-eyed beans (black-eye peas), drained

2 baby Lebanese cucumbers, or ½ English cucumber, halved and sliced

3 spring onions (scallions), finely sliced

2 tbsp chopped fresh mint

**Serves 4**

It's very easy to throw together, but classic *Rendang* does have a long cooking time and there is no way around this. The coconut milk must reduce so much and so slowly that it eventually separates into sediment and oil; the sediment is called "*blondo*". I promise you, it's worth the wait. Few vegetarian ingredients can stand up to the lengthy cooking time without disintegrating, however you could use fried tofu or tempeh (see page 249). Alternatively, you could cook the gravy separately and add vegetables later, as I've done with the kidney beans here.

This is an opportunity, however, to invite you to try green (unripe) jackfruit, readily available in cans in Asian food stores. The flesh has a fruity but not particularly sweet flavour, and the texture is the marvellous thing about it, being fibrous yet soft. It's advisable to use the canned – fresh jackfruit is difficult to tackle, it's huge, with a scaly green skin, large seeds and a sticky juice that stains clothes and fingers.

# Rendang Nangka
# Slow-cooked Jackfruit in Coconut

Sumatra

Place the shallots, garlic, ginger, chillies, galangal (if using) and turmeric in a blender with a splash of coconut milk and blend until smooth. Place in a large, heavy based saucepan and add the remaining coconut milk (I use some to slosh around the emptied blender, to get all remaining paste out.) Add the bay leaf, lemon grass, salt and jackfruit and bring to the boil.

Reduce the heat to medium and simmer rapidly for 2 hours, stirring occasionally. After 2 hours, the gravy will become very thick and more frequent stirring will be necessary. The objective is to cook until the gravy is so thick that it just coats the jackfruit, and a golden crust starts to form as it catches on the base of the pan. Use a metal spatula to keep scraping the crust and letting a new one form. When you have done this once or twice, add the kidney beans. Keep stirring and scraping a few more times. This will take another 30 minutes or so. Serve hot with rice and fresh green vegetables.

3 shallots, peeled and quartered

2 garlic cloves, degermed

2-cm/¾-inch piece fresh root ginger, peeled and coarsely chopped

½ tsp turmeric

3 fresh red chillies (chilies), de-seeded and coarsely chopped if large

1 tsp chopped galangal (optional)

3 x 400 g/14 fl oz cans coconut milk

1 bay leaf

1 lemon grass stalk, 1 outer layer removed

1 tsp salt

2 x 565 g/1 lb 2 oz cans green/young jackfruit in water, drained

1 x 400 g/14 oz can red kidney beans, drained

**To serve:**

Boiled rice

Fresh steamed green vegetables

The Philippines, according to Raymond Sokolov, is the "farthest-flung outpost of the Hispanic kitchen." The food is a curious mix of Asian and Spanish, and there are countless dishes of meat, fish and vegetables in "*adobo*". But not in the Spanish sense, where *adobo*, from the verb *adobar*, to marinate, is a sauce of wine and spice, or in the Mexican sense, where it's usually a thick tomato and chilli sauce. Filipino *adobo* is a clear garlic and vinegar sauce. This is one most delicious treatments of greens I have come across.

*Kangkong* is also known as water spinach or swamp cabbage, the favourite greens of the Philippines. Any delicate greens are suitable, including bok choy and choi sum. I've used the old faithful, spinach, below.

# Kangkong Adobo
# Greens in Sour Sauce Philippines

Place the prepared spinach in a large bowl and pour over boiling water to cover, stir and leave for a few minutes to wilt. Drain thoroughly – it should now have condensed considerably, making it easier to handle.

To make the sauce, mix the cornflour and water together in a bowl until smooth, then stir in the vinegar, lime juice, soy sauce and lots of black pepper.

Heat a wok or large saucepan over a medium-high heat and add the oil. Add the garlic and as soon as it is fragrant, stir the sauce mixture and pour into the pan. Stir while it thickens, and when thick and bubbly, stir in the wilted spinach quickly and serve as soon as it is heated through.

700 g/1½ lb fresh spinach (trimmed weight), large stems removed, thoroughly washed and coarsely chopped
1 tbsp cornflour (cornstarch)
1 tbsp water
4 tbsp cider vinegar
1 tbsp lime juice
3 tbsp dark soy sauce
Freshly ground black pepper
4 tbsp sunflower oil
6 garlic cloves, finely chopped

**Serves 4–6**

This is such a gorgeous dish that I can only think the mother-in-law was really out to impress her daughter's partner. Crisp-fried boiled eggs with hot and tangy tamarind sauce – a total revelation. It's very low on labour as well if you don't mind the deep-frying, which is the only way to achieve the required texture and appearance of the eggs, garnished with delectable crispy garlic and shallots – ambrosia! One egg is sufficient as a first course, two as the main course supplemented with rice and vegetables.

# Kai Look Koie
# Son-in-Law Eggs Thailand

First make the tamarind sauce. Place the tamarind in a small saucepan and pour over the boiling water. Bring to the boil and simmer for 10–15 minutes until the flesh falls off the seeds. Strain into a bowl, then return the tamarind water to the pan. Add the ginger, cumin, chilli and sugar and stir. Bring to the boil, then reduce to a simmer and cook until thick, about 10–15 minutes. Taste at this stage – tamarind can have a natural saltiness to it, so if you don't think it is salty enough, add soy sauce to taste. Remove the saucepan from the heat and set aside.

Meanwhile, place the eggs in a saucepan and cover with cold water. Bring to the boil and simmer for 8 minutes. Drain and cool under cold running water. When cool enough to handle, peel the eggs, rinse and dry them thoroughly.

Heat a 5 cm/2 inch depth of oil in a wok or large, deep saucepan until a piece of shallot sizzles immediately – the oil should be shimmering but not smoking. Alternatively, use a deep-fat fryer and heat the oil to 190°C/375°F. Have ready a plate lined with kitchen paper (paper towels). Add all the shallots to the oil and cook until just golden but not burnt, about 1–2 minutes. Remove with a slotted spoon and drain on kitchen paper (paper towels). Repeat with the garlic.

Next add the eggs to the oil. Deep-fry, rolling them gently with the slotted spoon for even cooking, until deep golden and crisp all over, about 5 minutes. Drain.

Line up the lettuce leaves on a plate and spoon the now tepid tamarind sauce inside them. Top with an egg and garnish with fried shallots and garlic.

6 organic eggs
Vegetable oil for deep-frying
6 shallots, finely sliced
6 garlic cloves, finely sliced
6 Little Gem (Boston) lettuce leaves

**For the tamarind sauce:**
100 g/3½ oz tamarind, about
　5 x 5-cm/2 x 2-inch piece (see page 222)
250 ml/8 fl oz/1 cup boiling water
1 tsp finely grated fresh root ginger
1 tsp ground cumin
1 small fresh red chilli (chili), sliced
2 tsp dark brown sugar
Light soy sauce to taste (optional)

**Serves 3–6**

Thai papayas grow to watermelon-size proportions, and unripe marrow-sized specimens are the key ingredient for this dish. There is an alternative which is a fine impersonator: the humble turnip. It shares the crisp texture of the green papaya and delivers all these intense flavours with finesse.

# Som Tum Hot and Sour Green Papaya Salad Thailand

To make the dressing, pound the garlic, chillies and salt to a paste in a heavy mortar, then whisk in the remaining ingredients. Alternatively, whiz everything in the blender. Taste for seasoning – there should be a good balance of sweet, sour, salty and hot.

For the salad, combine the grated papaya, green beans, pepper, tomato, spring onions, mint and half the peanuts. Stir the dressing through the salad, then sprinkle with the remaining peanuts.

**For the dressing:**
2 garlic cloves, peeled
2 fresh red chillies (chilies), stem removed
½ tsp coarse crystal sea salt
4 tbsp light soy sauce
4 tbsp lime juice
4 tbsp chopped palm sugar (jaggery) or light brown sugar

**For the salad:**
300 g/11 oz green papaya, peeled, de-seeded and grated, or use turnip or swede (rutabaga)

100 g/3 ½ oz green beans, diagonally sliced
1 red (bell) pepper, de-seeded and thinly sliced
1 medium tomato, de-seeded and cut into strips
4 spring onions (scallions), sliced
2 handfuls of fresh mint leaves
50 g/2 oz/⅓ cup toasted peanuts, ground

**Serves 4**

Typically this would not be served as an alternative to plain boiled rice. It is sweet and rich and is a gorgeous accompaniment to *Som Tum* (above), or steamed or stir-fried vegetables. This recipe is adapted from David Thompson's mind-bogglingly comprehensive *Thai Food*.

# Hung Kao Man Gati Coconut Rice Thailand

Rinse the rice, place in a bowl and cover with plenty of cold water. Leave to soak for at least 2 hours. Drain the rice and place in a heavy-based saucepan with a lid. Add the pandanus leaves, if using. In a bowl or measuring jug, combine the coconut cream, water, salt and sugar. Pour over the rice. Bring to the boil over a medium heat, stirring to prevent separation. When boiling, reduce the heat to a simmer, cover and leave to cook for 15 minutes. If cooked, remove from the heat and leave for 5 minutes before serving. If not yet cooked, stir, cover and cook for a few more minutes.

380 g/13½ oz/2 cups Thai jasmine rice
2 pandanus leaves (see page 249), tied in knots (optional)
500 ml/16 fl oz/2 cups coconut cream
250 ml/8 fl oz/1 cup water
Large pinch of sea salt
1 tbsp chopped palm sugar (jaggery), or golden caster (superfine) sugar

**Serves 4–6**

Thai curries are one of the quickest dishes to throw together once you have the paste ready – you simply chop and fry some vegetables in the paste, add some coconut milk and adjust the flavour – all done in 5–10 minutes. Store-bought Thai curry pastes almost invariably contain shrimp, although I have come across some special Thai pastes without. In any case, if you make it yourself as below, you'll have one mind-blowingly delicious curry instead of a middle-of-the-road one. The paste can be made ahead and kept for up to three days in the refrigerator, although the aromatics are more pungent if used sooner.

# Geng Gwio Green Curry Thailand

For the curry, place the chopped creamed coconut in a bowl and pour the boiling water over it. Leave for a couple of minutes, then stir until smooth.

To make the paste, whiz all the ingredients for the paste together in a blender, adding more water if necessary to get the blades moving, so a smooth, barely pourable paste results.

Heat a large, heavy-based saucepan or wok over a medium heat and add the paste. Stir until fragrant, then add the onion, beans and broccoli. Cook, stirring for a couple of minutes until slightly softened, then add the smooth coconut mixture and sugar and bring to the boil. Adjust the consistency to your preference, adding a little more water if you prefer a thinner gravy.

Add the bamboo shoots and bean curd and simmer for 5 minutes. Stir in the Thai basil leaves. Taste the gravy and adjust the seasoning, adding more light soy sauce or sugar to achieve a balanced flavour. You may even like to add a little more lime juice or chilli.

Serve each portion on a bed of rice with ½ tbsp coconut cream dribbled over the top and some shredded lime leaves.

200 g/7 oz block creamed coconut, chopped
500 ml/16 fl oz/2 cups boiling water
1 medium onion, halved and coarsely sliced from head to base
200 g/7 oz French (green) beans, cut into 2.5-cm/1-inch pieces
1 medium head of broccoli, cut into florets
2 tsp chopped palm sugar (jaggery), or golden caster (superfine) sugar
1 x 200 g/7 oz can shredded or sliced bamboo shoots, drained
300 g/11 oz fried bean curd, sliced
Large handful of fresh Thai sweet basil
Light soy sauce (optional)
Boiled rice, to serve

**For the paste:**

4 spring onions (scallions), coarsely chopped
2 garlic cloves
Large handful of fresh coriander (cilantro), coarsely chopped
3 lemon grass stalks, coarsely chopped
6 fresh thin green chillies (chilies)
2.5-cm/1-inch thumb of fresh root ginger, coarsely chopped
4 kaffir lime leaves, middle stem removed, coarsely chopped
2 tsp ground cumin
¼ tsp turmeric
4 tbsp light soy sauce
1 tbsp lime juice
1 tsp sea salt
1 tbsp sunflower oil
1–2 tbsp water

**To garnish (optional):**

2 tbsp coconut cream
4 kaffir lime leaves, middle stem removed, finely shredded

**Serves 4**

These fantastic little garlicky sweetcorn fritters use two types of flour in the batter: rice flour makes them super-crisp on the outside, while self-raising wheat flour gives them a light and fluffy texture inside. The fresh sweetcorn kernels burst with juice between the teeth – so it's very important to fry these over a mellow heat, to prevent the kernels getting over-excited and exploding in the pan.

Fresh sweetcorn is a seasonal ingredient and isn't always available. Frozen is the next best thing, and is actually a great product because the corn is frozen close to harvesting, thus retaining the sweetness. Use canned sweetcorn as a last resort. Cornflour can be substituted for rice flour if unavailable, as it has a similar ultra-starchy quality and fries very crisp.

# Tod Mun Kao Pode
# Curried Sweetcorn (Corn) Fritters Thailand

To prepare the fresh sweetcorn, stand each cob of corn upright in a large bowl and use a sharp knife to strip the kernels, shaving downwards.

If using frozen sweetcorn kernels, pour over boiling water to cover and leave for a minute or two, then drain.

Place the sweetcorn in a large bowl and stir in both flours. In a separate bowl, beat together the curry paste, crushed garlic, coriander, lime leaves, if using, egg and the water. Stir into the kernel mixture, season with salt and pepper, and combine thoroughly to form a thick batter.

Heat a shallow pool of oil in a non-stick frying pan over a low-medium heat, until a drop of batter sizzles immediately. Place level tablespoons of batter in the oil and smooth down to form little round cakes. Cook on both sides until golden brown, then drain on kitchen paper (paper towels). Serve with Fresh Sweet Chilli Sauce.

2 corn-on-the-cobs (ears fresh corn), husks stripped, or 250 g/9 oz/generous 2 cups frozen sweetcorn (corn) kernels

3 tbsp rice flour or cornflour (cornstarch)

3 tbsp self-raising (self-rising) flour

2 tbsp vegetarian red curry paste, from a jar, or fresh green curry paste (see *Geng Gwio* on page 261)

2 garlic cloves, crushed

Small handful of fresh coriander (cilantro), finely chopped

2 kaffir lime leaves, middle stem removed, very finely chopped

1 organic egg

50 ml/2 fl oz/¼ cup water

Sunflower oil for frying

Fresh Sweet Chilli (Chili) Sauce (see page 250), to serve

**Makes 20**

My friend Tou, a Thai chef, showed me how to make this soup after I begged for the recipe, having eaten it in her restaurant. This is one instance where I will not resort to the convenience of canned coconut milk. The canned stuff will make a decent soup, but the simple method below using dried coconut makes an outstanding soup, memorable for its delicate, fragrant character. Tou always makes coconut milk this way and uses it in all her coconut-based dishes, including curries. Now I do too, when I have the time.

Straw mushrooms are a South-east Asian favourite, but you are far more likely to find them in cans than fresh, available in Asian food stores. Served whole, they are rather alarmingly eyeball-like and I much prefer to slice them in half, to drain the liquid captured inside and to reveal the adorable premature mushroom figure framed inside the outer capsule. If you can't find straw mushrooms, use fresh button (white) mushrooms instead.

# Tom Kha Hed
# Coconut Soup with Mushrooms Thailand

Place the coconut in a bowl and pour over the boiling water. Leave to cool. Purée with a hand-held mixer or in a blender, then push through a sieve (strainer), squeezing out as much coconut milk as possible. Just under 1 litre/1¾ pints/4 cups should remain.

Slice the galangal or ginger and lemon grass (doing this now will maximize the flavour; these will infuse the broth but will not necessarily be eaten) and place in a saucepan with the coconut milk, soy sauce and sugar.

Bring to the boil and simmer for 10 minutes, stirring occasionally. Add the mushrooms, return to the boil and simmer for 3 minutes. Taste for seasoning, adding more soy sauce or sugar as desired. Ladle into small bowls. Squeeze lemon juice into each bowl and top with coriander leaves. Serve.

250 g/9 oz/2½ cups unsweetened desiccated (dry) coconut

1.2 litres/2 pints/5 cups boiling water

4-cm/1 ½-inch thumb fresh galangal or fresh root ginger, peeled

2 pieces lemon grass, trimmed

2 tbsp light soy sauce, or to taste

1 tbsp chopped palm sugar (jaggery) or light brown sugar

100 g/3½ oz/½ cup canned straw mushrooms, drained and halved

50 g/2 oz/½ cup oyster mushrooms, sliced

1 tbsp lemon juice

Handful of fresh coriander (cilantro) leaves

This is one of the most astonishingly addictive dishes I have come across in this culinary quest. The super-sweet "fondue" is a pleasurable assault on the sense of taste, a four-pronged attack on the receptors of sweet, sour, salty and hot – and the cool fruit and cucumber are the perfect vehicles for this. You can also serve this as a fruit salad with the dip as a dressing, though spearing the cold fruit and dunking it in the fiery syrup completes a totally ambrosial experience. This is more of a snack than a dessert, though it does make a cracking finish to a meal. Or try it as a canapé or appetizer – it really stimulates the appetite.

# Penang Rojak
# Sweet Chilli Fondue with Fruit and Cucumber Malaysia

Place the fruit and cucumber in a bowl and pour over enough cold water to cover. Dissolve the salt in the water and leave to chill in the refrigerator for at least 30 minutes or up to 2 hours.

Crush the chilli and sea salt to a paste in a mortar with a pestle. Alternatively, wearing gloves, chop the chilli very fine, then grind the salt through it with the side of your knife. In a bowl or in the mortar, combine the chilli paste with the brown sugar, lime juice and water. Stir very thoroughly until the sugar has mostly dissolved into a thick syrup. Add a little more water if necessary.

Scoop the fondue into a small glass or a vessel which is slightly more upright than an ordinary bowl, to provide depth for dipping.

Drain the fruit thoroughly and pile into a bowl. Place some bamboo skewers in the bowl to use for skewering, then serve with the fondue.

1 large, firm, underripe mango, peeled and cut into bite-sized chunks

1 star fruit (carambola), sliced

1 baby or ½ regular pineapple, peeled and cored, cut into bite-sized chunks

½ English cucumber, cut into bite-sized chunks

1 tsp salt

**For the fondue:**

1 small fresh red chilli (chili), stem removed

½ tsp coarse sea salt

100 g/3½ oz/½ cup soft brown sugar

1 tbsp lime juice

1 tbsp water

**Serves 4–6**

By now you may be getting your *sambal/sambol/sambars* all mixed up, so just to clarify, they all share a common ingredient: chilli, and usually red chilli. Red chilli is sweeter than green chilli, as it has ripened and the starches have converted to sugars. *Sambal* will normally be a slightly sweet, hot, red sauce, often with tomato, and often containing another *sambal* as an ingredient – *sambal oelek* – this is a tangy Indonesian chilli paste, which is a very useful item to have in the refrigerator for instant heat injection, and widely available. *Sambar* is the red-hot South Indian soup, similar to *Dal* (see page 235). *Sambol* is a coconut chutney spiked with red chilli (see *Hoppers with Sambol* on page 225). This *Sambal* is very quick and easy and even tofu-sceptics are likely to love it.

# Tofu Sambal
# Tofu in Spicy Tomato Sauce Malaysia

Place the tofu in a bowl and pour over the soy sauce. Leave to marinate for 20–30 minutes, then drain thoroughly.

Heat a wok or large saucepan with a lid over a medium-high heat and add the oil. Add the tofu and fry – stand back as it may splutter – turning with tongs, until golden on all sides. Drain on kitchen paper (paper towels), leaving the remaining oil in the wok.

Add the onion to the wok and stir-fry for 1–2 minutes, or until slightly softened, then add the garlic and ginger and fry until fragrant, about 1 minute. Add the remaining ingredients and stir. Stir in the tofu, cover and simmer for 2–3 minutes. Serve hot with rice.

250 g/9 oz firm tofu, drained and cut into 2.5-cm/1-inch cubes

125 ml/4 fl oz/½ cup light soy sauce

4 tbsp sunflower oil

1 large onion, finely sliced

2 garlic cloves, chopped

2.5-cm/1-inch piece fresh root ginger, peeled and finely chopped

1 tbsp *sambal oelek* (Indonesian chilli (chili) paste/sauce) or other chilli sauce, to taste

1 tbsp tomato purée (paste)

½ tsp sea salt

2 tsp chopped palm sugar (jaggery), or light brown sugar

2 plump vine-ripened tomatoes, about 275 g/10 oz, finely chopped

80 ml/3¾ fl oz/scant ⅓ cup water

Boiled rice, to serve

**Serves 4**

This classic dish is part soup, part salad, part noodle dish – so there's only really one word to describe it, and that's *laksa*. The recipe has several separate stages, but fear not, they are all easy and come together to create one fabulous meal-in-a-bowl. The distinctive perfume of fresh lemon grass and lime leaves make up part of this spice paste, but if you have difficulty acquiring them don't be put off, just leave them out. You could also use a store-bought *laksa* paste or Thai curry paste instead, though bear in mind that they often contain ground shrimp.

# Laksa
# Curried Coconut Noodle Soup Malaysia

First cook the pumpkin. Place in a saucepan with the water and a little salt. Bring to the boil and simmer until tender, about 10 minutes. Do not overcook or it may turn mushy. Drain and reserve the cooking water.

Meanwhile, make the spice paste by whizzing everything to a smooth purée in a spice grinder or blender. Add a little extra water if necessary to get the blades moving freely.

Heat the sunflower oil in a frying pan to a depth of 1 cm/½ inch. Add the tofu and fry until golden and crisp all over. Drain on kitchen paper (paper towels).

Dissolve the chopped creamed coconut in the boiling water. Heat a wok or large saucepan over a medium heat and add 2 tbsp of the sunflower oil. Add the spice paste and fry for 2 minutes to release the flavours, then add the coconut milk, bean curd, soy sauce and sugar. Add the pumpkin water to the wok. Taste for seasoning. Bring to the boil and simmer for 10 minutes.

Place the noodles in a bowl and pour over boiling water. Leave to soak until tender, about 5 minutes, then drain. Place 4 serving bowls in the oven to warm, and assemble the remaining ingredients.

When the coconut broth is cooked, take the bowls from the oven and align in a row. Place in each a nest of noodles, some pumpkin, a nest of beansprouts and 2 tomato wedges. Use tongs to place a piece of tofu in each bowl, then ladle over the hot coconut broth. Top each bowl with cucumber sticks, mint leaves, coriander sprigs and chopped spring onion. Eat with knife, fork and spoon.

250 g/9 oz/2 cups cubed pumpkin, or orange-fleshed squash such as butternut or kaboucha

600 ml/1 pint/2½ cups water

Sea salt

Sunflower oil for frying

300 g/11 oz tofu, patted dry and cut into 4 triangles

200 g/7 oz block creamed coconut, chopped (2 x 400 ml/14 fl oz cans coconut milk can be substituted)

600 ml/1 pint/2½ cups boiling water

4 tbsp light soy sauce

2 tsp sugar

150 g/5 oz rice vermicelli noodles

150 g/5 oz/2 cups beansprouts

1 medium tomato, cut into 8 wedges

5-cm/2-inch piece of cucumber, cut into short thin sticks

Generous handful of fresh mint leaves

8 fresh coriander (cilantro) sprigs

2 spring onions (scallions), chopped

**For the spice paste:**

2 garlic cloves, coarsely chopped

2 fresh fleshy red chillies (chilies), de-seeded and coarsely chopped

5-cm/2-inch thumb of fresh root ginger, peeled and finely grated

1 small onion or ½ medium onion

½ tsp turmeric

2 lemon grass stalks, sliced

4 fresh lime leaves, middle stem discarded, chopped

3 tbsp water

**Serves 4**

An exquisite treatment of cucumbers, where they become an assertive vegetable in a starring role. This is one case where a larger cucumber is the only one for the job – delicate baby cucumbers would be overwhelmed by the cooking and spicing. Serve with *Bahn Xeo* (see opposite), *Jakut Murab* (page 255), *Tofu Sambal* (page 266) and rice or noodles.

## Thanhat
# Spicy Cooked Cucumber Salad

Myanmar (Burma)

Peel the cucumbers, cut in half lengthways and scoop out the seeds. Cut each half in two crossways, forming 8 pieces. Place in a saucepan and pour over boiling water to cover. Add 3 tbsp of the vinegar and place over a medium heat. Cover and bring to the boil, then simmer for about 15 minutes, by which time the cucumbers should have become somewhat translucent. Drain, return cucumbers to the pan, sprinkle with the salt and set aside to cool.

Heat a large frying pan over a medium heat and add oil. Add the onions and garlic and fry until golden, then remove with a slotted spoon. Remove the frying pan from the heat and leave the oil to cool slightly. Stir the turmeric, sugar, remaining vinegar and black pepper into the oil. Pour over the cucumbers and toss to coat. Empty the contents of the pan on to a plate. Scatter the onions and garlic over the cucumbers. Chill thoroughly before serving.

2 large English cucumbers
6 tbsp rice vinegar
1 tsp salt
125 ml/4 fl oz/½ cup sunflower oil
2 medium onions, halved and thinly sliced
4 garlic cloves, sliced
1 tsp turmeric
1 tsp sugar
Freshly ground black pepper

**Serves 4**

This delectable yolk-yellow pancake with fragrant and crunchy vegetables makes a fine snack or part of a feast, here with its minimal filling of beansprouts. It can easily be turned into a fabulous main course by adding a few fried shiitake mushrooms and tofu with the sprouts. I've been served this pancake both fried crisp and soft like a crêpe – of course the latter is easier on the waistline – but for a crispy pancake simply use more oil.

# Banh Xeo
# Coconut Pancake with Beansprouts

Vietnam

Preheat the oven to 120°C/250°F/Gas Mark ½ for keeping warm.

To make the pancake batter, place the flour, eggs, coconut milk, turmeric and salt in a blender and whiz until smooth. Heat a medium non-stick frying pan over a medium heat and add 1 tsp of the oil. Pour in a quarter of the batter in a thin layer and swirl the pan to coat the base. Sprinkle with spring onions before it sets. When golden underneath, flip over and cook until golden. Remove to a plate and keep warm. Make 3 more pancakes.

Place the beansprouts in a bowl and pour boiling water over them to cover. Leave for 2 minutes, then drain thoroughly.

To serve, place a handful of beansprouts on one half of each pancake and fold over. Serve with cucumber, coriander and mint sprigs and lettuce. To eat, roll all together and dip in the nuoc cham sauce.

**For the pancakes:**

4 tbsp flour

3 organic eggs

100 ml/3½ fl oz/generous ⅓ cup canned coconut milk

¼ tsp turmeric

Large pinch of salt

4 tsp sunflower oil

4 spring onions (scallions), sliced

**To serve:**

200 g/7 oz/4 cups beansprouts

½ cucumber, sliced

4 fresh coriander (cilantro) sprigs

4 fresh mint sprigs

Few lettuce leaves

1 x quantity *nuoc cham* dressing (see Hot and Sour Noodle Salad, see page 271)

**Serves 4**

This gorgeous, light main course salad sings the harmony of the fragrant exotic herbs against a backdrop of intense, five-pronged flavour from the dressing – it just epitomizes Southeast Asian food and all that's so desirable about it. A fabulous summer lunch, this is an impressive little number for entertaining, though I recommend you plate it up individually – the noodles can be a bit unruly for self-service, and the concluding garnishes should be artistically finessed by the cook.

# Bún Dau Xào Xa
# Hot and Sour Noodle Salad with Tofu and Lemon Grass

Vietnam

To make the dressing, combine all the ingredients thoroughly, stirring until the sugar dissolves. Set aside.

Slice the tofu into 2.5 x 5-cm/1 x 2-inch strips. Heat a shallow pool of oil in a large frying pan until a tiny piece of tofu sizzles immediately. Add the tofu and fry on both sides, turning with tongs, until golden and crisp. Drain on kitchen paper (paper towels).

Place the rice vermicelli and beansprouts in a large bowl and pour over enough boiling water to cover. Leave to stand until the noodles are cooked, about 4 minutes. Drain thoroughly. Return the noodles and beansprouts to the dry bowl and add the lemon grass, herbs and spring onions. Using clean hands, mix together thoroughly until evenly combined. Divide between 4 serving plates or bowls. Top with clusters of fried tofu, tomatoes and cucumber. Pour the dressing over the salads and sprinkle with peanuts.

200 g/7 oz fresh firm tofu, drained and patted dry

Sunflower or vegetable oil, for frying

125 g/4 oz rice vermicelli or thin rice sticks

100 g/3½ cups/2 cups beansprouts

2 lemon grass stalks, trimmed and sliced very finely (see page 248)

Generous handful of fresh coriander (cilantro), chopped

Generous handful of fresh sweet Thai basil, chopped (see page 249) or fresh mint, chopped

2 spring onions (scallions), finely sliced

2 vine-ripened tomatoes, cored and cut into wedges

½ cucumber, cut in thin batons (short thin sticks)

50 g/2 oz/⅓ cup roasted peanuts (2 handfuls), chopped

**For the *nuoc cham* dressing:**

80 ml/3¾ fl oz/scant ⅓ cup fresh lime juice

80 ml/3¾ fl oz/scant ⅓ cup light soy sauce

4 tbsp caster (superfine) sugar

½ tsp dried chilli (dried red pepper) flakes, or to taste

2 garlic cloves, crushed

3 tbsp coarsely grated carrot

**Serves 4**

# chapter eleven Australasia

The cuisine of Australia and New Zealand is almost completely bereft of a vegetarian tradition. Before the first English and Scottish immigrants – mostly exiled convicts – arrived in the late 1700s, the native Aborigines in Australia were eating some wild plants, but mostly insects, reptiles and game, and the New Zealand Maoris, descendents of Polynesians, had a few cultivated plants but thrived mostly on birds and seafood. As the flow of immigration began to increase in the 1800s, colonial cooks started using indigenous foods, but much of it was meat-based and vegetable cookery remained unimaginative. Cakes, pies, scones, biscuits (cookies) and puddings, however, became a national obsession and the baking tradition remains strong to this day.

Being a clean slate in the area of gastronomy, this region was ripe for a revolution. The turning point came in the early 1980s, first in Australia and later in New Zealand, when innovative photographers such as Geoff Lung began taking pictures of food that actually made you salivate. Writers in major magazines started enthusing about restaurant chefs and turning them into celebrities for the first time. These factors, combined with the proximity of Asia, the quality and abundance of ingredients, and the knowledge and passion of Mediterranean and Asian immigrants, provoked an eruption, which precipitated a confident, experimental and stylish cuisine. This chapter is unlike any other, as it celebrates contemporary food – it is fitting to finish on this note, with one foot in the future of a culinary paradise.

"(Australian food) bows to the past, sends kisses to Europe, shakes hands with Asia, and is happy at home in its own back yard." Jill Dupleix, *New Food*

# meet the expert:
# Nadine Abensur – Australian Cuisine

Nadine Abensur is author of *The Cranks Bible – A Timeless Collection of Vegetarian Recipes*, among many other vegetarian cookbooks. She was born in Casablanca to French-Jewish parents who loved entertaining; during these formative years, she absorbed a huge amount of culinary knowledge. She has travelled extensively in Australia, and has now made it her home.

Cranks Restaurant was a vegetarian institution in the UK, which started in the 1960s. When Nadine became Food Director, it still had a rather old-fashioned image, which she transformed through her innovative menus and cookbooks. Cranks has now closed its doors and Nadine has moved on to sunnier climes. While she was back in the UK for a visit, I asked her how vegetarianism is viewed in Australia today. "Well, I have to say that I never hear the word! Which isn't to say that people don't like their greens – quite the opposite – but vegetarian food is very well integrated into cooking and eating," says Nadine. "I live in Byron Bay – hippy-ville *par excellence* – but there isn't a single vegetarian restaurant. The mainstream restaurants do a good job of catering to vegetarian needs – having said that, many people who call themselves vegetarian do eat fish."

Australia may be the land of the "barbie" (barbecue), but with such a contemporary food style, hospitable climate and strong Asian influence, Aussie food that is vegetarian must be at its best. "With the varied influences affecting Australian food right now, it's rare to find a restaurant or cafe that doesn't have its version of a 'veggie stack', or several warm salads with some sort of roasted vegetable at its core," says Nadine. "But people don't like the proselytizing that goes hand-in-hand with the 'ism' in 'vegetarianism', so it's all veggo food or veggie food." I agree wholeheartedly – I've long been in favour of trading in what I call "The V word" for a more modern term.

"Sweet potatoes, avocados, pumpkin, mangoes and macadamia nuts pop up in many dishes, as they grow so prolifically there," says Nadine. "I've lost track of the number of the times I've been stopped in a supermarket when I've had celeriac (celery root), artichokes or fennel in my basket. People are fascinated – they want to know what to do with them. From my own perspective, I was brought up on an extremely varied diet, which took in the influences of Morocco and the Mediterranean. The cooking of my childhood was exceptionally refined and cooked by true masters of their art, which gave me a visceral understanding of food that I've never lost." Nadine perceives Oz as a burgeoning food culture, and it seems people are hungry for more. "When a newspaper ran an article about my veggie classes, I was inundated with calls, and still am," she says.

The "meat-and-two-veg" mentality is still a lingering leftover from the British settlers, but it is swiftly being replaced. "The arrival first of Greek and Italian immigrants, then later the Asians, has had a huge impact. Australian food right now is incredibly eclectic and cosmopolitan with a rare and often successful element of daring. Fusion cooking gets a bad press but when it is done well, it is truly marvellous."

# focus on ingredients

**Medjool Dates**

Dates – The fruit of the date palm is thought to be native to the Middle East and India and has a long history – the ancient Egyptians made wine out of them and the Romans used them as an all-purpose sweetener instead of sugar. They are a favourite

**Star Anise**

throughout the Islamic world, especially at Ramadan, when they are eaten as a metabolism-boosting fast-breaker at the end of daylight hours. Because of their extremely high sugar content, they make delectable desserts as well as perking up savoury dishes. The Australian classic Sticky Date and Toffee Pudding is legendary, as are the Dates Stuffed with Vodka-Spiked Roquefort (see page 293). There are many varieties; some are sold compacted into blocks, which are destined for cooking, others are sold very fresh and are best peeled. Plump dessert dates such as medjool are the finest. Always remove the stone (pit) before eating – it's rare but occasionally little critters have found their way into the centre of the date!

Star anise – Probably the most beautiful looking spice, the star-shaped, rusty-brown pod usually has 8 points encasing flat, glossy seeds. It is the fruit of an evergreen shrub native to the Far East. Usually it is not ground because of its delightful appearance, except when it is one of the spices in Chinese "five-spice" powder along with fennel, cloves, cinnamon or cassia, and Szechuan pepper. Used whole, it infuses its aniseed- (anise-) like flavour into syrups, sauces, marinades and coatings (see Baked Ricotta on page 276), and though it is not botanically related to aniseed (anise), it contains the same oil called anethole, which gives it the distinctive liquorice flavour.

Macadamia nuts – With the highest fat content of all nuts, these buttery morsels are native to Australia and grow on trees. They are an asset to sweet recipes, especially biscuits (cookies), brownies and chocolates and they make an unbelievably good brittle. As with all nuts, they are also wonderful in savoury dishes, especially sprinkled over salads, and their flavour is maximized by a light toasting and salting. Most macadamia nut cultivation today takes place in Hawaii.

Soy sauce – This may seem like an odd chapter for this essential ingredient to land, as it's originally from China, but in Australia it is without a doubt the most important condiment, a reflection of how

Asian food has been absorbed into their culture. Manufacture involves a several month-long process of fermenting soya beans (soybeans) with wheat and salt. The Japanese have developed particularly flavourful varieties of soy sauce such as shoyu and tamari, which is made without wheat. Light soy sauce has less of a fermented character in the flavour and is used where a dark colour is not wanted. Ketjap Manis is an Indonesian version, which is very sweet and syrupy.

## Soba noodles
– This Japanese staple has been almost as enthusiastically embraced by the Australians as the Japanese. Soba noodles are made from buckwheat and wheat – two crops which were easier to grow than rice in Japan – buckwheat especially, as it only takes 75 days from sowing to harvest. Soba alone is not elastic enough to make noodles, which is why some wheat is added. The thin, mushroom-coloured noodles cook in about 4 minutes and they are best served chilled as a salad or decorative nests, cooled under running water as soon as they are cooked, or served in broth – however they do not take well to stir-frying.

## Blue cheese
– Australians love blue cheese in salads, sauces, burgers and tarts. The world's great blues including Stilton, Roquefort and Gorgonzola all have unique characteristics and are a bit of an acquired taste, but once acquired, it can become an obsession. Australia and New Zealand produce their own blue cheeses by the traditional method of injecting a mould into the cheese and allowing it to age under controlled conditions.

## Sweet Potato
– kumara, yam - It is actually inappropriate to call a sweet potato a yam as the Americans do – a true yam, a huge, brown-skinned, white-fleshed African vegetable, is unrelated. Sweet potatoes are an important world food source, being easy to grow, versatile, high in energy-giving carbohydrate and very delicious. Orange-fleshed varieties have a smooth brown skin and velvety sweet flesh; pink-skinned, white-fleshed varieties (kumara) are slightly less sweet. They can be baked in their jackets, boiled and mashed, or grilled (broiled) (see page 295) and they make delicious soup and desserts. Sweet potatoes are botanically unrelated to potatoes.

**Macadamia Nuts**

## Avocado
– avocado pear – Nature's butter-fleshed gift to Man is a fruit native to Mexico, where it got its name from the Aztec word *ahuacatl* meaning "testicle". In the tropics it's referred to as "poor man's butter"; in Australia it thrives in the subtropical climate and is used prolifically in many simple and gourmet dishes. There are many types – Hass, with a nearly black knobbly skin, are considered one of the best. Giant West Indian avocados are the size of melons and are also delicious, but it is of utmost importance that avocados are eaten fully ripe or else they are quite inedible. They are ripe when the flesh just yields under the gentle pressure of the thumb, especially near the stem end. They should not be stored in the refrigerator. Once the flesh is exposed to the air it turns brown quickly and must be dressed in lemon or lime juice to prevent this; also if part of the avocado is to be saved, if the stone (pit) is left in it seems to decelerate discoloration. Although the smooth, rich quality of avocados means they taste good just slightly warmed, it is easy to overdo it and if they end up cooked they completely lose their appeal. Avocados may be high in fat, but it's a good type of fat (monounsaturated) and they are also an excellent source of vitamin E – they are considered a super food, so eat up!

Aussies love ricotta almost more than the Italians do. If you can possibly get to a proper Italian deli, you should be able to acquire a real ricotta, which is miles better than a mass-produced version. Failing that, even a supermarket tub will turn out delicious with this treatment. Serve this hot from the oven with a loaf of fresh crusty bread, a simple salad, and there you have it – lunch.

# Baked Ricotta with Garlic and Star Anise Australia

Heat the oven to 190°C/375°F/Gas Mark 5. Line a baking sheet with foil or baking paper (parchment) and turn the ricotta out on to it.

Mix the chilli, garlic, spices, thyme and oil together. Spoon over the ricotta, dribbling the oil over the sides. Top with the Parmesan, salt and pepper. Bake in the oven for 20–25 minutes, basting halfway through, until slightly crusty on top and around the edges. Serve right away, straight from the foil, or slide on to a serving plate.

250 g/9 oz/1⅛ cups ricotta cheese, drained
1 fresh red chilli (chili), de-seeded if large, finely sliced
2 garlic cloves, sliced
3 star anise
½ tsp fresh thyme leaves
½ tsp coriander seeds, lightly crushed
3 tbsp olive oil
½ tbsp freshly grated Parmesan cheese
Pinch of sea salt
Freshly ground black pepper

**Serves 4**

Tantalizingly sweet caramelized onions and strong, edgy blue cheese turn out to be the perfect foil for each other. It's an eternally good combination, which first came to my attention in the form of a tartlet, from the Sydney restaurant that produced *The Bather's Pavilion Cookbook* by Victoria Alexander and Genevieve Harris. My simplified version here disposes of the need for tartlet moulds and delivers a classy little savoury pastry in true Australian style in minutes. A firm, dry cheese such as Danish Blue or Stilton works best.

# Caramelized Onion and Blue Cheese Galette Australia

Heat a large frying pan over a low heat and add the oil. Add the onions and cook gently for about 30 minutes until meltingly soft. When they start to turn golden, add the sugar and salt and fry attentively until well golden and caramelized. Leave to cool slightly.

Preheat the oven to 220°C/425°F/Gas Mark 7. Beat the mascarpone, blue cheese and egg together in a bowl.

Lay out the chilled pastry and cut it into 6 pieces, about 10-cm/4-inch square. Use the tip of a knife to score the pastry, drawing an inside border about 1 cm/½ inch inside the edge, like a picture frame. Place on a baking sheet.

Divide the onion between the pastries, spreading it inside the "frame". Top with a bit of chopped rocket, then spoon the cheese mixture on top. It's fine if it's piled up quite high, as it sinks into the pastry in the oven.

Bake in the oven for 15 minutes, or until the pastry is golden and puffed, and the cheese mixture is shiny, puffed and patched with gold. Serve warm or cold.

4 tbsp olive oil

3 medium onions, about 500 g/1 lb 2 oz, thinly sliced

1 tbsp golden caster (superfine) sugar

½ tsp sea salt

75 g/3 oz/⅓ cup mascarpone

180 g/6½ oz blue cheese such as Danish Blue or Stilton

1 egg

375 g/13 oz puff pastry, ideally ready-rolled, chilled

30 g/1 oz/½ cup rocket (arugula), chopped

**Serves 6**

Damper bread is probably a descendant of soda bread from Ireland, and this is one of the few recipes in this chapter which glances back to the days of the Australian pioneers. How industrious they were – with no yeast and no oven, they could mix up flour, fat, water and a bit of leavening in the flour sack, and without even a surface to knead on, the bread could be pulled together, then baked in the ashes of the fire. The modern addition of a little cheese and sage turns this into one blinding loaf, especially eaten hot with a smudge of butter in a cosy house full of the aromas of home-baking – divine.

# Cheese and Sage Damper Australia

Preheat the oven to 220°C/425°F/Gas Mark 7. Mix the flour and salt together in a large bowl. Rub in the butter with your fingertips until crumbly. Alternatively, whiz in a food processor until crumbly.

Add both cheeses and the sage and mix thoroughly. Gradually stir in the milk until you have a dough. If the mixture is sticky, add a little more flour. If the mixture seems too dry and isn't holding together, moisten with a little more milk until cohesive but not sticky.

Turn out on to a clean work surface and knead until fairly smooth, about 2–3 minutes. Squash the dough into a flattened circle, about 18 cm/ 7 inches diameter and 4 cm/1½ inches thick. Place on a lightly oiled baking sheet. Use a long, sharp knife to cut almost all the way through the dough 4 times, making 8 wedges.

Brush the top surface with milk and sprinkle with poppy seeds. Bake in the oven for about 25 minutes, or until golden and firm. Leave to cool on a wire rack and eat warm, cold or toasted, with butter.

335 g/11½ oz/2 cups self-raising wholemeal (self-rising whole wheat) flour
½ tsp salt
30 g/1 oz/2 tbsp soft butter
90 g/3¼ oz/1 loose cup grated Gouda cheese
3 tbsp freshly grated Parmesan cheese
2–3 tbsp chopped fresh sage leaves, or 1 tbsp dried sage
250 ml/8 fl oz/1 cup milk, plus extra for glazing
2 tsp poppy seeds
Butter, to serve

**Serves 8**

This chapter would not be complete without paying some kind of homage to the magnificent Donna Hay, who has almost single-handedly delivered the best of contemporary Australian cuisine to the doorsteps of the world through the brilliant, simple style of her books and her work for *Marie Claire* magazine. Before she was a style icon, she was already prolific, having written 25 cookbooks by the age of 25. One of her early books, *At My Table* from 1995, contains this clever little recipe, where thin slices of aubergine become the half-moon shaped cases for the spicy filling. This is a bit of a fiddly job, but the result is stunning. Rather than serve these as part of a meal, I think these work best as a canapé, which merits the effort and gives them the attention they deserve without the interference of any sauce or side dish.

# Aubergine (Eggplant) Ravioli Australia

Slice the aubergine into discs as thin as you can possibly manage – about 2 mm/⅛ inch is perfect. Lay the slices in a colander, sprinkling salt lightly between the layers. Leave to drain for 30 minutes. Pat dry thoroughly.

Place the cumin seeds in a dry frying pan over a medium heat and toast for 2 minutes, shaking the pan, until fragrant but not burned. Leave to cool briefly, then stir into the ricotta. Add the chilli and thyme and mix well.

To assemble the ravioli, place a level tsp of filling on half of each aubergine slice. Fold over and press to seal.

Preheat the oven to 110°C/225°F/Gas Mark ¼. Heat a large frying pan over a medium heat and add a shallow pool of olive oil. Fry the ravioli in batches for 2–3 minutes on both sides, until golden. Keep warm in the oven while you cook the next batch. Serve as soon as possible.

1 medium long, thin aubergine (eggplants), or 2 small aubergines, about 250 g/9 oz
Sea salt
1 tsp cumin seeds
180 g/6¼ oz/¾ cup ricotta cheese
1 fresh red chilli (chili), de-seeded if large, very finely chopped
2 tsp fresh thyme leaves, very finely chopped
Olive oil, for frying

**Makes 30–40, serves 8–10 as a canapé**

Cookery writer Jill Dupleix published this recipe in her *Times* column in the UK as an example of typical Australian food. Though she's lived in London for a while now, she returned from a trip to Sydney and Melbourne to declare, "Oz food...is, indeed, different – brighter, crisper, crunchier and wilder than northern hemisphere food; part-Asian, part-Mediterranean and part cake." This dish, more salad than pizza, is similar to something she ate at the legendary Melbourne restaurant Pearl – a very simple modern classic.

# Bottomless Pizza Australia

Place the peppers in a saucepan with a lid with the oil and a little salt and pepper. Place over a low heat and once hot, leave to stew for about 10–15 minutes, or until soft but not brown. Leave to cool until barely warm.

Using a slotted spoon, arrange the peppers over a serving plate (reserve the juices). Tear the parsley slightly and scatter over the peppers. Tear the mozzarella cheese into long shreds and dot them around the plate. Scatter over the olives and capers and finish with the reserved pepper juices trickled over the plate.

2 red (bell) peppers and 2 yellow (bell) peppers, cored, cut into postage-stamp sized squares

2 tbsp extra virgin olive oil

Sea salt and freshly ground black pepper

Handful of fresh flat-leaf parsley leaves

200 g/7 oz/2 balls fresh buffalo mozzarella cheese, drained and patted dry

Handful of high-quality olives such as Kalamata

1 tbsp capers in vinegar, drained

**Serves 4**

With a heavenly mild scent of garlic and herbs suspended in creamy velvet, these fancy timbales are an exciting way to start a meal, or can be served as the main event supplemented with salad. Either way, bread is a must. Adapted from *The Cook's Companion* by Stephanie Alexander, an essential book by one of Australia's culinary Grand Dammes.

# Garlic and Goat's Cheese Custards with Fresh Tomato Sauce Australia

Place the garlic cloves in a small saucepan and cover with cold water. Bring to the boil and simmer for 1 minute, then drain, cover in fresh water, boil, simmer and drain again. Next combine the garlic with the milk, bay leaf and thyme in the pan, bring to the boil, then reduce the heat to a simmer and cook for 10 minutes. Transfer the milk with the garlic and herbs to a bowl and leave to cool completely.

While it cools, you can prepare the tomato sauce. Heat the grill (broiler) to its highest setting. Cut the tomatoes in half and scoop out the seeds, then place on a baking sheet. Sprinkle with a little salt, pepper, sugar, olive oil and vinegar. Grill (broil) until softened and slightly charred, about 10 minutes. Remove the skins, then place in a small saucepan, crush slightly and set over a medium heat. Simmer until slightly thickened, about 1–2 minutes. Set aside.

Once the milk is cool, preheat the oven to 160°C/325°F/Gas Mark 3. Generously grease 4 individual ramekins or pudding moulds. Scoop out the herbs and place the milk and garlic in the food processor with the goat's cheese, eggs, salt, pepper and nutmeg and whiz until smooth. Add the chilled cream and pulse until just mixed, but do not overbeat.

Lay a tea (dish) towel or a piece of newspaper in a roasting dish and stand the ramekins or moulds on it. Divide the custard mixture between them. Pour boiling water in the dish to come halfway up the moulds. Place carefully in the oven and bake for 25–35 minutes, or until set and firm to the touch. Leave to cool slightly, while you reheat the tomato sauce. Run a sharp knife around the edges of the custards and turn out on to warmed plates. Top with a spoonful of sauce and serve right away.

Butter, for greasing

**For the custards:**
12 garlic cloves
300 ml/10 fl oz/1¼ cups milk
1 bay leaf
1 fresh thyme sprig
120 g/4¼ oz fresh, rindless goat's (goat) cheese
2 organic eggs, beaten
Sea salt and freshly ground black pepper
Generous grinding of nutmeg
150 ml/5 fl oz/⅔ cup double (heavy) cream, chilled (important)

**For the sauce:**
4 plump vine-ripened tomatoes
Sea salt and freshly ground black pepper
Sugar
Olive oil
Balsamic vinegar

**Serves 4**

From the Land of Cake – savoury cheesecake! This is a rather indulgent little number featuring sweet potato shavings as a crown. It makes an impressive centrepiece as part of a festive feast, and only takes about 5 minutes to throw together. Alternatively, serve as a light lunch with a large crisp salad.

# Herb Cheesecake with Shaved Kumara Australia

Preheat the oven to 150°C/300°F/Gas Mark 2. Brush the springform cake tin generously with olive oil.

Place the ricotta, Parmesan and eggs in a food processor and whiz until smooth. Add the rocket, herbs, salt, pepper and nutmeg and process until very well blended, then pour into the prepared tin.

Peel the sweet potato, then shave it into as many long ribbbons as you can manage. Place in a bowl and pour over the 1 tbsp of olive oil. Toss with your hands to coat each ribbon evenly, then arrange on top of the cheese mixture. Bake in the oven for 1 hour–1 hour 10 minutes, checking that it does not burn; some of the sweet potato shavings may get quite dark and crisp, which is fine. If it wobbles slightly when you remove it from the oven, remember it will continue to set as it cools. Leave to cool completely, then serve just barely warm or at room temperature.

1 tbsp olive oil, plus extra for brushing
750 g/1 lb 10 oz fresh ricotta cheese
200 g/7 oz/1 ¾ cups freshly grated Parmesan cheese
4 organic eggs
50 g/2 oz/2 cups rocket (arugula) leaves, coarsely chopped
2 tbsp chopped fresh rosemary
2 handfuls/½ cup fresh flat-leaf parsley leaves
1 tsp sea salt
Freshly ground black pepper
Generous grinding of nutmeg
1 large sweet potato, about 250 g/9 oz

25-cm/10-inch springform cake tin (pan)

**Serves 6–8**

Rice-paper wrappers, also referred to as rice skins or rice sheets, are made from a dough of rice flour, water and salt, which is rolled paper-thin and dried. They often come from Vietnam, where they are called *bahn trang*, and are usually used for spring rolls, but these are a contemporary treat – I've also seen these square Aussie-style parcels wrapped around a piece of fish. The wrappers are brittle and delicate and have the appearance of frosted glass, with marks from the bamboo trays where they were left to dry. Usually they are round, (square ones are also available), and come in a range of sizes, some as large as an LP record, though for this recipe, you want the smallest size. Handle them carefully as they break easily – though typically they're sold in packets of at least 100, so you have leeway for a few casualties. They can be eaten raw or steamed, but here they crackle in hot oil and deliver a toothsome treat.

# Crackling Rice-paper Parcels with Hoisin Tofu Australia

Drain the tofu and wrap in several layers of kitchen paper (paper towels) to dry off for a few minutes. Unwrap and cut into 8 flat pieces, measuring about 5 cm/2 inches square and 1 cm/⅓ inch thick.

Mix the hoisin sauce, sesame oil and water together in a small bowl. Dip each piece of tofu in the marinade to coat and leave on a plate in the refrigerator for 30 minutes to allow the flavour to develop.

Fill a largish bowl with warm water. Place 2 rice-paper wrappers at a time into the water and leave until totally soft and pliable, about 2 minutes. Lay one wrapper flat on the work surface and place a coriander leaf, greener-side-down, in the middle. Lay a piece of tofu on top of the leaf. Fold the wrapper over the tofu, forming a neat envelope. Place seam-side down on a plate and repeat with remaining ingredients. Leave the parcels to self-seal, about 10–15 minutes in the refrigerator.

Prick each parcel a few times with a pin. Heat a 2.5 cm/1 inch depth of oil a wok or heavy-based saucepan until a tiny bit of wrapper, dry or wet, sizzles immediately. Deep-fry 2–3 parcels at a time on each side until golden and crackly. Drain on kitchen paper. Serve warm with chilli sauce, if desired.

200 g/7 oz firm tofu
2½ tbsp hoisin sauce (see page 197)
1 tsp sesame oil
2 tsp water
8 small rice-paper wrappers (skins),
   16 cm/6¼ inches in diameter
8 whole fresh coriander (cilantro) leaves
Sunflower or vegetable oil, for deep-frying
Fresh sweet chilli (chili) sauce (see page 250)
   or bottled Thai sweet chilli sauce,
   to serve (optional)

This is my personal homage to Oz. Its contemporary cooking style has given me huge inspiration and confidence in my culinary creativity ever since I first picked up a vegetable knife. Every Australian cook makes Pumpkin Soup; no doubt somebody makes it just like this one – a little bit of Asia fused with a little Mediterranean flair, using indigenous ingredients to impressive effect. This soup is drop-dead gorgeous and gets a dinner party off to a great start.

# Pumpkin and Coconut Soup with Macadamia Pesto Australia

Heat a large saucepan with a lid over a medium heat and add the oil. Add the onion and fry until soft and translucent, then add the garlic and ginger and cook until fragrant, about 1 minute. Add the pumpkin, stir, cover and cook for 5 minutes to release the juices.

Add the cumin and stir for 1 minute, then add the coconut milk and vegetable stock. Bring to the boil and taste for seasoning, adding salt if necessary. Reduce the heat to a simmer and cook for 15–20 minutes, or until the pumpkin is very soft. Cool briefly, then purée, ideally with a hand-held blender, until completely smooth.

When ready to eat, make the pesto. Pound everything together in a mortar until a coarse paste results. Alternatively, whiz in the food processor.

Reheat the soup and serve each bowl with a teaspoon of pesto on top.

1 tbsp olive oil

1 medium onion, finely chopped

3 garlic cloves, finely chopped

3-cm/1¼-inch piece fresh root ginger, peeled and finely chopped

700 g/1½ lb pumpkin or orange-fleshed squash, peeled, de-seeded and cubed (trimmed weight)

1 tsp ground cumin

1 x 400 ml/14 fl oz can coconut milk

700 ml/1¼ pints/3 cups vegetable stock

Salt (optional)

**For the pesto:**

12 large basil leaves

1 tbsp olive oil

30 g/1 oz/½ cup roasted salted macadamia nuts

2 tsp lemon juice

**Serves 4–6**

A ravishing display of glistening orange squash against a fortifying green canvas, this salad is a real head-turner, with a rich, sweet character. Serve as part of a spread of Mediterranean-inspired *meze* – pitta (pita) bread, Beetroot Hummus (see page 293), Greek salad and olives.

# Pumpkin and Avocado Salad Australia

Preheat the oven to 200°C/400°F/Gas Mark 6. Place the pumpkin on a baking sheet and drizzle with the oil, then use your hands to give each piece an even coating. Bake in the oven for 10–15 minutes, or until soft. While still hot, release from the baking sheet by loosening with a spatula. Set aside to cool.

To make the dressing, mix all the ingredients together in a bowl and taste for seasoning. Thin with a little water if necessary to achieve a pourable consistency.

When ready to serve, peel and slice the avocado and dress lightly in lemon juice. Arrange the baby salad leaves on a platter and the pumpkin and avocados over them. Drizzle the dressing over the salad and serve right away.

500 g/1 lb 2 oz pumpkin or orange-fleshed squash, peeled, de-seeded and sliced about 7 mm/⅓ inch thick (trimmed weight)

1 tbsp olive oil

2 perfectly ripe avocados

Lemon juice

100 g/3½ oz baby salad leaves (greens), washed and dried

**For the dressing:**

125 ml/4 fl oz/½ cup yogurt

3 tbsp chopped fresh mint

1 tbsp runny honey

1½ tsp ground cumin

Salt and freshly ground black pepper

**Serves 4–6**

A fresh and practically instantaneous bowl of pasta which just screams "summer"! Lemon zest is the key to the flavour here, and it is so very important when removing the zest that you only remove the outermost yellow layer where the succulent oils dwell. Beneath this layer is the white pith, which is bitter and unpleasant and must be avoided. If possible use a razor-sharp grater such as a Microplane, and move it across each section of the lemon once – never saw back and forth.

# Lemon and Fresh Herb Fettuccine

Australia

Bring a large saucepan of water to the boil and salt it well. Add the pasta and cook until *al dente*, about 9–10 minutes, or follow the packet (package) instructions.

Meanwhile, finely grate the zest of the lemons, taking care to only remove the outer layer. Squeeze the juice and measure 4 tbsp. In a bowl, beat the zest, lemon juice, rocket, herbs, spring onions, garlic, crème fraîche (or sour cream), olive oil and salt together.

Drain the pasta quickly, retaining some moisture, and return it to the saucepan. Stir through the sauce mixture and distribute as evenly as possible – it may help to use tongs to toss it through. Serve immediately, in warmed bowls with plenty of freshly grated Parmesan cheese and black pepper.

350 g/12 oz fettuccine or spaghetti

**For the sauce:**
4 lemons, unwaxed, or scrubbed under a hot tap
30 g/1 oz/½ cup rocket (arugula), finely chopped
30 g/1 oz/½ cup fresh parsley, finely chopped
30 g/1 oz/½ cup fresh coriander (cilantro), chopped
4 spring onions (scallions), chopped
1 plump garlic clove, crushed
4 tbsp crème fraîche (or sour cream)
2 tbsp olive oil
1 tsp salt

**To serve:**
Freshly grated Parmesan cheese
Freshly ground black pepper

**Serves 4**

Australians have adopted Asian ingredients with tremendous flair and soba noodles are an all-time favourite. The delightfully slippery texture of the mushrooms, paired with the deeply nutty flavour of sesame seeds and sesame oil make ideal companions for the cold noodles, and the crunchy green beans lift and balance the flavour and texture for one first-class lunch dish.

# Soba Noodle Salad with Mushrooms Australia

Bring a medium-sized saucepan of water to the boil. Add the noodles, return to the boil and simmer for 3–4 minutes, or until tender. Drain and run cold water over them until completely cool. Leave to drain for a few minutes, then place in a bowl and stir through the sesame oil, followed by the soy sauce. Set aside.

To cook the mushrooms, heat a large frying pan or wok over a medium-high heat and add the sunflower oil. Add the garlic and chilli and stir-fry until fragrant, about 30 seconds, then add the mushrooms and salt. Stir-fry until the mushrooms are wilted, shiny and soft, about 3 minutes. Remove from the pan and leave to cool.

Place the sesame seeds in a dry frying pan and toast over a medium heat, stirring and shaking until golden and popping. Remove from the pan and leave to cool.

Cook the beans by steaming in the microwave with a little water for 2 minutes, or by blanching in boiling water, or by steaming. Cool under cold running water and drain thoroughly.

When all components of the salad are prepared and cooled, assemble at the last minute by mixing the mushrooms and beans through the noodles. Stir the sesame seeds through last.

200 g/7 oz soba noodles

1 tbsp sesame oil

1 tbsp dark soy sauce

375 g/13 oz mushrooms, shiitake (stems removed) and oyster, torn or sliced (trimmed weight)

2 tbsp sunflower oil

2 garlic cloves, finely chopped

1 fresh red chilli (chili), de-seeded if large, finely chopped

½ tsp sea salt

3 tbsp sesame seeds

120 g/4¼ oz/1 cup French (green) beans, trimmed and cut into 1-cm/½-inch pieces

**Serves 4–6**

Italian–Australians were instrumental in the gastronomic revolution that occurred in recent decades, applying their passion and culinary knowledge to re-create traditional dishes with the exceptional local ingredients. This is the just the sort of dish that represents that ingenuity. This makes a fairly small quantity and works as a light lunch, perhaps with a salad accompaniment, or as a stylish first course.

# Sweetcorn (Corn) Risotto with Tarragon Australia

Bring the stock to the boil in a saucepan. Add the sweetcorn and cook for 1 minute until tender. Remove with a slotted spoon and set aside. Reduce the heat to a simmer.

Heat a large heavy-based saucepan over a medium heat and add the butter. When melted, add the onion and cook until soft and translucent. Add the rice and stir until evenly coated. Pour in the vermouth or wine and cook, stirring, until it is absorbed. Add a ladleful of stock and cook, stirring, until it is absorbed. Continue adding the stock gradually in this way. After about 15 minutes, the rice should have absorbed the stock and should be tender, yet firm to the bite and not chalky.

Stir in the grated Parmesan cheese and chopped tarragon. Cover and leave to stand for 2–3 minutes, then serve with extra Parmesan cheese, grated or shaved.

1 litre/1¾ pints/4 cups well-flavoured vegetable stock
125 g/4 oz/scant 1 cup fresh sweetcorn (corn) or frozen sweetcorn kernels
30 g/1 oz/2 tbsp butter
1 medium onion, chopped
175 g/6 oz/scant 1 cup Arborio risotto rice
100 ml/3½ fl oz/generous ⅓ cup vermouth or white wine
2 tbsp freshly grated Parmesan cheese, plus extra to serve
3 tbsp chopped fresh tarragon

**Serves 4**

More of a trick than a dish, this instant party-starter is now so ubiquitous in Australia, the cheese manufacturer has even packaged it ready-made. Its simplicity is its greatest asset, but you can elevate it to gourmet status by making the chilli sauce, which is simply a matter of stirring five ingredients together. See Fresh Sweet Chilli Sauce on page 250.

# Sweet Chilli Philly Australia

Invert the cheese on to a small serving plate, squeezing the container slightly to release (or unwrap). Use kitchen paper (paper towels) to gently mop up any liquid. Smooth the edges with a butter knife if it hasn't come out in a clean shape. Pour the chilli sauce over the top, letting it dribble down the sides. Scatter the basil over and finish with a good grinding of black pepper. Serve with crackers.

200 g/7 oz/⅞ cup tub or block cream cheese

4 tbsp/¼ cup Thai sweet chilli (chili) sauce, or Fresh Sweet Chilli Sauce (see page 250)

6 large fresh basil leaves, torn or finely shredded

Freshly ground black pepper

Plain rice crackers or rye crackers, to serve

**Serves 6–8**

Australians, with their fondness for cakes, would typically bake this in a cake tin (pan), which is perfectly acceptable, but I prefer it thinner and cut into squares. If cooked in a gratin dish, this rich and delicious savoury cake can be also cut into small pieces when cool and served at parties. This is a downright classic from *Australian Women's Weekly*, an institution of great home cooking championed by generations of housewives.

# Zucchini (Courgette) Slice Australia

Preheat the oven to 180°C/350°F/Gas Mark 4 and brush a casserole or gratin dish, measuring about 20 x 30 cm/8 x 12 inches with olive oil.

In a large bowl, combine the courgettes, onion, cheese, flour and oil. Beat the eggs with the smoked paprika, salt and pepper. Combine thoroughly with the courgette mixture. Pour into the prepared dish and bake in the oven for 30–40 minutes, until well browned and firm. Serve hot, warm or cold.

125 ml/4 fl oz/½ cup olive or sunflower oil, plus extra for brushing

3 medium/2 large courgettes (zucchini), about 400 g/14 oz, coarsely grated

1 large onion, finely chopped

75 g/3 oz/¾ cup grated Cheddar cheese

140 g/4½ oz/scant 1 cup self-raising (self-rising) flour

5 organic eggs

½ tsp smoked paprika (pimentón)

1 tsp salt, or to taste

Freshly ground black pepper

**Serves 6**

These party nibbles have a knock-out flavour, not for the faint-hearted – they get the sense of taste very excited, as all good party food should do. Roquefort is the king of blue cheeses, with the perfect creamy texture and acidity to balance the queen of dates, the Medjool (see page 274).

# Dates Stuffed with Vodka-spiked Roquefort Australia

In a small bowl, mash the cheese with the vodka until smooth. Use a teaspoon to fill the centre of the dates. Nestle in a walnut half on top. These can be chilled in the refrigerator for up to 4 hours before serving.

100 g/3½ oz Roquefort cheese
1 tbsp vodka
10 Medjool dates, stoned (pitted)
10 walnut halves

**Serves 6–8**

An Aussie friend tells me that they have a real fondness for pink food "down under". They also have a real knack for entertaining, and this generous bowl of scrumptious, rather outrageous looking fuchsia-coloured dip makes fabulous cocktail food. I've always been one to spice up ready-made hummus with a bit of lemon, cumin and chilli, but this takes it to a new dimension. Serve with crostini, warm pitta (pita) or breadsticks.

# Beetroot (Beet) Hummus Australia

Heat a frying pan over a medium heat and add the oil. Add the onion and fry until translucent. Leave to cool slightly.

Place the cooled onion, hummus, beetroot, cumin, lemon juice, garlic, cayenne and salt in a food processor and whiz to a smooth purée.

1 tbsp olive oil
1 medium onion, finely chopped
300 g/11 oz/1½ cups ready-made hummus
300 g/11 oz cooked beetroot (beet), about 5 small ones, peeled
2 tsp ground cumin
1 tbsp fresh lemon juice
1 garlic clove, de-germed, crushed
⅛–¼ tsp cayenne pepper, to taste
½ tsp salt, or to taste

**Serves 8–10**

The New Zealand sweet potato or kumara, pronounced "kum-eyra", is typically pink-skinned and white-fleshed. The skin is much tougher and the flesh slightly less sweet that the orange type, and it also has a tendency to appear slightly grey when cooked. Orange-fleshed varieties are slightly better from an aesthetic point of view. This classy treatment of sweet potatoes, as a side dish or as a vegetable for dipping, is inspired by Peter Gordon's *The Sugar Club Cookbook*.

# Grilled Kumara
# Char-grilled Sweet Potato New Zealand

Gently scrub the sweet potatoes, but don't peel them. Place them in a saucepan and cover with cold water. Add 1 tbsp of salt. Cover and bring to the boil. Cook for 15–20 minutes, by which time they should be nearly cooked but still firm. A sharp knife or skewer should meet a little resistance towards the core but should still penetrate. Drain and leave to cool.

Heat a char-grill pan (stove-top grill pan) over a high heat for at least 5 minutes. Slice the sweet potatoes into 1-cm/½-inch circles. Brush with olive oil and char-grill on both sides until striped with black and slightly crisp. Serve with plenty of freshly ground black pepper.

2 orange-fleshed sweet potatoes, weighing about 350 g/12 oz each
Sea salt
Olive oil, for brushing
Freshly ground black pepper, to serve

**Serves 4**

Cheese-on-toast for kids and adults alike, these are left to go cold and nibbled out of the cookie jar. Vegemite® is essential, according to my Kiwi friend Camille, but if you must, use a different type of yeast extract (see page 67).

# Mousetraps New Zealand

Heat the grill (broiler) to its highest setting. Lightly toast the bread in a toaster. Cut the crusts off, then spread each slice with a thin smear of yeast extract. Cut into strips or "soldiers", place on a baking sheet and cover lightly with grated cheese. Bake in the oven until melted, then leave to cool. Store in an airtight container.

4 square slices of bread
Yeast extract (see page 67)
50 g/2 oz/½ cup Cheddar cheese, grated

**Serves 4**

Where else in the world would they think of barbecuing a lettuce? I found this idea in Auckland-based Julie Le Clerc's *More Simple Café Food*, a book just bursting at the seams with good ideas. Flashing the cos lettuce on the char-grill or barbecue penetrates it with a smoky flavour and turns it into a wonderfully juicy vegetable. Here it's paired up with my own vegetarian Caesar dressing, but it's equally good with a simple balsamic vinaigrette. The important thing is to serve it right away while it still has its hot and smoky appeal.

# Char-grilled Caesar Salad New Zealand

For the dressing, place the eggs in a small saucepan of cold water and bring to the boil. Boil for 5 minutes, drain and rinse under cold running water until cool, then peel.

To make the croûtons, preheat the oven to 190°C/375°F/Gas Mark 5. Place the cubed bread in a bowl and drizzle with the olive oil. Stir to coat evenly. Spread the bread out on a baking sheet and bake until golden and crisp, about 10 minutes, checking frequently that they are not burning.

Cut the lettuces in half from top to base. Rinse under cold running water, then leave to drain.

To make the dressing, mash the peeled eggs well in a small bowl. Add the Parmesan cheese, vinegar, Worcestershire sauce, chives and salt and pepper to taste and whisk thoroughly. Gradually whisk in the olive oil until blended. Set aside.

Heat a char-grill pan (stove-top grill pan) over a high heat for at least 5 minutes. Place the lettuce on the grill, cut-side down, and scorch until slightly wilted and blackened, about 1–2 minutes. Alternatively, flash briefly on the barbecue. Arrange on a serving plate, pour the dressing over and scatter with the croûtons. Eat immediately.

2 hearts of cos (romaine) lettuce

**For the dressing:**
2 organic eggs
4 tbsp freshly grated Parmesan cheese
2½ tbsp white wine vinegar
1 tsp vegetarian Worcestershire sauce or light soy sauce
Small handful of chives, snipped
Salt and freshly ground black pepper
4 tbsp olive oil

**For the croûtons:**
2 thick slices of white bread, cubed
1 tbsp olive oil

**Serves 4-6**

Every Kiwi I asked mentioned sweetcorn fritters as a classic recipe, so I confidently turned to *The Sugar Club Cookbook*. New Zealand-born chef, food writer and restaurateur extraordinaire Peter Gordon's recipe must be the very embodiment of the sweetcorn fritter. These are surprisingly soft and sweet, nothing like their crisp Thai counterparts *Tod Mun Kao Pode* (Curried Sweetcorn Fritters on page 262), though they also appreciate the company of a little Fresh Sweet Chilli Sauce (see page 250) or Fresh Tomato Sauce (see page 282). Serve as party food, as a first course, or as the starch component of a balanced meal. Do cook over a low-medium temperature and stand well away, as fresh sweetcorn can have a habit of bursting out of the pan.

# Sweetcorn (Corn) Fritters New Zealand

To prepare the fresh sweetcorn, stand each cob of corn upright in a large bowl and use a sharp knife to strip the kernels, shaving downwards.

If using frozen sweetcorn, pour boiling water over them and leave for a minute or two, then drain.

Mix the sweetcorn with the eggs, polenta, cornflour, crème fraîche (or sour cream), spring onions, salt and pepper to form a thick batter.

Heat a large non-stick frying pan over a medium heat and add a small amount of oil. Fry dessertspoons of batter until golden on both sides, turning carefully. Drain on kitchen paper (paper towels) and serve.

4 fresh corn-on-the-cobs (ears fresh corn), or 420 g/14¾ oz/3 cups frozen sweetcorn (corn)

4 eggs

40 g/1 ½ oz/generous ¼ cup polenta (cornmeal)

30 g/1 oz/¼ cup cornflour (cornstarch)

125 ml/4 fl oz/½ cup crème fraîche (or sour cream)

4 spring onions (scallions), finely chopped

½ tsp sea salt

Freshly ground black pepper

Sunflower oil, for frying

**Makes 15–20, serves 4–6**

# Index

Index

301

# Bibliography

Abensur, Nadine, *Cranks Light*, Weidenfeld & Nicolson, 2000

Alexander and Harris, *The Bather's Pavilion Cookbook*, Ten Speen Press, 1995

Anderson, E.N., *The Food of China*, Yale University Press, 1988

Ayrton, Elisabeth, *The Cookery of England*, Penguin, 1974

Barber, Kimiko, *The Japanese Kitchen*, Kyle Cathie, 2004

Bayley, Monica, *Black Africa Cookbook*, Determined Productions, 1971

Berriedale-Jonhson, Michelle, *The British Museum Cookbook*, British Museum Press, 1987

Betar, Yasmine, *Finest Recipes from the Middle East*, Self-published, 1957

Blashford-Snell, Brooks Brown, Ferrigno, Joyce, *One Year at Books for Cooks Number Three*, Pryor Publications, 1998

Canadian Home Economics Association, *The Laura Secord Canadian Cookbook*, Whitecap, 2001

Canter, Canter and Swann, *The Cranks Recipe Book*, Panther Books, 1985

Carper, Jean, *The Food Pharmacy*, Bantam Press, 1988

Chela, Iglesias, and Marrero, *50 Essential Recipes of Canarian Cuisine*, Cabildo de Tenerife, 2004

Corbitt, Helen, *Helen Corbitt's Cookbook*, Riverside Press, 1957

Cotter, Denis, *Parasido Seasons*, Atrium, 2003

Couffignal, Huguette, *The People's Cookbook*, Macmillan, 1979

Cross Media, *Healthy Tofu Recipes*, Cross Media, 2001

Cross Media, *Miso*, Cross Media, 2002

David, Elizabeth, *French Provincial Cooking*, Penguin, 1960

Davidson, Alan, *The Oxford Companion to Food*, Oxford University Press, 1999

Davies, Gilli, *Tastes of Wales*, BBC Books, 1990

Del Conte, Anna, *Gastronomy of Italy*, Pavilion, 2001

Devi, Yamuna, *The Art of Indian Vegetarian Cooking*, Angus & Robertson, 1987

DeWitt, Willan, and Stock, *Hot and Spicy and Meatless*, Prima Publishing, 1994

Elliot, Rose, *The Bean Book*, Fontana, 1979

Eren, Neset, *The Art of Turkish Cooking*, Doubleday, 1982

Farmer, Fannie Meritt, *The Boston Cooking-School Cookbook*, Little, Brown and Co, 1951

Gluck and Rowe, *Supergrub*, Collins, 2004

Goldstein, Darra, *The Georgian Feast*, University of California Press, 1993

Gomes, Michele, *Sushi Made Easy*, New Holland, 1999

Gordon, Peter, *The Sugarclub Cookbook*, Hodder & Stoughton, 1997

Grigson, Jane, *Fruit Book*, Penguin, 1982

Grigson, Jane, *Vegetable Book*, Penguin, 1978

Hachten, Harva, *Best of Regional African Cooking*, Hippocrene Books, 1970

Hahn, Emily, *The Cooking of China*, Time-Life, 1969

Haroutunian, Arto Der, *The Yoghurt Book*, Penguin, 1983

Hay, Donna, *At My Table: Fresh and Simple Food*, Barbara Beckett, 1995

Hazan, Marcella, *The Essentials of Classic Italian Cooking*, Knopf, 1992

Hazelton, Nika Standen, *The Cooking of Germany*, Time-Life, 1969

Hekmat, Forough, *The Art of Persian Cooking*, Mehr-e Amin, 2001

Hsuing, Deh-Ta, *Chinese Vegetarian Cooking*, Apple Press, 1985

Jaffrey. Madhur, *Eastern Vegetarian Cooking*, Jonathan Cape, 1983

Jaffrey. M., *The Essential Madhur Jaffrey*, Ebury, 1999

Jones, Bill, *Sublime Vegetarian*, Douglas & McIntyre, 1999

Junior League of Denver, *Colorado Cache*, C7C Publications, 1978

Kabir, Siddiqua, *Bangladeshi Curry Cookbook*, Taj Publishing, 1984

Kalra, J Inder Singh, Prashad: *Cooking with Indian Masters*, Allied Publishers Ltd., 1986

Kouki, Mohamed, *La Cuisine Tunisienne*, Tunis, 1967

Kraus, Barbara, *The Cookbook of the United Nations*, United Nations Association of the USA, 1964

Kujore, Adesumbo, *African Delights*, Fieldfair Press, 1996

Le Clerc, Julie, *More Simple Café Food*, Penguin, 2000

Leeming and Kohsaka, *Japanese Cookery*, Rider Books, 1984

Levy, Paul, *The Penguin Book of Food and Drink*, Penguin, 1996

Linford, Jenny, *Food Lovers' London*, Metro, 2003

Lo, Kenneth H C, *Chinese Vegetarian Cooking*, Pantheon Books, 1974

Lo, Kenneth H C, *New Chinese Cookery Course*, Little Brown, 1989

Luard, Elisabeth, *The Flavours of Andalucia*, Collins & Brown, 1991

Madison, Deborah, *The Savoury Way*, Bantam Press, 1990

Man and Weir, *The Compleat Mustard*, Constable, 1988

Margvelashvili, Julianne, *The Classic Cuisine of Soviet Georgia*, Prentice Hall, 1991

McDermott, Nancie, *Real Vegetarian Thai*, Chronicle Books, 1997

McGee, Harold, *On Food and Cooking: The Science and Lore of the Kitchen*, Fireside, 1984

Medearis, Angela Shelf, *The Ethnic Vegetarian*, Rodale Press, 2004

Merkato Market, *Taste of Ethiopia*, Merkato Publications, 1991

Milliken and Feniger, *Mesa Mexicana*, Morrow, 1994

Mongrain-Dontigny, Micheline, *A Taste of Maple*, Quebec Cooking Collection, 2003

Moore, Isabel, *The Food Book*, BBC Worldwide, 2002

Moosewood Collective, *Sundays at Moosewood Restaurant*, Simon & Schuster, 1990

Morse, Kitty, *The Vegetarian Table: North Africa*, Chronicle Books, 1996

New Mexico Federation of Business and Professional Women, *License to Cook New Mexico Style*, Penfield Press, 1988

Nickels, Harry G. , *The Cooking of the Middle East*, Time-Life, 1970

Oetker, Dr. August , *Dr. Oetker's German Home Cooking*, JD Broelemann, 1963

Orga, Irfan, *Turkish Cooking*, Andre Deutsch, 1958

Ortiz, Elisabeth Lambert, *Caribbean Cookery*, Penguin, 1973

Owen, Sri, *Indonesian Regional Food and Cookery*, Frances Lincoln, 1994

Owen, Sri, *The Rice Book*, Frances Lincoln, 1993

Padmanabhan, Chandra, *Dakshin: Vegetarian Cuisine from South India*, Harper Collins, 1992

Pupella, Eufemia Azzolina, *Sicilian Cookery*, Casa Editrice Bonechi, 1999

Rau, Santha Rama, *The Cooking of India*, Time-Life, 1970

Redon, Sabban, and Serventi, *The Medieval Kitchen*, University of Chicago Press, 1991

Roden, Claudia, *A Book of Middle Eastern Food*, Penguin, 1968

Roden, Claudia, *Mediterranean Cookery*, BBC Books, 1987

Roden, Claudia, *The Book of Jewish Food*, Penguin, 1996

Root, Waverley, *The Cooking of Italy*, Time-Life, 1969

Rozin, Elisabeth, *Blue Corn and Chocolate*, Ebury, 1992

Segall, Pickford and Hammick, *A Handful of Herbs*, Ryland, Peters & Small, 2001

Siauw and Rath, *Eating in Paradise: Cooking in Bali and Java*, Dumont Monte, 2001

Simonds, Nina, *Asian Noodles*, Morrow, 1997

Singh, Dharamjit, *Indian Cookery*, Penguin, 1970

Sokolov, Raymond, *Why We Eat What We Eat*, Summit Books, 1991

Spayde, Jon, *Japanese Cookery*, Century, 1984

Spencer, Colin, *The Adventurous Vegetarian*, Cassell, 1989

Spencer, Colin, *The Heretic's Feast: A History of Vegetarianism*, Fourth Estate, 1994

Spieler, Marlena, *The Flavour of California*, Thorsons, 1992

Sreedharan, Das, *The New Tastes of India*, Headline, 2001

Sreedharan, Das, *Fresh Flavours of India*, Conran Octopus, 1999

Steinberg, Rafael, *Pacific and Southeast Asian Cooking*, Time-Life, 1970

Steingarten, Jeffrey, *The Man Who Ate Everything*, Headline, 1997

Stow, Josie, *African Kitchen*, Interlink Pub Group Inc, 2000

Thai, Kim Lan, *Chinese Cooking*, Aura Books, 1990

Thompson, David, *Thai Food*, Pavilion, 2002

Time-Life, *Recipes: African Cooking*, Time-Life, 1970

Treuille and Blashford-Snell, *Canapes*, Dorling Kindersley, 1999

*Vogue Entertaining Cookbooks*, Conde Nast, 1999/00

Waldo, Myra, *The Complete Book of Oriental Cooking*, Bantam Press, 1960

Wangmo and Houshmand, *The Lhasa Moon Tibetan Cookbook*, Snow Lion Publications, 1999

Weekes, Annette Norma, *Vegetarian Cooking Caribbean Style*, Angela Royal Publishing Ltd., 1996

Wells, Patricia, *At Home in Provence*, Kyle Cathie, 1997

Wells, Troth, *The New Internationalist Food Book*, New Internationalist Publications Ltd., 1990

Weschsberg, Joseph, *The Cooking of Vienna's Empire*, Time-Life, 1968

Wise, Victoria, *The Vegetarian Table: Japan*, Chronicle Books, 1998

Yen and Feng, *The Joy of Chinese Cooking*, Faber & Faber, 1964

## Dedication  For Daniel, Captain of my Ship

## Acknowledgements

This book only exists because of the generous, passionate people who offered their knowledge, contributed recipes and ideas, and helped to steer me on my path. All those people are simply too numerous to mention, and to anybody whose name does not appear here, you know who you are – thank you.

Infinite thanks to the talented and indispensible team of recipe testers and assistants in my test kitchen: Alice Hart, Chrissy, Adrienne O'Callaghan, Rebecca Rains, Tanya Sadourian, Victoria Sedley and Blanca Valencia.

My deepest heartfelt gratitude to my expert interviewees, who donated their valuable time: Marlena Spieler, Sofia Craxton, Denis Cotter, Jenny Chandler, Kevin Gould, Anissa Helou, Rita Pankhurst, Kimiko Barber, Das Sreedharan, Sri Owen and Nadine Abensur. And special thanks to Jenni Muir for added insight.

At Pavilion, thanks to Kate Oldfield for your vision, for enthusiastically providing the means to turn my idea into hard copy, and for suggesting the title. Emily Preece-Morrison, you are a real dynamo who kept the motor running on this project with composure and reassurance – thank you so much for your hard work and patience, as always.

Food stylist Jane Suthering, you are a magician. I am so lucky that you took on this project, and along with talented designer Mark Latter and brilliant photographer Gus Filgate – thank you for creating the beauty on these pages. It's an honour and a blessing to have had such a diamond-studded team!

To the Childwickbury gang, thanks for your ebullient appetites. Christiane, Tracy and Paula, thanks for all your support. Sorry I had to abandon you for a while to get this done.

Dad, Mom, Amy, Beth, Jess, Michael and Tess, your love keeps me going! Mark, thanks for the beets! Paulie, Jeanne, Rupert, Jessica, and James, thank you all for testing and tasting. And Inna, thank you so much for all your Russian inspiration.

To the team at Books for Cooks: Rosie, Eric, Sally, Marie Louise, Camille, Jesh, Mary Lou and Alma, thanks a million times over for your continuing support.

Warm thanks to the following for your suggestions, contributions, translations: Etel Barborka, Liselotte Bohlin, Riitta Bonstow, Stephan Brallet, Ying Chang, Charlotte @ The Colour of People, Samira Cherrouk, Chung @ Green Papaya, Darius the Magician, Roz Denny, Di, Mo and Zubeneisa, Carole Dulude, Richard Ehrlich, Bernd Einhorn, Lewis Esson, Susie Fairfax, Rickie Garza, Hakim and Ben, Roy Hall, Geraldine Hartley, Mary Hope, Shriti Karia, Kurshid Khan, Mary Jane Knudsen, Tzu Ann Leong, Cathy Lowis, Manju Mahli, Michael and Joy Michaud, Mario Montaño, Margarita Padilla, Gels and Antonio Picciuto, Pat Rowbottom, Silvena Rowe, Angelique Schoop, Liz Seeber, Mariamna Soudakoff, Liisa Sular, Edith Taylor, and Lexo Zatiashvili. Big love.

First published in Great Britain in 2005 by PAVILION BOOKS

An imprint of **Chrysalis** Books Group plc

The Chrysalis Building, Bramley Road, London W10 6SP
www.chrysalisbooks.co.uk

© Pavilion Books, 2005
Text © Celia Brooks Brown, 2005
Photography © Gus Filgate, 2005, apart from selected images credited below

The moral right of the author has been asserted.

All rights reserved. No part of this publication may be reproduced, stored in a retrieval system, or transmitted in any form or by any means, electronic, mechanical, photocopying, recording, or otherwise, without the prior written permission of the copyright owner.

Commissioning Editor: Kate Oldfield
Senior Editor: Emily Preece-Morrison
Copy Editor: Kathy Steer
Designer: www.pinkstripedesign.com
Photographer: Gus Filgate
Home Economist: Jane Suthering
Prop Stylist: Penny Markham
Cartographer: William Smuts
Indexer: Patricia Hymans

ISBN 1 86205 677 3

A CIP catalogue record for this book is available from the British Library.

10 9 8 7 6 5 4 3 2 1

Printed and bound by CT Printing Ltd, China.
Reproduction by Mission Productions Ltd, Hong Kong

Chrysalis Books Group Plc is committed to respecting the intellectual property rights of others. We have therefore taken all reasonable efforts to ensure that the reproduction of all content on these pages is done with the full consent of copyright owners. If you are aware of any unintentional omissions please contact the company directly so that any necessary corrections may be made for future editions.

**TL**= Top left, **TR** = Top right, BL=Bottom left, **BR**=Bottom right
**11TR** Getty Images/Donovan Reese; **37BR** Photolibrary/Index Stock Imagery/ Peter Adams; **64TL** Corbis/Wolfgang Kaehler; **91BR** Alamy Images/Hortus; **117BR** Alamy Images/Israel Images/ Yasha Mazur; **143BR** Getty Images/Jean Du Boisberranger; **168BR** Alamy Images/ImageState/ David South; **195TR** Alamy Images/Neil McAllister; **220BL** Alamy Images/Peter Adams Photography; **246TL** Photolibrary/Index Stock Imagery/ Peter Adams; **273TR** Alamy Images/Gondwana Photo Art.